Deception Tips
Revised And Expanded

ALSO BY SPENCER COFFMAN

A Guide To Deception
Relax And Unwind
Work Less Live More
A Healthier You!
Affiliate Marketing Expert
More Facebook Everything
365 Days Of Devotion For Everyone
YouTube Takeover
Find Us On Pinterest
Start Affiliate Marketing

DECEPTION TIPS

101 Cues To Detecting Deception Revised
And Expanded

BY
SPENCER COFFMAN

While every precaution has been taken in the preparation of this book, the author and/or publisher assumes no responsibility for errors or omissions, or for damages resulting from the use of the information contained herein.

DECEPTION TIPS: 101 CUES TO DETECTING DECEPTION REVISED AND EXPANDED

First edition. January 2019.

ISBN: 978-1-7294309-0-3 (Paperback)
ISBN: 978-1-3860441-0-9 (Digital)

Written by Spencer Coffman.
SpencerCoffman.com

So you think you're pretty good at reading people?

Wanna be better?

Continue learning the language everyone knows yet very few understand.

Body Language.

You don't have to be in the dark always wondering if someone actually means what they are saying.

Now you can know. Body language always tells the truth and you have the power to never be deceived again!

No more scams, cons, or getting the wool pulled over your eyes.

It's time for you to learn MORE about how to detect deception!

How many more times will you wonder whether or not your child is telling the truth?

How often will you fall for the same old story in your relationships?

When's the next time you'll miss out on a sale because you

couldn't quite read your target?

The Answer...

NEVER AGAIN!!!

Body language is present everywhere and if you can read it, you will be much better able to see exactly what someone really wants to say.

So how can you read it?

Introducing

Deception Tips

Revised And Expanded

101 Cues To Detecting Deception

Yeah, that's right.

Revised AND Expanded.

This book goes in depth. You are going to learn MORE about lies and deceit.

WHY?

Well, because.

Lies and deception can really take a toll on your emotions and you need to be able to protect yourself and recognize what people are really saying.

When you are able to understand body language you'll live a more enlightened life!

You'll finally be able to...

Protect yourself from emotional damage.

Know whether or not you are about to get ripped off.

Start knowing what people are truly saying and learn what they really mean.

Increase your sales capability.

Understand what your kids are saying.

Give your customers exactly what they want but are afraid to ask.

Recognize the needs of your spouse.

The list goes on!

I created this book because people loved Deception Tips, which I created because people loved the Deception Tips

Blog, which I created because people loved A Guide To Deception.

Now you have a truly incredible resource in one handy location. You have many of the tips from A Guide To Deception, all of the tips from the blog, and from Deception Tips, explained in detail, in one great location!

The question is: what would you be willing to pay for such a valuable resource.

How much is this knowledge worth to you?

Deception Tips Revised And Expanded is packed with 101 images that you can learn from and review on a daily basis. It also has an explanation of each deception tip so you can fully understand it!

In fact, the value is truly priceless.

The good news is I want you to learn. I want you to have this book.

Even though it could easily be sold at high cost textbook price.

It's yours for this very special price.

Yes! I'm ready to sharpen my body language skills and start reading people like never before!

Send my copy of "Deception Tips Revised And Expanded" so I can learn even MORE about body language right away!

Claim Your Copy Today!

Deception Tips
Revised And Expanded

Table of Contents

Introduction

101 Cues To Detecting Deception

Conclusion

About The Author

Introduction

Reading people is an incredible topic. People love to try and understand body language and are fascinated with micro-expressions. Everyone wants to know what other people are thinking. People love to learn how to read people. Body language is the language that everybody speaks and very few people understand. However, you have a pretty good understanding of it.

Body language is the ONLY language in the world that always speaks the truth. Every other language is filled with lies and, deep down, people want the truth. It is a natural state. We cannot help it. Our unconscious mind is always truthful. It always tells and wants the truth.

You can train your deceptive conscious mind to recognize lies and find the truth. It is there, in your unconscious and in the unconscious behaviors of other people. That is the purpose of this book. It is to help you dig deeper and learn more about reading people and detecting deception.

As you know, this is a sequel. It is the second book. The first was Deception Tips, which was a book based on the Deception Tips Blog. That was a book filled with images. This book is the revised and expanded edition. That means, instead of only images, this book is filled with descriptive text as well. You will not only see the deception tip, but you'll also get an explanation of the tip.

I guess this is actually more of a third book in a "greater" series. It all started with A Guide To Deception. Then the Deception Tips Blog and the Deception Tips eBook. After that, the Deception Tips

Deception Tips Revised And Expanded

Podcast began along with the Deception Tips Videos. Now, here it is Deception Tips Revised And Expanded.

It seems like people always want more and I have no doubt that once I've finished the podcast and the videos that there will be more books or other podcasts. People always want to find the truth and as long as they are seeking a method of finding it then I will continue to help them learn. I will continue to help you learn.

Therefore, be sure to check out the other books I've written on body language and deception. Take a look at the Deception Tips Blog, the Deception Tips Podcast, and the Deception Tips Videos. I've even created a website where you can conveniently find each podcast episode and video. It's cleverly called deceptiontips.com.

Thank you for your interest in this topic. Without you, I would be unable to continue exploring my passion of teaching others how to read people and detect deception. I truly hope you'll take advantage of the other resources I have to offer and that you'll enjoy this book.

101 Cues To Detecting Deception

Spencer Coffman

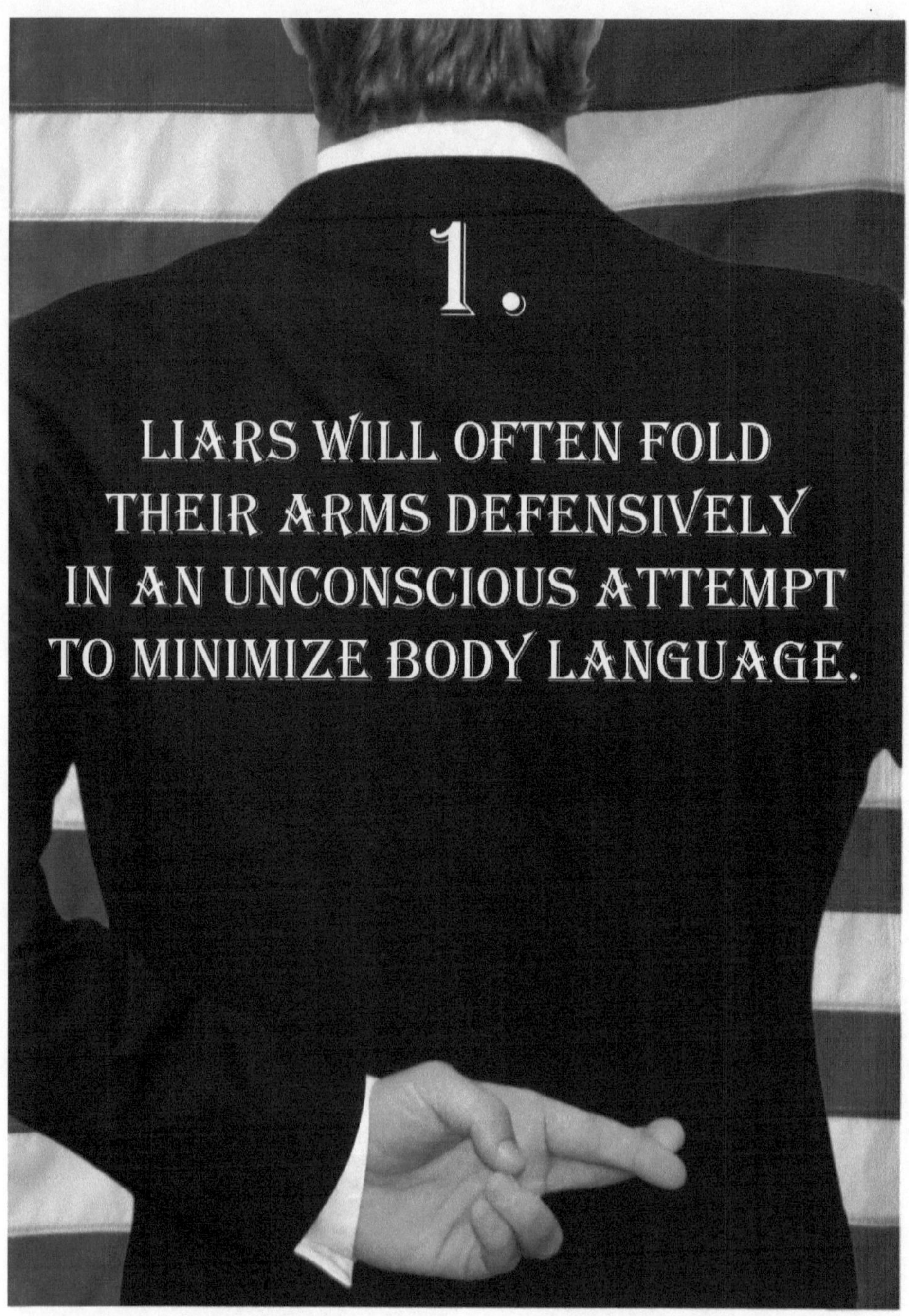

1.
LIARS WILL OFTEN FOLD
THEIR ARMS DEFENSIVELY
IN AN UNCONSCIOUS ATTEMPT
TO MINIMIZE BODY LANGUAGE.

Deception Tip 1 – Folding Arms

Liars will often fold their arms defensively in an unconscious attempt to minimize body language.

Folding arms is a gesture that can have several different meanings. For this reason, it is essential that you look for patterns, and clusters, of behavior rather than relying on any individual behavior. When someone folds his or her arms, it doesn't always mean that the person is being deceptive. Look at the tip again. It says defensiveness and minimizing body language.

People are defensive when they feel attacked, which may not always be due to not being believed. In addition, some people may minimize their body when they are cold. Another important aspect of arm folding is that men and women fold their arms differently.

Women, due to their anatomy, will fold their arms lower on the torso, usually across the belly. Men, on the other hand, fold their arms higher, usually across the chest. Therefore, if you see women folding their arms higher or men folding their arms lower there could be a different meaning. Perhaps bashfulness for women or stomach pain for men, for example.

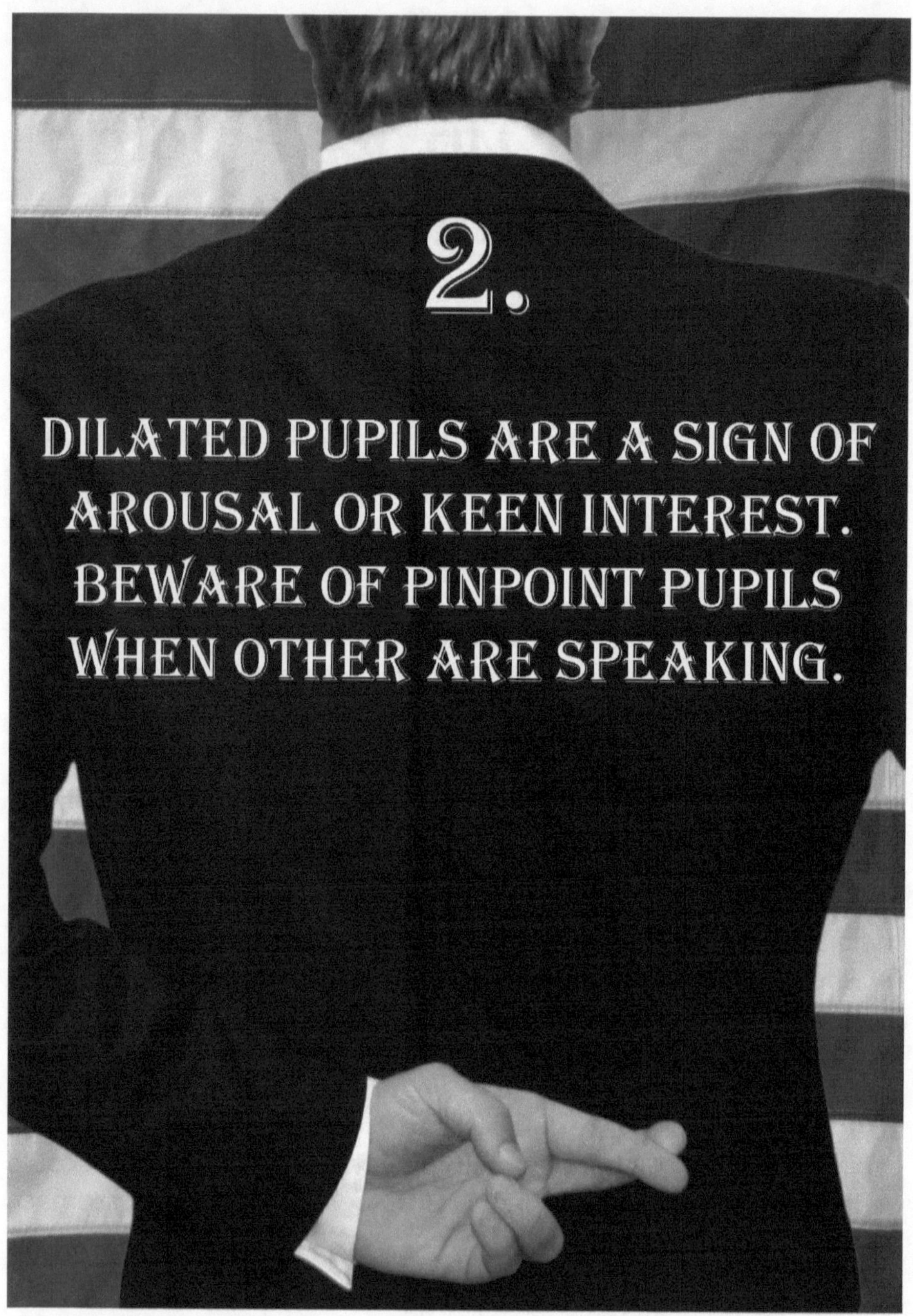
2.
DILATED PUPILS ARE A SIGN OF
AROUSAL OR KEEN INTEREST.
BEWARE OF PINPOINT PUPILS
WHEN OTHER ARE SPEAKING.

Deception Tip 2 – Dilated Pupils

Dilated Pupils are a sign of arousal or keen interest. Beware of pinpoint pupils when others are speaking.

Pupils are great to watch when speaking with someone. They can tell you so much about what is going on inside his or her mind. Remember the old saying, "the eyes are the windows to the soul"? It is true when it comes to body language. The eyes will give you some great information about how a person really feels.

There are a couple of things to watch for when looking at the pupils and they both fall into one category so it will be easy for you to remember. That is dilation. You need to watch for the dilation of the pupils. This doesn't mean normal dilation. No, you need to watch for extreme dilation.

When they are extremely dilated, the person likes what he or she is experiencing. When they are extremely narrow, the person doesn't like what he or she is experiencing. Of course, you also need to be conscious of possible chemical or environmental factors that may cause the pupils to dilate such as drugs, fumes, et cetera.

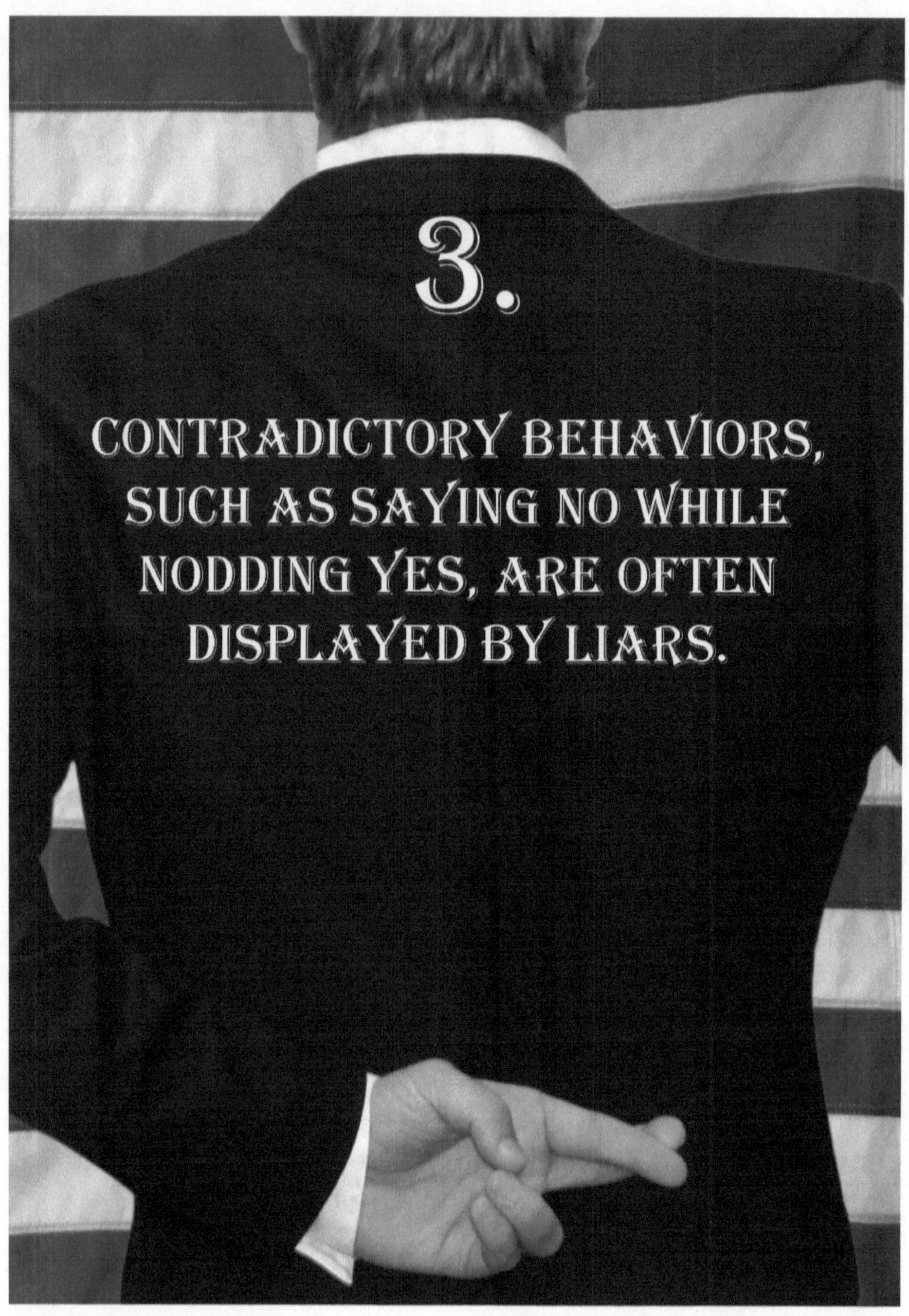
3.

CONTRADICTORY BEHAVIORS,
SUCH AS SAYING NO WHILE
NODDING YES, ARE OFTEN
DISPLAYED BY LIARS.

Deception Tip 3 – Contradictory Behaviors

Contradictory behaviors, such as saying no while nodding yes, are often displayed by liars.

Contradictory behaviors can occur when people lie. This is usually caused by the internal battle that is taking place between the conscious and the unconscious mind. When people lie, the unconscious wants to tell the truth. The conscious wants to get away with the lie. As a result, the unconscious will leak some truthful behaviors, and these behaviors may contradict the behaviors displayed by the conscious.

Therefore, watch for signs that appear unnatural. You are looking for things that are a little bit odd but not outwardly noticeable. Remember they are unconscious. That means they are unconsciously displayed by the liar and they are also unconsciously seen by you. You need to train yourself to start consciously seeing them.

These contradictions can be between speech and body language, speech alone, or body language alone. Therefore, you need to be on alert at all times. People can say no and nod yes, which would be a contradiction between speech and body language. In addition, they could also nod their head yes while gesturing no with a hand or finger, which is a contradiction between body language alone. There are numerous examples and the best way to learn and understand them is to pay attention in everyday conversation.

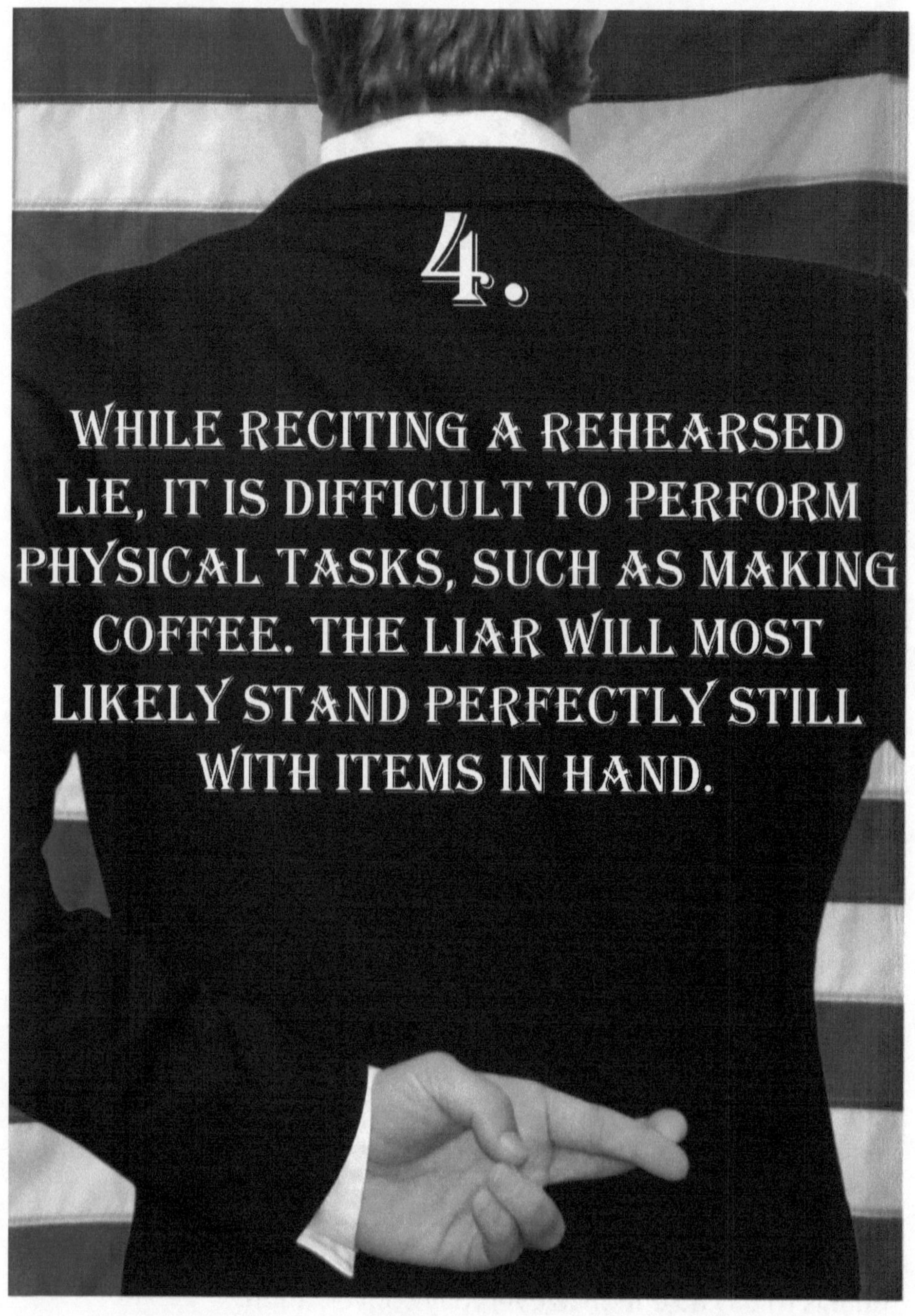

4.

WHILE RECITING A REHEARSED LIE, IT IS DIFFICULT TO PERFORM PHYSICAL TASKS, SUCH AS MAKING COFFEE. THE LIAR WILL MOST LIKELY STAND PERFECTLY STILL WITH ITEMS IN HAND.

Deception Tip 4 – Physical Tasks

While reciting a rehearsed lie, it is difficult to perform physical tasks, such as making coffee. The liar will most likely stand perfectly still with items in hand.

Telling lies can be mentally straining and challenging for some people. Keeping all of the lies straight can require a lot of brainpower. This often means that a person will be so focused on the lie that he or she may not know what is happening around them. This means that sometimes, the liar may not be able to perform basic physical tasks.

Remember there is a battle going on between the conscious and the unconscious. The conscious is fighting to get the lie out and the unconscious is fighting to reveal the truth. In some cases, when the conscious starts telling a lie, the unconscious stops all other unconscious behavior to try to fight the lie. In doing so, a sign of leakage is displayed.

Notice how I said 'stops all other unconscious behavior'. This means that the behavior that someone is doing needs to be somewhat of a habit. It needs to be something that they can do almost unconsciously. A behavior like making coffee, which many people can do in their sleep, is a great example.

5.
GUILTY PEOPLE OFTEN AVOID
USING CONTRACTIONS AS IF TO
EMPHASIZE THEIR INNOCENCE.
EXAMPLE:
USING DID NOT INSTEAD OF DIDN'T.

Deception Tip 5 – Contractions

Guilty people often avoid using contractions as if to emphasize their innocence. Example: using did not instead of didn't.

When people tell lies, they want to sound truthful. They want people to believe their lie as if it was the truth. This means they may overemphasize what they are saying. The liar will want to make sure that people hear that he or she is innocent. As a result, liars will usually break apart contractions and say each word individually.

This is a little unusual because one would think that a liar would want to get the lie out and over with as soon as possible. Following that reasoning, it would seem that contractions would help serve that purpose. However, that is not the case. A liar may very well want to get the lie out as soon as possible. In addition, they may want to use contractions but the unconscious has other plans.

Remember, the unconscious is very truthful. Therefore, it will break up the contractions in hopes that others will notice the oddity of the liar's speech and catch the conscious in the lie. So pay attention to people when they speak and see if you notice any broken contractions. It is natural to speak with contractions so when you hear them split apart, some form of deception might be going on.

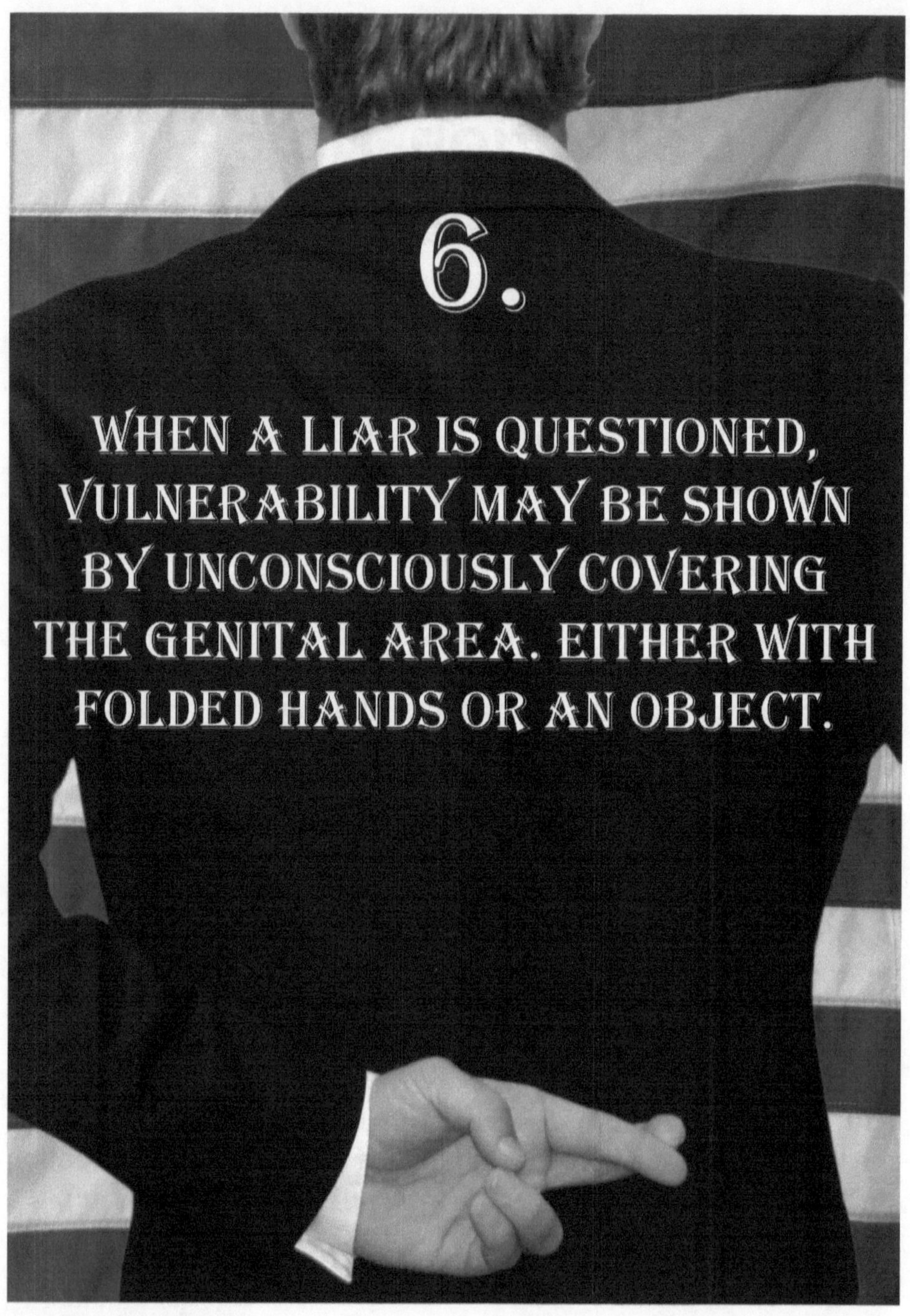
6.
WHEN A LIAR IS QUESTIONED,
VULNERABILITY MAY BE SHOWN
BY UNCONSCIOUSLY COVERING
THE GENITAL AREA. EITHER WITH
FOLDED HANDS OR AN OBJECT.

Deception Tip 6 – Covering Genitals

When a liar is questioned, vulnerability may be shown by unconsciously covering the genital area. Either with folded hands or an object.

When someone lies, he or she is nervous and anxious about being caught. They want to get the lie over with as quickly as possible. Therefore, when a liar is challenged, he or she may feel vulnerable. Sort of like when you catch your dog tearing up the trash or a kid with their hand in the cookie jar. They feel ashamed.

If you've ever been to a hypnotist then you may have witnessed some members of the crowd become hypnotized. Occasionally, the hypnotist will tell these people that they are naked. Almost instantly, many of them begin to hide and cover up as if they really were naked. They feel shame. They feel vulnerability.

When a liar is challenged, the same feeling may be experienced. As a result, he or she may cover these private or sensitive areas. In reality, there is no reason to cover up because they are already wearing clothing. The fact that he or she is covering means that the person is feeling vulnerable, which could be due to feeling caught in a lie.

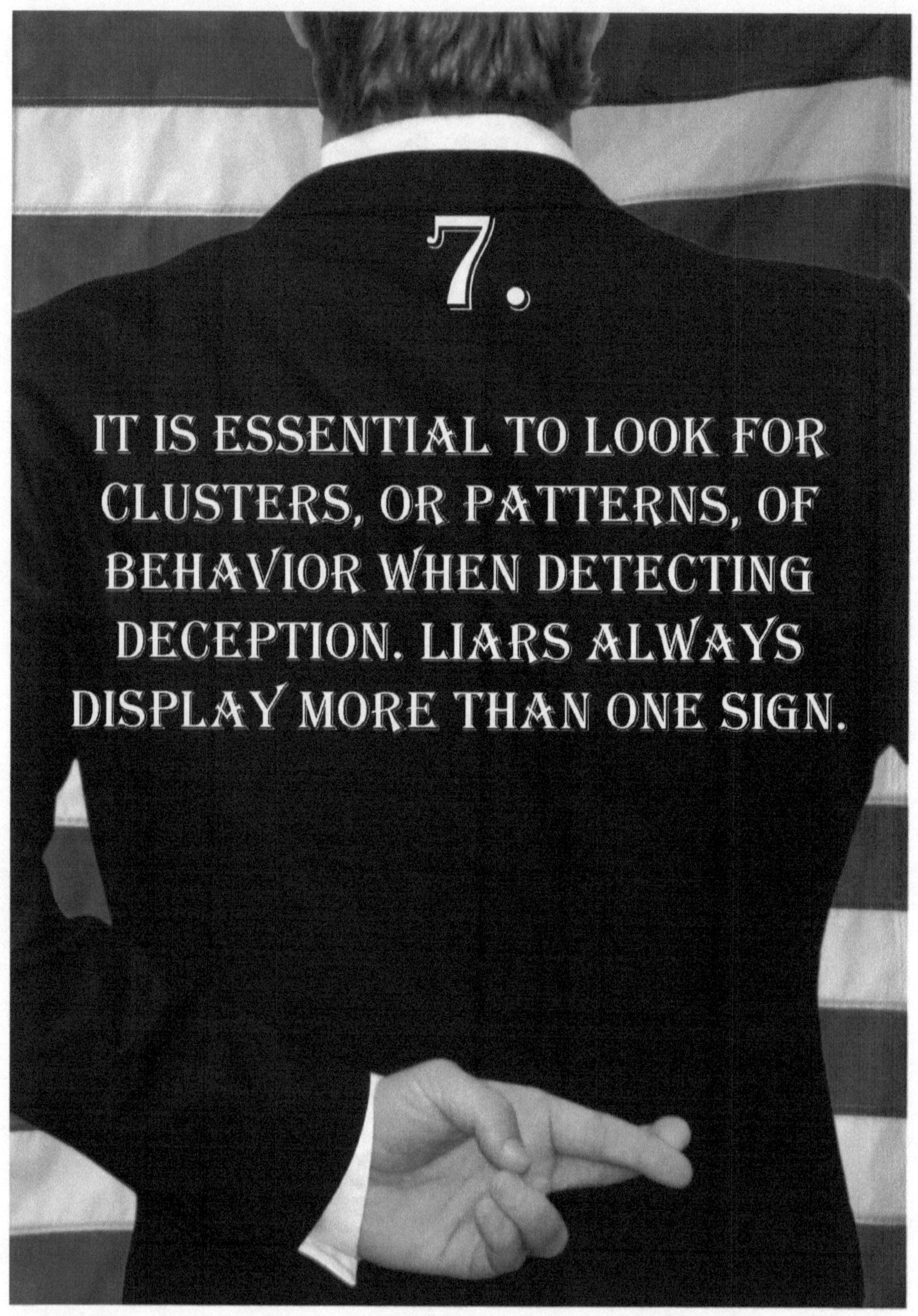
7.
IT IS ESSENTIAL TO LOOK FOR
CLUSTERS, OR PATTERNS, OF
BEHAVIOR WHEN DETECTING
DECEPTION. LIARS ALWAYS
DISPLAY MORE THAN ONE SIGN.

Deception Tip 7 – Clusters of Behavior

It is essential to look for clusters, or patterns, of behavior when detecting deception. Liars always display more than one sign.

There are many different signs of deception. In addition, nearly all of these signs can have more than one meaning. This means that any one sign is not directly indicative of deception. This can be troublesome if you are trying to detect deception. How can you be certain that the body language you are observing means that someone is lying?

The answer is simple. You look for clusters, or patterns, of behavior. You need to pay attention to each individual sign of deception. Notice everything and make a mental note of it. However, don't immediately classify it as a deceptive gesture. Yes, it could be a sign of deception, however, you need to continue to watch for other signs to confirm your suspicion.

When people lie, they will always display more than one sign of deception. This is because there is a constant battle going on between the conscious and the unconscious. The conscious wants to get away with the lie and the unconscious wants to expose the truth. That means there will be multiple unconscious signs of leakage.

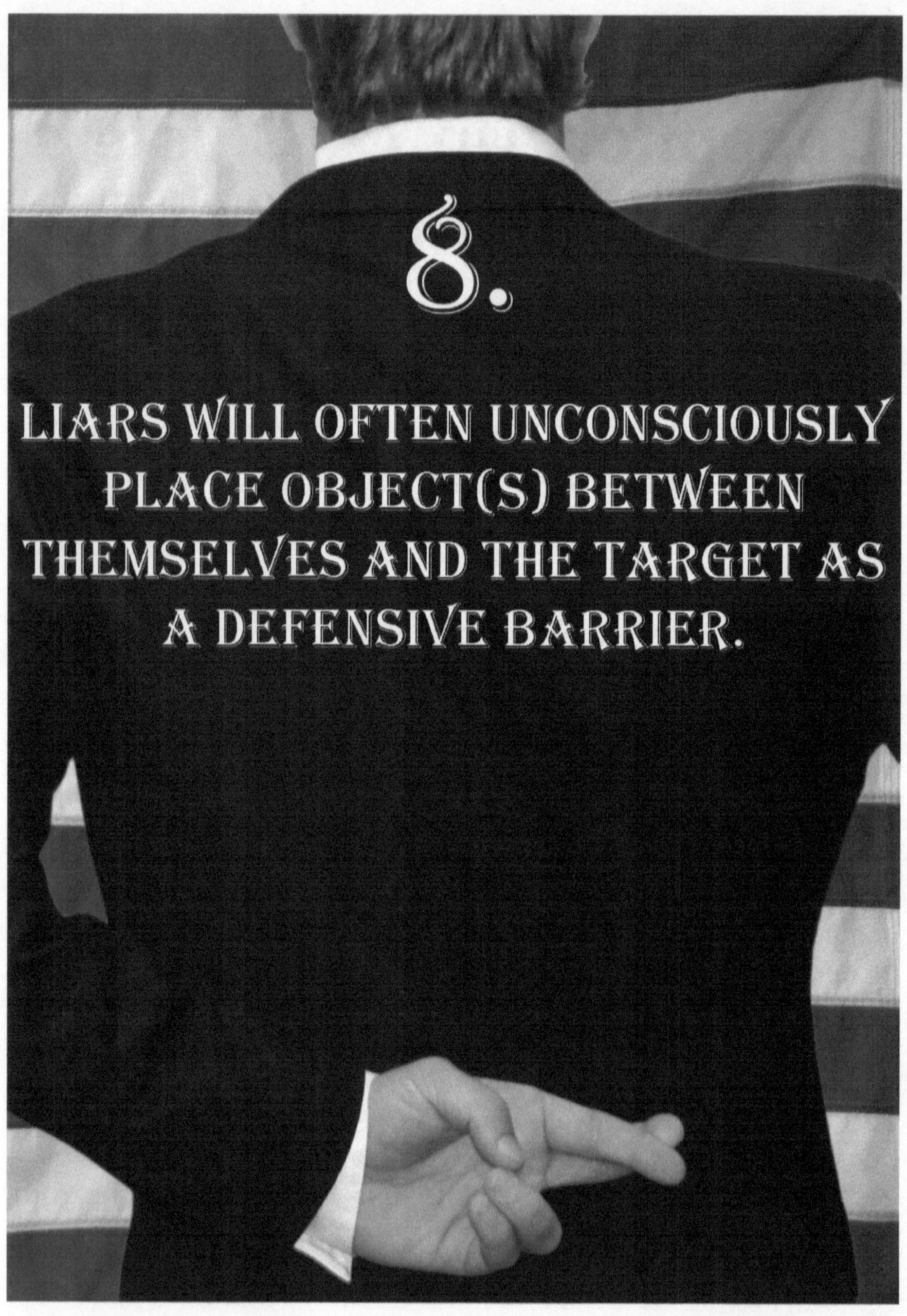

8.
LIARS WILL OFTEN UNCONSCIOUSLY PLACE OBJECT(S) BETWEEN THEMSELVES AND THE TARGET AS A DEFENSIVE BARRIER.

Deception Tip 8 – Defensive Barriers

Liars will often unconsciously place object(s) between themselves and the target as a defensive barrier.

When people lie, the unconscious is trying to reveal the truth. This means that if you pay attention, you will be able to spot lies and detect deceit. It also means that the conscious knows that the unconscious is leaking behaviors to try and expose the truth. Sometimes, it will try to stop this leakage thinking that it will prevent the unconscious from exposing the truth. Usually, the unconscious is one step ahead and often allows these behaviors.

Remember that most liars do not enjoy lying. They often feel uncomfortable telling lies. Unless someone is psychologically sick, their conscience will make them feel bad about lying. Since people feel bad about lying they will often want to hide their bodies. Sort of like the shame felt when they try to cover their genitals as mentioned in Deception Tip 6.

This time, instead of covering the genitals, the liar tries to cover entire areas of the body. The conscious wants to block others from seeing body language and the unconscious allows it because it is a sign of deception in and of itself. Anything can be a defensive barrier. People can use object, desks, chairs, monitors, et cetera.

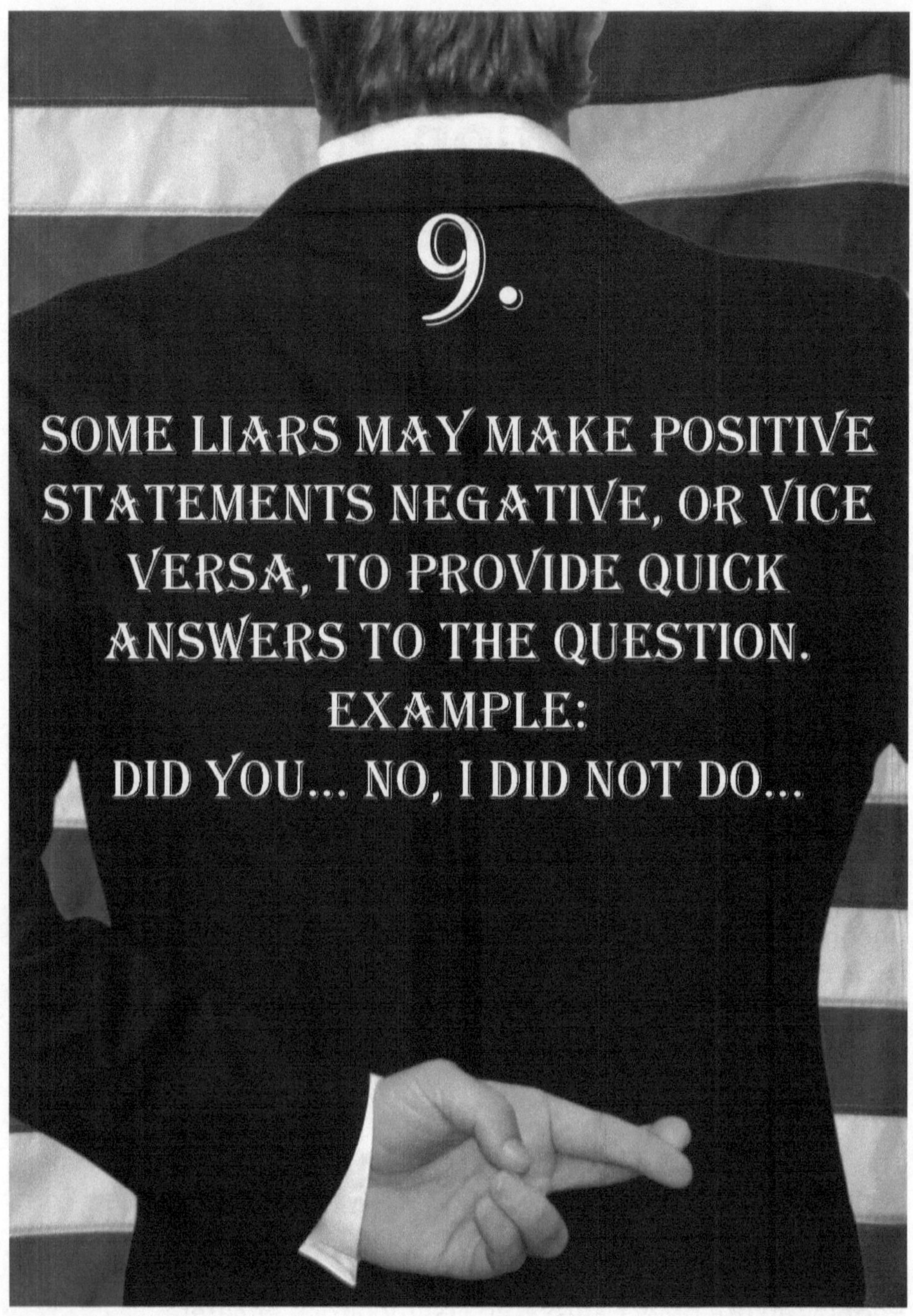
9.
SOME LIARS MAY MAKE POSITIVE STATEMENTS NEGATIVE, OR VICE VERSA, TO PROVIDE QUICK ANSWERS TO THE QUESTION.
EXAMPLE:
DID YOU... NO, I DID NOT DO...

Deception Tip 9 – Converting Statements

Some liars may make positive statements negative, or vice versa, to provide quick answers to the question. Example: Did you… No, I did not do…

This is probably one of the most difficult to understand deception tips. Therefore, I really suggest you listen to episode 9 of the podcast and watch the videos. Both can be found on spencercoffman.com/deception-tip-9 and on deceptiontips.com. In addition, read over this a couple of times. I'm going to break it down in an effort to make it as easy as possible for you to understand.

Liars can either make positive statements negative or negative statements positive. In any case, the response that they give will not make any sense at all. Provided you think about it, that is. For example, positive statements would be something like "did you" and negative statements would be something like "you didn't… did you". Take a look at this table for a general outline.

The following are taking a positive statement and making it something else.

Did you… No, I did not do Positive – Negative – Negative
Did you… Yes, I did it Positive – Positive – Positive
Did you… No, I did Positive – Negative – Positive

Deception Tips Revised And Expanded

Did you... Yes, I did not Positive – Positive – Negative

The following are taking a negative statement and making it something else.

You didn't... Yes, I did not do Negative – Positive – Negative
You didn't... No, I did Negative – Negative – Positive
You didn't... Yes, I did Negative – Positive – Positive
You didn't... No, I did not do Negative – Negative – Negative

As you can see, it can be a little confusing. However, simply create your own questions using the statements and responses provided. You will soon understand how it works. In addition, you'll notice that some of the responses make absolutely no sense.

39

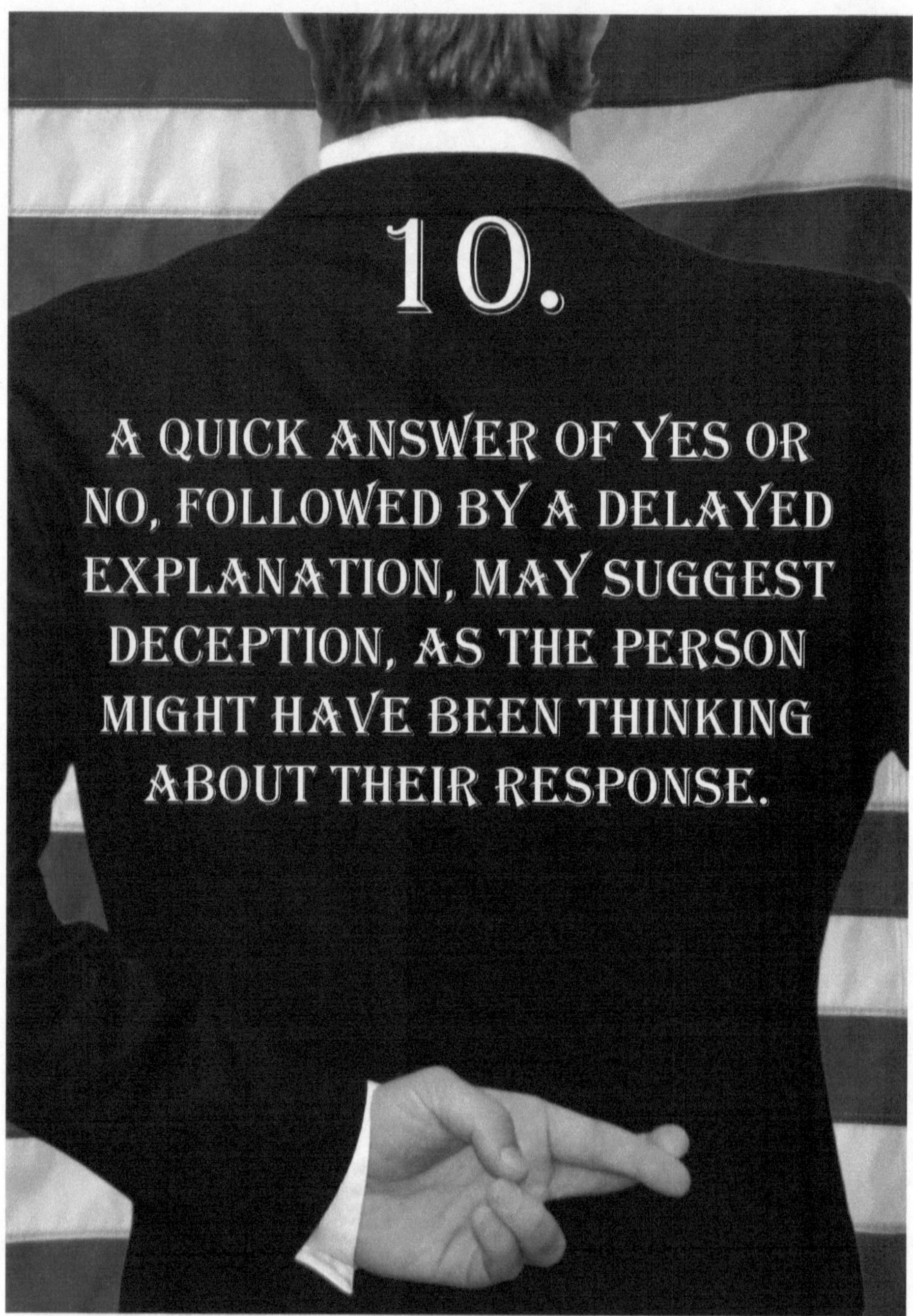

10.

A QUICK ANSWER OF YES OR NO, FOLLOWED BY A DELAYED EXPLANATION, MAY SUGGEST DECEPTION, AS THE PERSON MIGHT HAVE BEEN THINKING ABOUT THEIR RESPONSE.

Deception Tip 10 – Quick Answers

A quick answer of yes or no, followed by a delayed explanation, may suggest deception, as the person might have been thinking about their response.

When people answer quickly and then take a little extra time to explain, you need to be on your guard. This could mean that he or she was thinking about the best way to convince you of whatever the answer was. Often times, liars will give a quick answer followed by an explanation so that it doesn't seem like they are delaying the response. However, what you may not realize is that this is a stalling tactic done to give them more time to think about the response.

When someone answered with "yes" or "no" that is all there is. What more is needed? If the question was a good question then the response can be either "yes" or "no". Therefore, when someone responds quickly and then begins to explain you need to watch out. He or she is trying to justify the response and make it more believable.

Of course, this doesn't always mean that someone is lying. However, it could be a sign of deception so you should be on alert. Watch for other signs that may appear and use them to put together a cluster of behaviors. Never let any one sign be the determining factor. Always base your judgments on clusters, or patterns, of behavior.

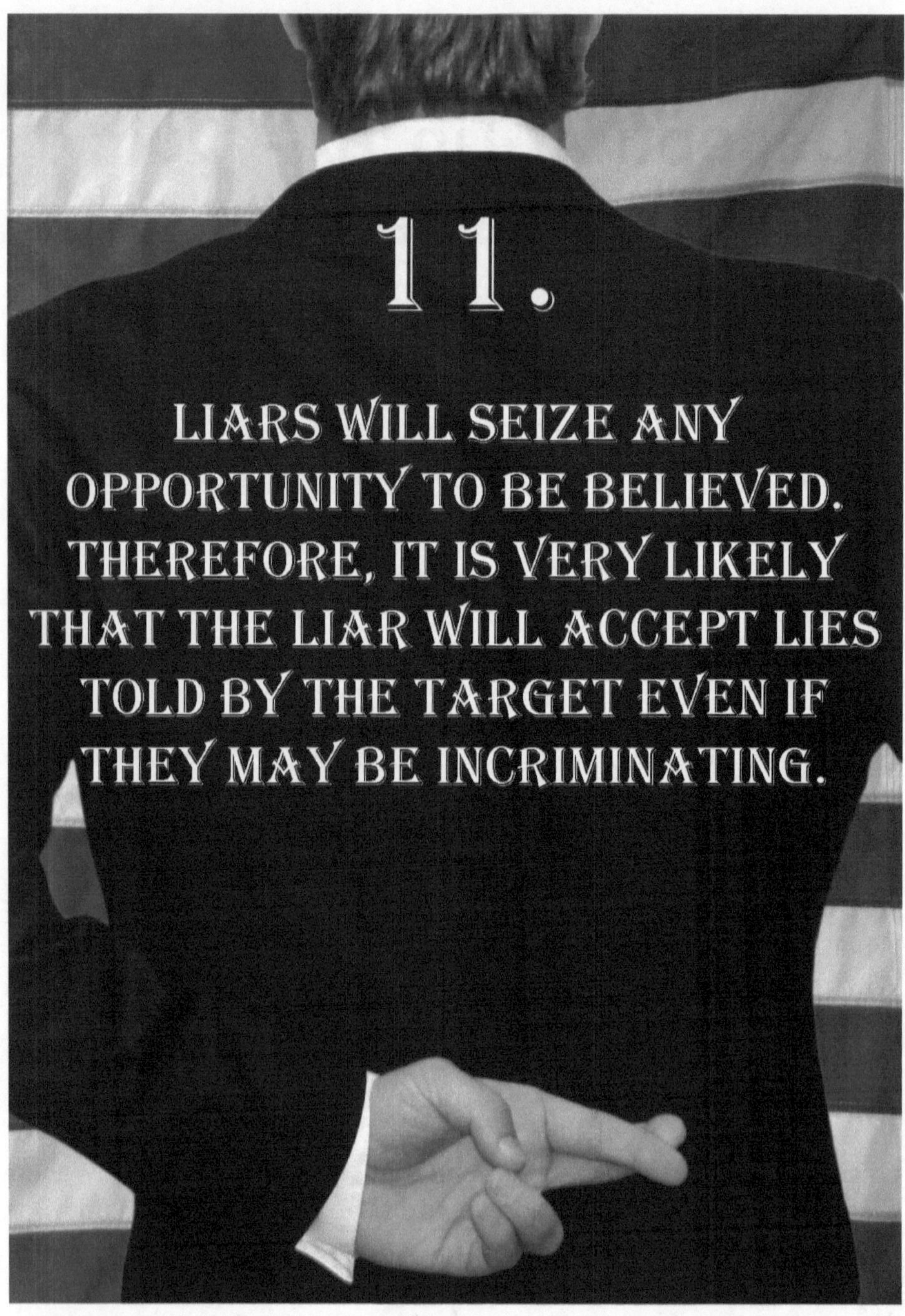
11.

LIARS WILL SEIZE ANY
OPPORTUNITY TO BE BELIEVED.
THEREFORE, IT IS VERY LIKELY
THAT THE LIAR WILL ACCEPT LIES
TOLD BY THE TARGET EVEN IF
THEY MAY BE INCRIMINATING.

Deception Tip 11 – Accepting Lies

Liars will seize any opportunity to be believed. Therefore, it is very likely that the liar will accept lies told by the target even if they may be incriminating.

When people tell lies they usually have one main goal in mind. That is, to get other people to believe their lie. Liars want to be believed. Think about it, getting someone to believe their lie is their main goal. Yes, of course, they are probably lying to cover up something or to avoid blame. However, that isn't the main purpose of the lie. It is the second purpose. Being believed is the first purpose because if people don't believe the lie then covering something up or avoiding blame no longer matters because the liar got caught.

You can use this to your advantage. Since you know that liars desperately want to be believed, you can feed them information and see if they agree with it. Give them some lies of your own for them to work into their story. If they incorporate them, then you know that he or she is being deceptive. However, if they don't use your false material, then he or she may be telling the truth.

As always, use other tactics and techniques when detecting deception. In addition, be sure to watch for other signs as well. Remember Deception Tip 7? Liars will always display more than one sign so there will be plenty for you to see.

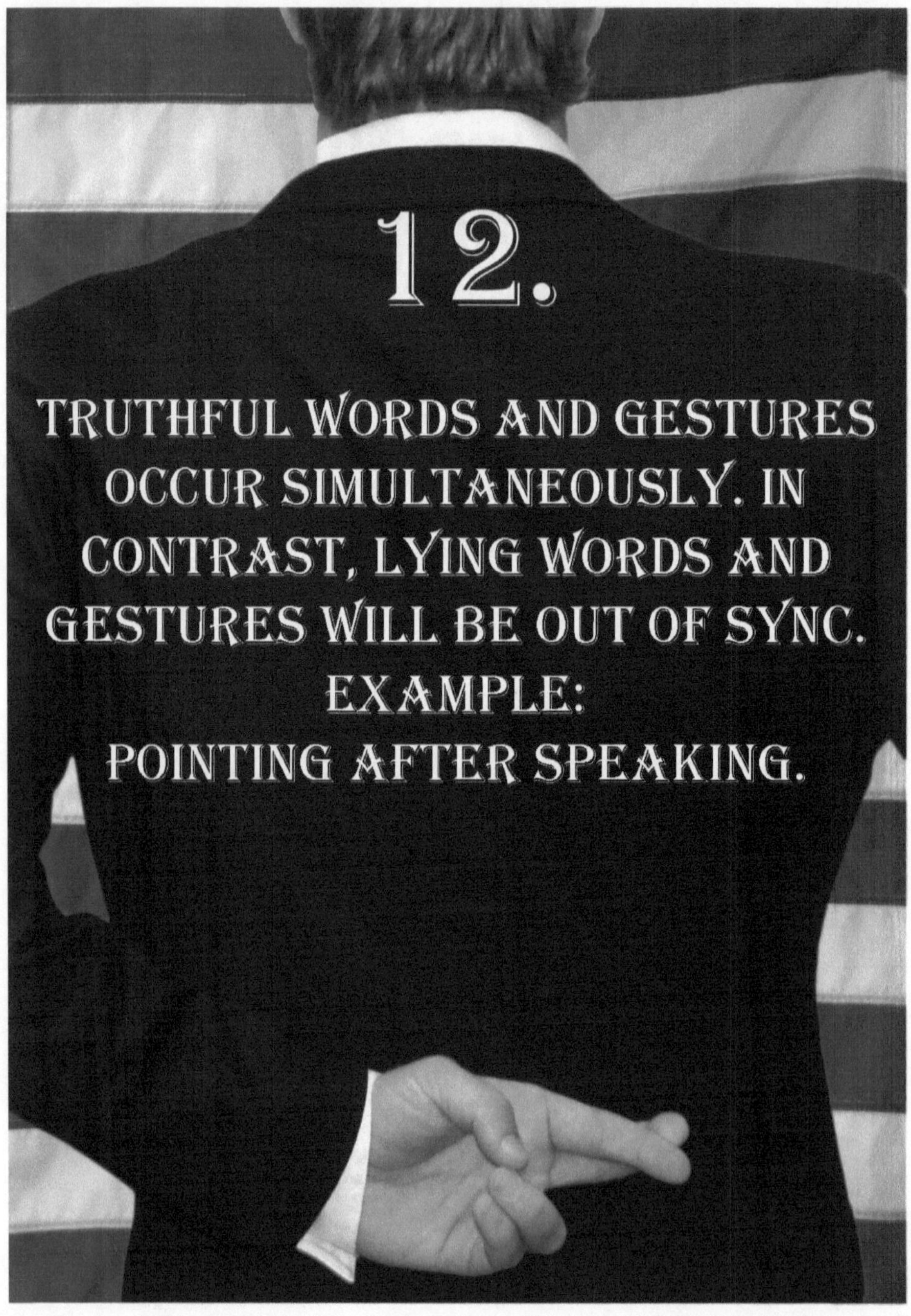

12.

TRUTHFUL WORDS AND GESTURES OCCUR SIMULTANEOUSLY. IN CONTRAST, LYING WORDS AND GESTURES WILL BE OUT OF SYNC. EXAMPLE: POINTING AFTER SPEAKING.

Deception Tip 12 – Simultaneous Gestures

Truthful words and gestures occur simultaneously. In contrast, lying words and gestures will be out of sync. Example: Pointing after speaking.

When people are being truthful, their gestures should occur simultaneously with their speech. Everything should be in harmony and have a nice natural look to it. Their gestures and speech should be fluid and in sync with one another. On the other hand, when people lie, their gestures may not occur simultaneously with their speech. They will not appear natural and fluid. Rather, they will be unnatural and delayed.

A great example of this occurs when someone is displaying anger but he or she really isn't upset about the situation. The person may shout and smack the table or stop a foot. This type of behavior directly represents anger so you may be curious as to how it relates to deception. Well, when someone shouts and smacks the table or stomps a foot, anger is definitely prevalent as long as the gesture is synchronized with the speech.

However, if the gesture is delayed and comes after the shout, then it is indicative of deception. It is important to note that the difference will be less than a second or two. That means it will be very slight and tough to notice. Therefore, pay attention. If you think you notice it, then watch for other signs as well.

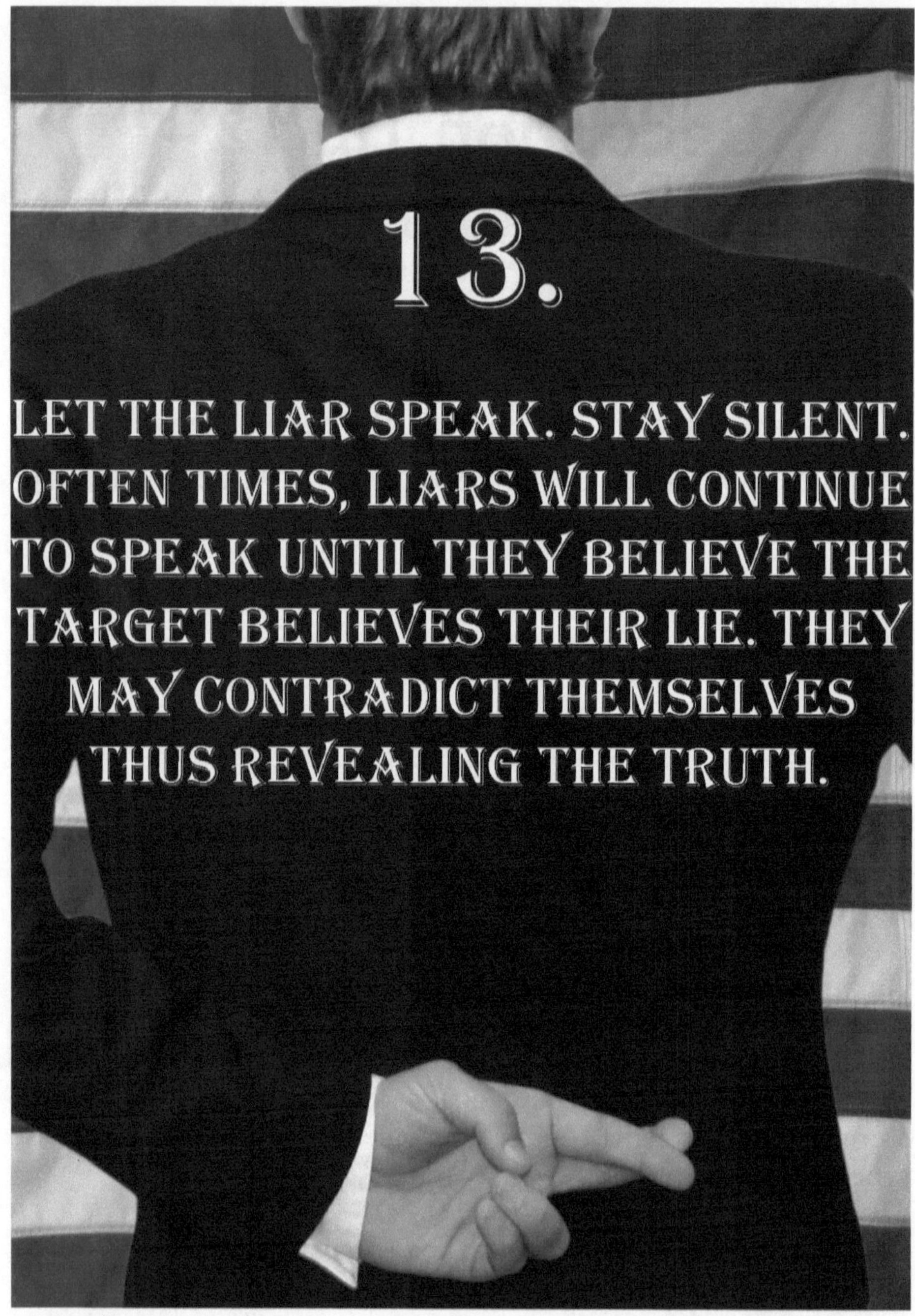
13.

LET THE LIAR SPEAK. STAY SILENT.
OFTEN TIMES, LIARS WILL CONTINUE
TO SPEAK UNTIL THEY BELIEVE THE
TARGET BELIEVES THEIR LIE. THEY
MAY CONTRADICT THEMSELVES
THUS REVEALING THE TRUTH.

Deception Tip 13 – Stay Silent

Let the liar speak. Stay silent. Often times, liars will continue to speak until they believe the target believes their lie. They may contradict themselves thus revealing the truth.

There is a lot of stress and anxiety that goes into telling a lie. Most people don't like feeling stressed and anxious and would like those feelings to go away as soon as possible. This means that if lying makes a person feel that way, then that person would want to tell the lie and get rid of those feelings as fast as they can.

Therefore, if you allow a liar to speak, then he or she may continue to talk in an effort to rid themselves of the stress and anxiety involved in telling a lie. They need to talk, and if you allow them to, then they will eventually trip over their tongue and mess up. If you are paying attention, then you'll be able to catch them in their lie.

Another important point to note is that when people lie, they want to be believed. Thus, they are looking for your approval. They are looking for you to approve what they said and accept it as truth. Therefore, if you stay silent and say nothing, the liar will become even more anxious and continue to speak to fill the awkward silence you've created. He or she will talk until they convince themselves that you approved, or believed their lie.

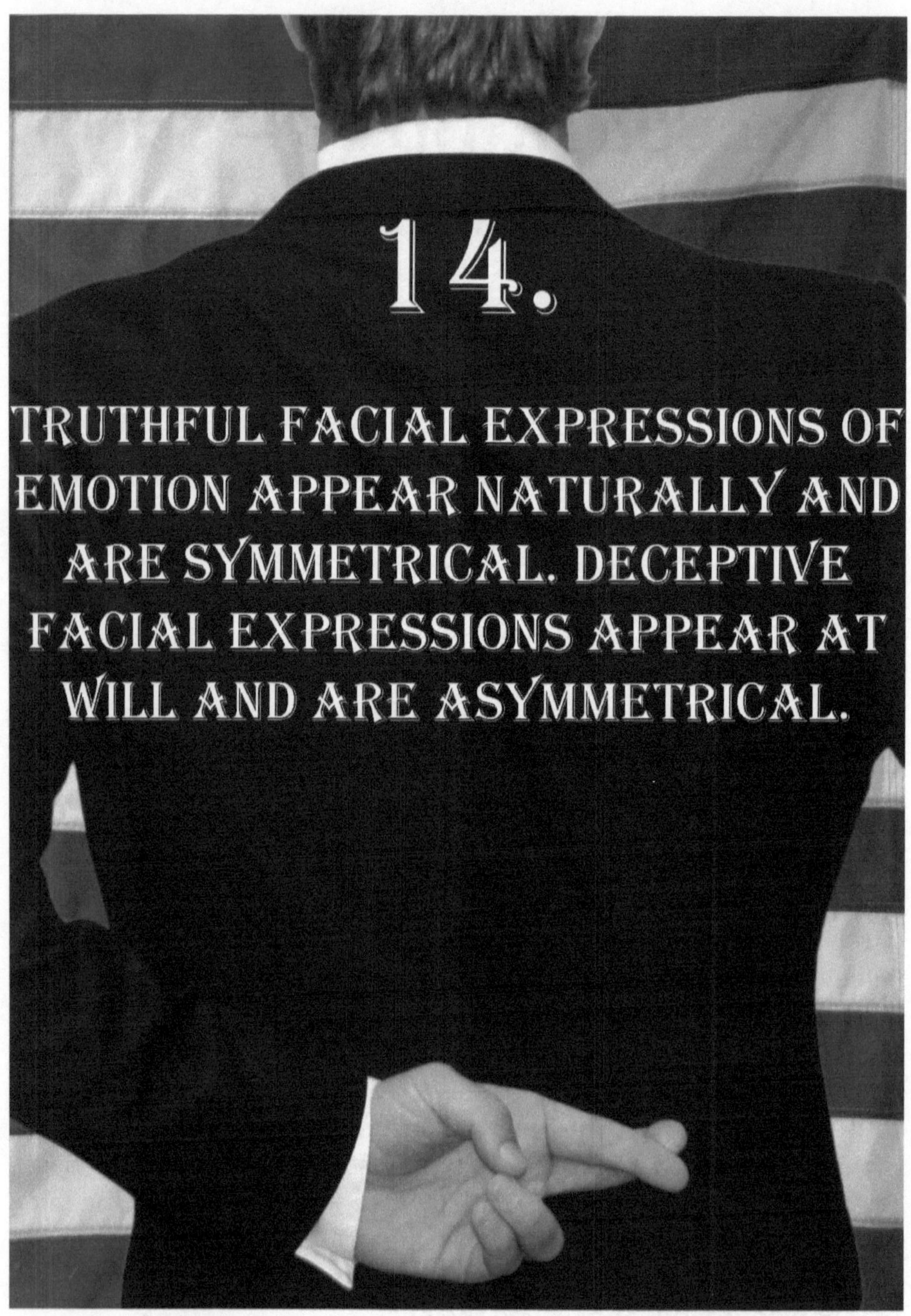
14.
TRUTHFUL FACIAL EXPRESSIONS OF EMOTION APPEAR NATURALLY AND ARE SYMMETRICAL. DECEPTIVE FACIAL EXPRESSIONS APPEAR AT WILL AND ARE ASYMMETRICAL.

Deception Tip 14 – Symmetrical Expressions

Truthful facial expressions of emotion appear naturally and are symmetrical. Deceptive facial expressions appear at will and are asymmetrical.

When people talk, the expressions that they display should happen on both sides of the face. There is only one exception to this rule and that is when people display contempt, which is primarily displayed on the right side of the face. Remember that when people are telling the truth their behaviors must not contradict each other as mentioned in Deception Tip 3 and their gestures should be simultaneous as mentioned in Deception Tip 12.

Smiles are another tricky aspect of this deception tip. Often times, you may see people smile more on one side of the face than the other. This is usually because the person is not feeling genuine enjoyment. That means he or she is lying. That person is faking a smile, which is why the smile is asymmetrical.

Different areas of the brain control the emotional expressions on our faces. However, in general, the left side of the brain controls the right side of the body and the right side of the brain controls the left side of the body. When you see these asymmetrical expressions, you'll notice that they are predominant on the left side of the face. That means that the right brain is more prominent in deception.

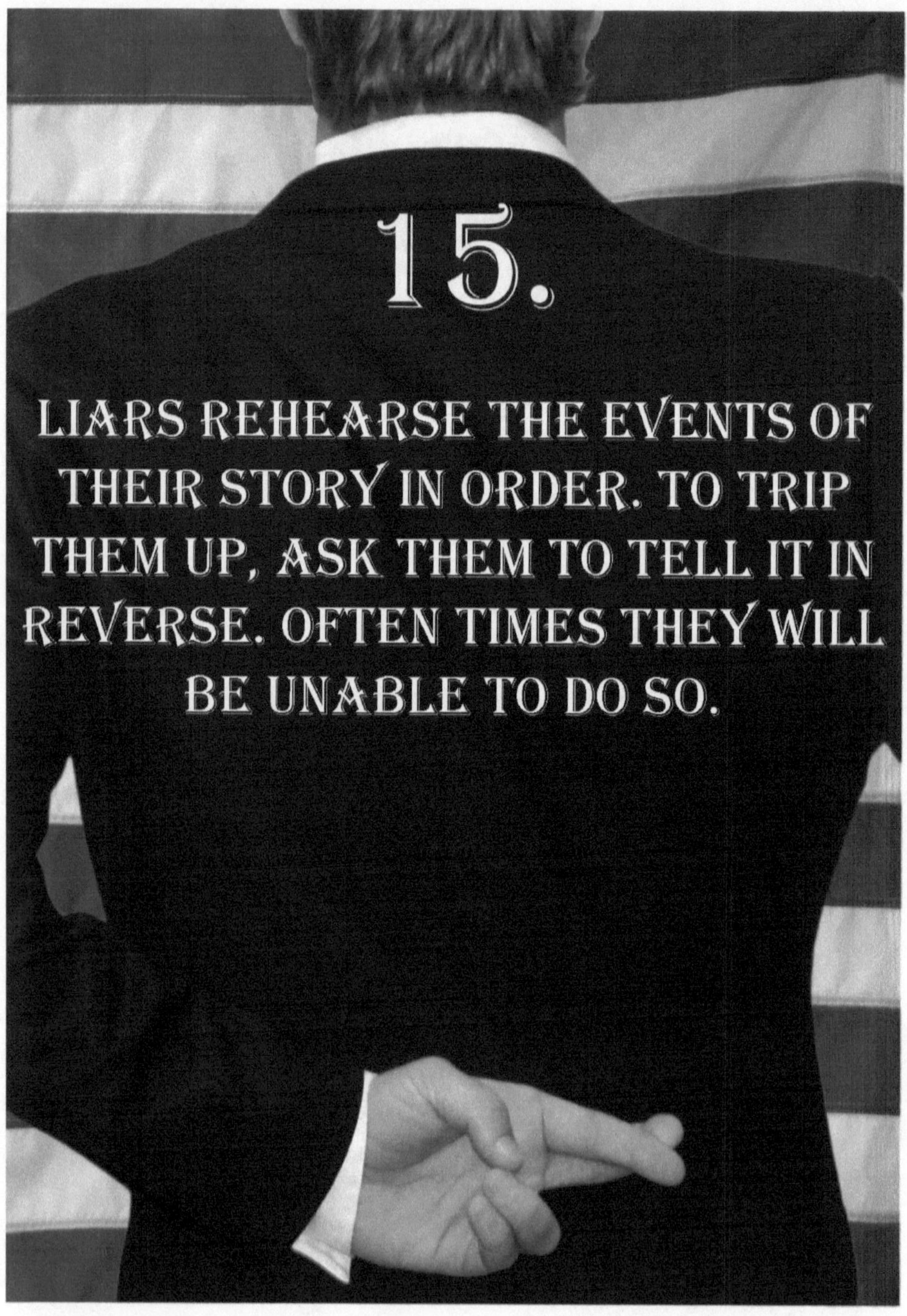
15.
LIARS REHEARSE THE EVENTS OF THEIR STORY IN ORDER. TO TRIP THEM UP, ASK THEM TO TELL IT IN REVERSE. OFTEN TIMES THEY WILL BE UNABLE TO DO SO.

Deception Tip 15 – Rehearsed Stories

Liars rehearse the events of their story in order. To trip them up, ask them to tell it in reverse. Often times they will be unable to do so.

Lying requires a lot of memory. There are a lot of little facts and details that a liar has to keep straight. One little slip and the entire lie comes crashing down like a house of cards. Due to the complexity of lying, liars tend to rehearse their stories in order. They memorize them in a linear fashion almost like a narrative. First, this happened, then this, et cetera.

Although this seems completely normal, our minds don't work in a linear fashion. When you remember things, do you remember them in the exact order they happened? Of course not. Our memories are always missing bits of information and remembering them later. They are imperfect and therefore don't remember exact sequences of events. So if someone is telling you an exact order based on a memory then, unless it is directions, you better watch out.

Once you've noticed that red flag and are on alert for deception, you can confirm your suspicion by asking the person to tell his or her story in reverse. If it is something that they memorized, then they will be unable to do so. This is because they memorized the story in order. Not in reverse. However, when we remember things, we will be able to reverse the process because it is a real memory.

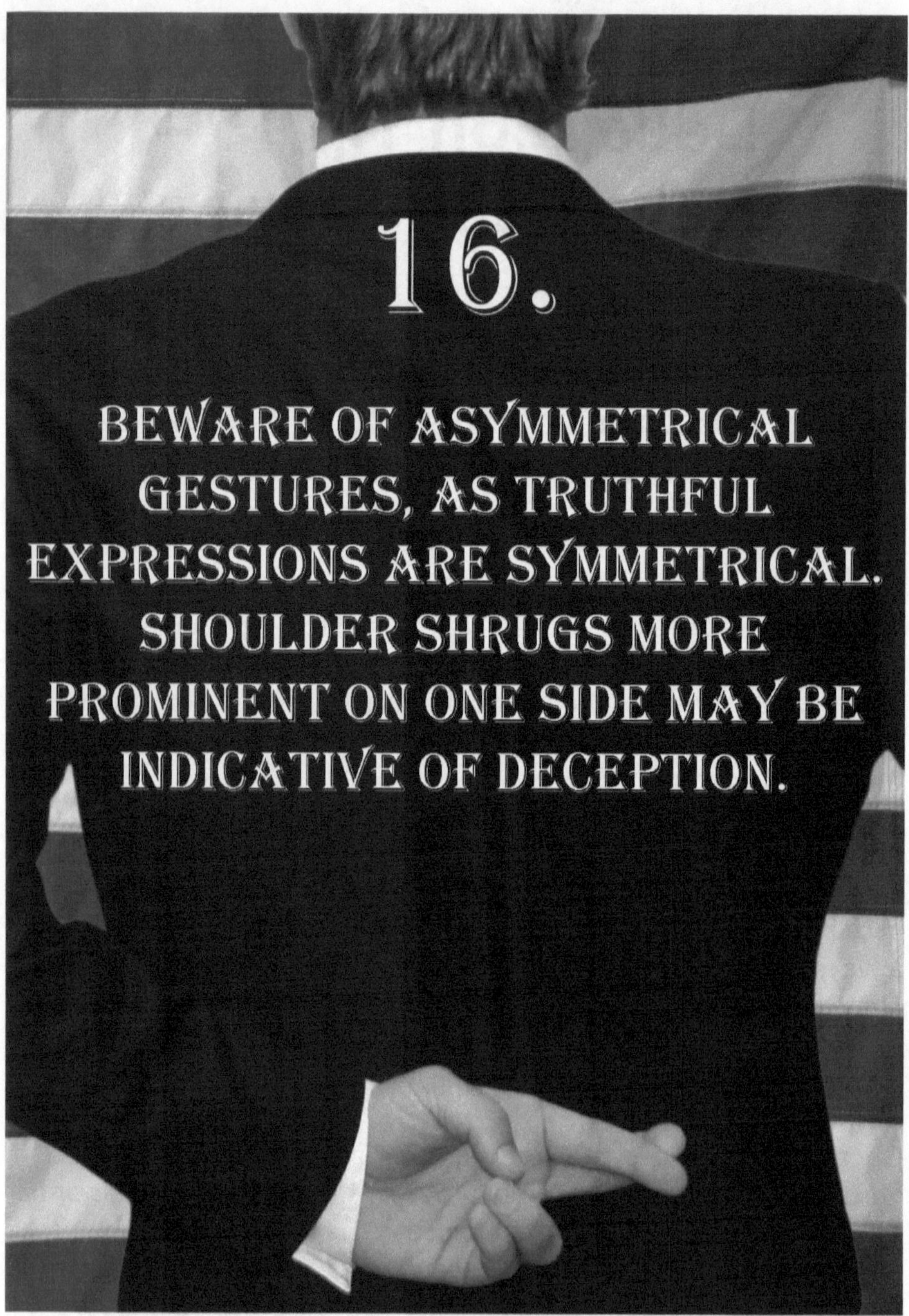
16.
BEWARE OF ASYMMETRICAL
GESTURES, AS TRUTHFUL
EXPRESSIONS ARE SYMMETRICAL.
SHOULDER SHRUGS MORE
PROMINENT ON ONE SIDE MAY BE
INDICATIVE OF DECEPTION.

Deception Tip 16 – Symmetrical Gestures

Beware of asymmetrical gestures, as truthful expressions are symmetrical. Shoulder shrugs more prominent on one side may be indicative of deception.

This tip goes along with a few tips we've had before. Deception Tip 3 Contradictory Behaviors, Deception Tip 12 Simultaneous Gestures, and Deception Tip 14 Symmetrical Expressions. Hopefully, you are beginning to notice a constant theme. Facial expressions, gestures, and speech should all be symmetrical and congruent with each other.

When people more prominently display expressions or gestures on one side of the body compared to the other, then there is a pretty good chance they are being deceptive. Picture the person who turns one hand upward in an "I don't know" type gesture. In addition, think of the person who shrugs one shoulder instead of both of them. Both of these people know more than they are sharing.

Anytime you notice that speech, facial expressions, or gestures are not symmetrical then you need to be on the lookout for lies. That means both if they are not symmetrical within themselves, such as on both sides of the body, or congruent with each other, like speech and body language. In any case, watch for more signs of deception.

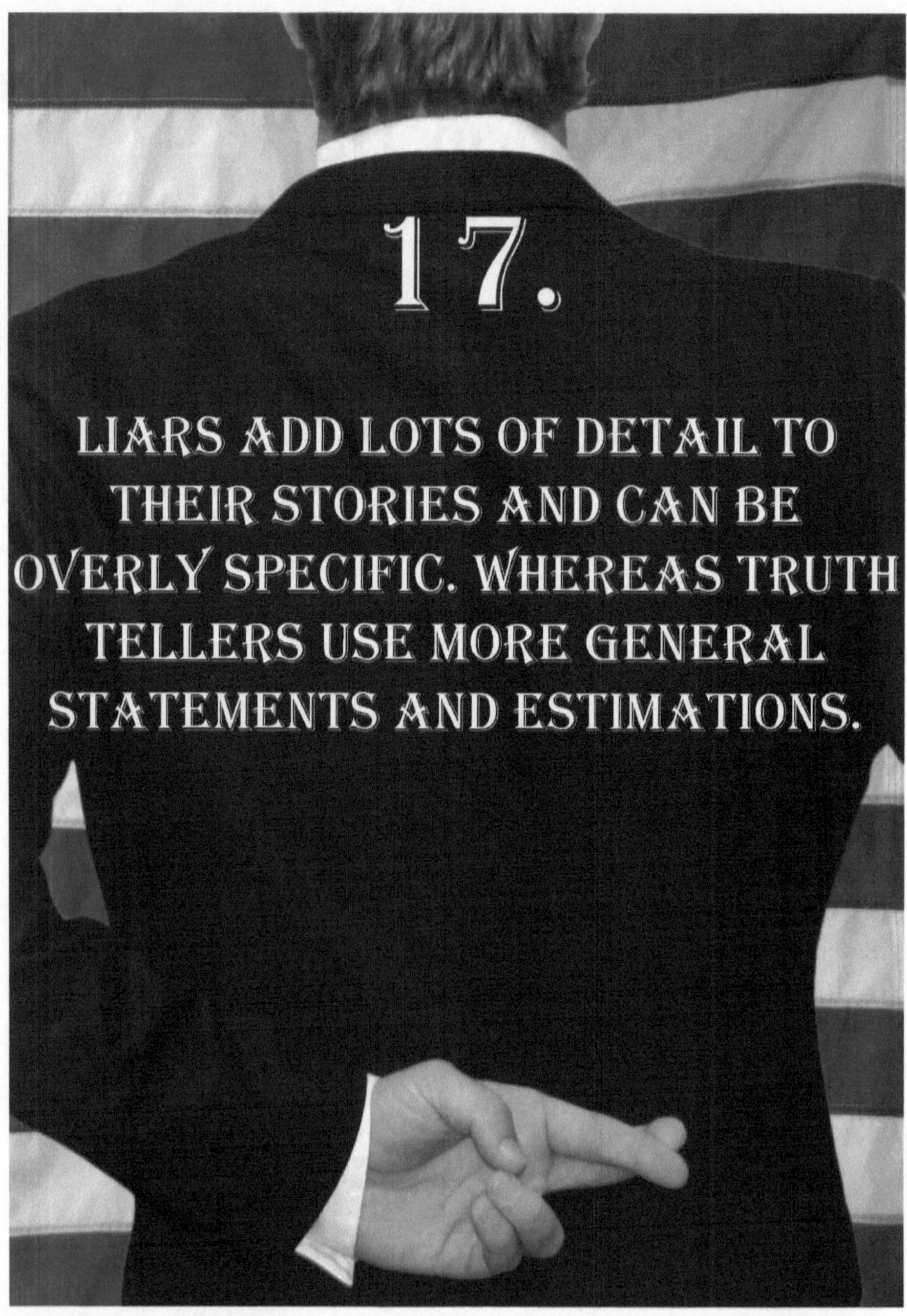
17.
LIARS ADD LOTS OF DETAIL TO THEIR STORIES AND CAN BE OVERLY SPECIFIC. WHEREAS TRUTH TELLERS USE MORE GENERAL STATEMENTS AND ESTIMATIONS.

Deception Tip 17 – Detailed Stories

Liars add lots of detail to their stories and can be overly specific. Whereas truth tellers use more general statements and estimations.

Liars want to be believed. Their primary goal is to convince you that what they are saying is true. They want you to believe the lie. That means they will often use more detail so that they sound more believable. The addition of these added specifics and statistics may make them sound more credible and like they are telling the truth.

However, this is not the case. When people start throwing around details that are that specific, then there is a pretty good chance they are lying. This is because anytime people spout off statistics they usually have them memorized. Further, when people are telling their story of events, it should be coming from memory, not memorization.

As you know, memory is imperfect. We often forget details, times, dates, et cetera. Therefore, when telling a story of what happened, there is a good chance that some details will be left out and some estimation will be used. When people tell their story using lots of detail it is very possible that they have memorized some of the events.

18.

LIARS OFTEN USE DISTANCING LANGUAGE WHEN SPEAKING ABOUT SOMEONE THEY WOULD LIKE TO AVOID BEING ASSOCIATED WITH. EXAMPLE: THAT MAN INSTEAD OF HIS NAME.

Deception Tip 18 – Distancing Language

Liars often use distancing language when speaking about someone they would like to avoid being associated with. Example: That man instead of his name.

Anytime someone is being deceptive, that person will often want to avoid associating with anyone who could make him or her appear guilty. That means they will not want to incriminate themselves through association. Many times, they will be so worried about being associated with a particular person or place that they will use distancing language to try and separate themselves.

This is something to watch for because most people would simply refer to people by their names or titles. In addition, we would refer to places by their names or locations as well. However, when people use distancing language they refer to people and places using more general terms. Often times, the pronouns are preceded by the word 'that'.

Some popular examples would be "that place", "that man/woman", "that person", et cetera. Usually, the liar will have a certain tone of voice that lets you know that he or she is frustrated or irritated. Keep in mind that this doesn't always mean the person is being deceptive. Perhaps he or she is simply upset with the other person and is using distancing language because of that anger.

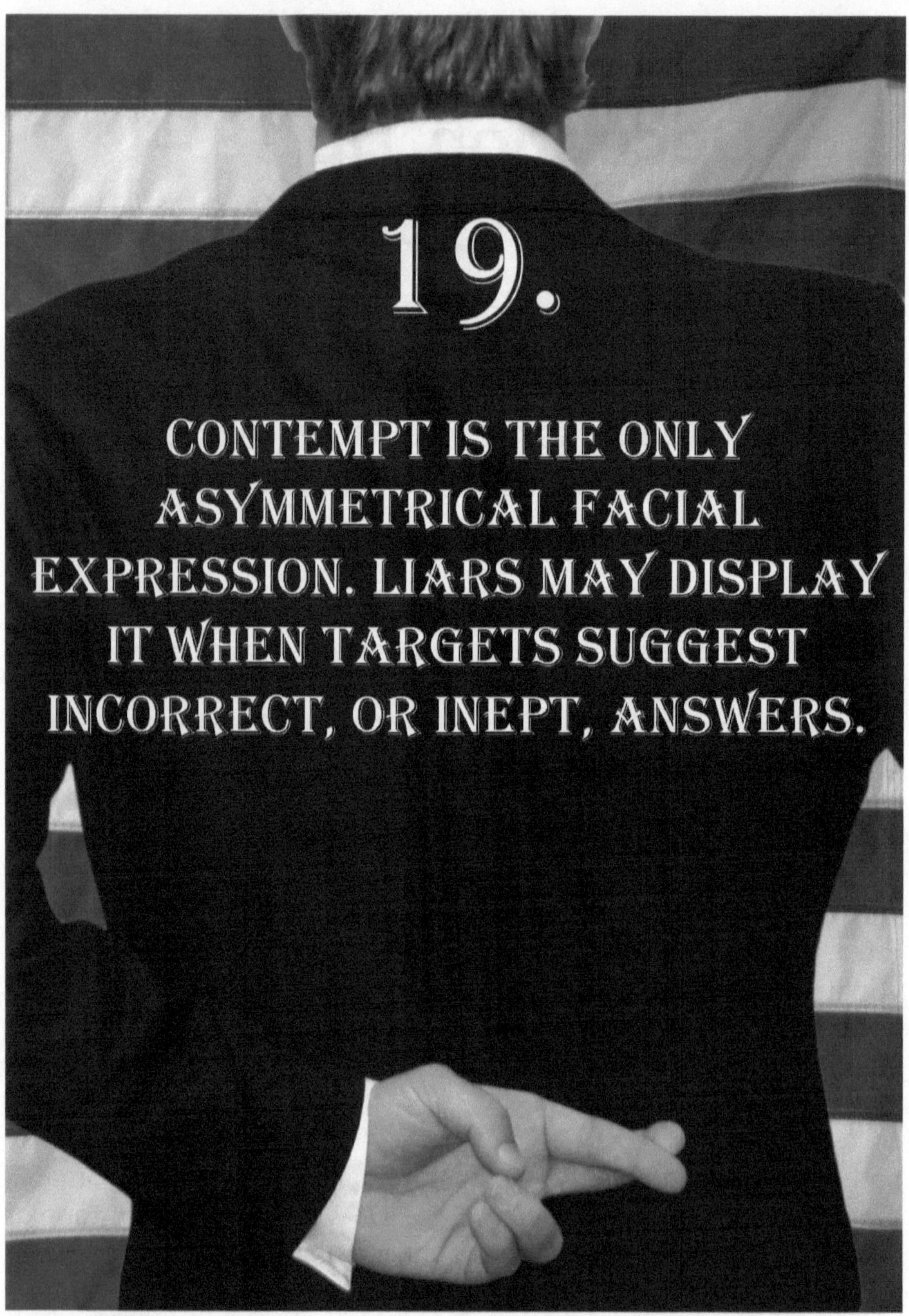

19.

CONTEMPT IS THE ONLY
ASYMMETRICAL FACIAL
EXPRESSION. LIARS MAY DISPLAY
IT WHEN TARGETS SUGGEST
INCORRECT, OR INEPT, ANSWERS.

Deception Tip 19 – Contempt

Contempt is the only asymmetrical facial expression. Liars may display it when targets suggest incorrect, or inept, answers.

Contempt is an unusual emotion. It is displayed when someone thinks they are better than you. They give you a contemptuous look. Noticing contempt can be very helpful when you are trying to find the truth. Usually, this will happen once you have determined that someone is lying or withholding information. You are trying to find out that information and may see contempt when they believe you are incorrect.

Therefore, purposefully suggest some outcomes that are completely off base. Make sure they think you are serious, and if you witness contempt on his or her face then you know that whatever you are suggesting is not correct. Use that to move to other possibilities and narrow down your search. Often times, you can find the truth rather quickly.

Remember that contempt isn't only shown when people are withholding information. It is shown when someone thinks that he or she is better than you. Therefore, when you see it, pay attention to what you were saying or doing when you witnessed the expression. You will learn a lot about what others think of you.

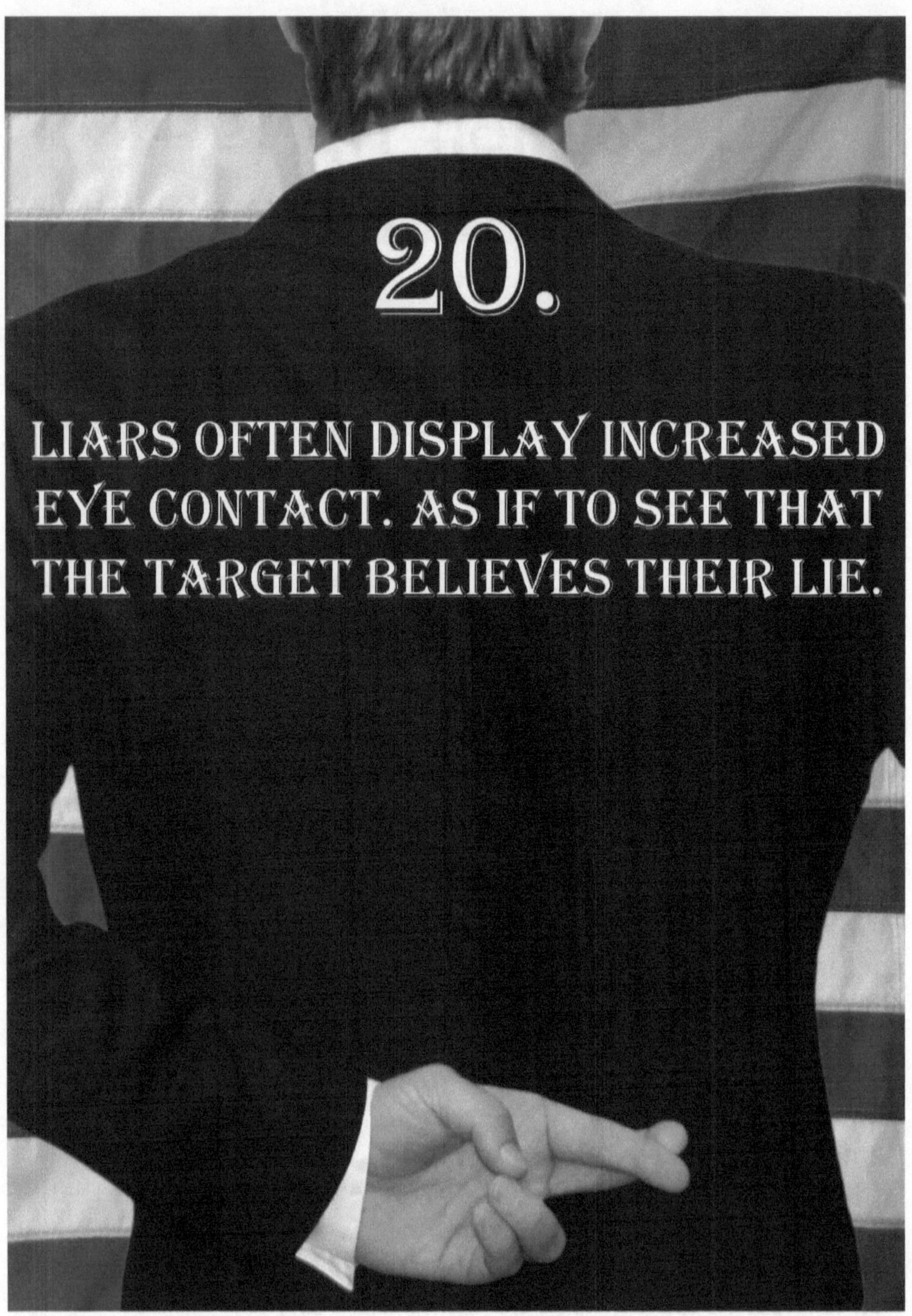
20.
LIARS OFTEN DISPLAY INCREASED
EYE CONTACT. AS IF TO SEE THAT
THE TARGET BELIEVES THEIR LIE.

Deception Tip 20 – Eye Contact

Liars often display increased eye contact. As if to see that the target believes their lie.

Eye contact is something that you're told to maintain in conversation. It is also a sign of politeness and respect when speaking with someone. You are to maintain good eye contact so that you engage your listeners. However, when it comes to lie detection, maintaining good eye contact can hinder your ability.

Think about it. If you are always maintaining good eye contact then you aren't able to see all of the leakage that may be happening on the rest of the body! In addition, how often have you heard someone say "look me in the eye so I know you're telling the truth"? It happens all of the time.

People believe that when you look directly into someone's eyes that you will be better able to tell whether or not that person is lying. However, this is a myth. When you are only focused on the eyes, then you miss everything else. In addition, most liars want to watch you believe their lie. Remember, getting you to believe them is their primary goal. Therefore, they will be happy to look you in the eye when speaking with you.

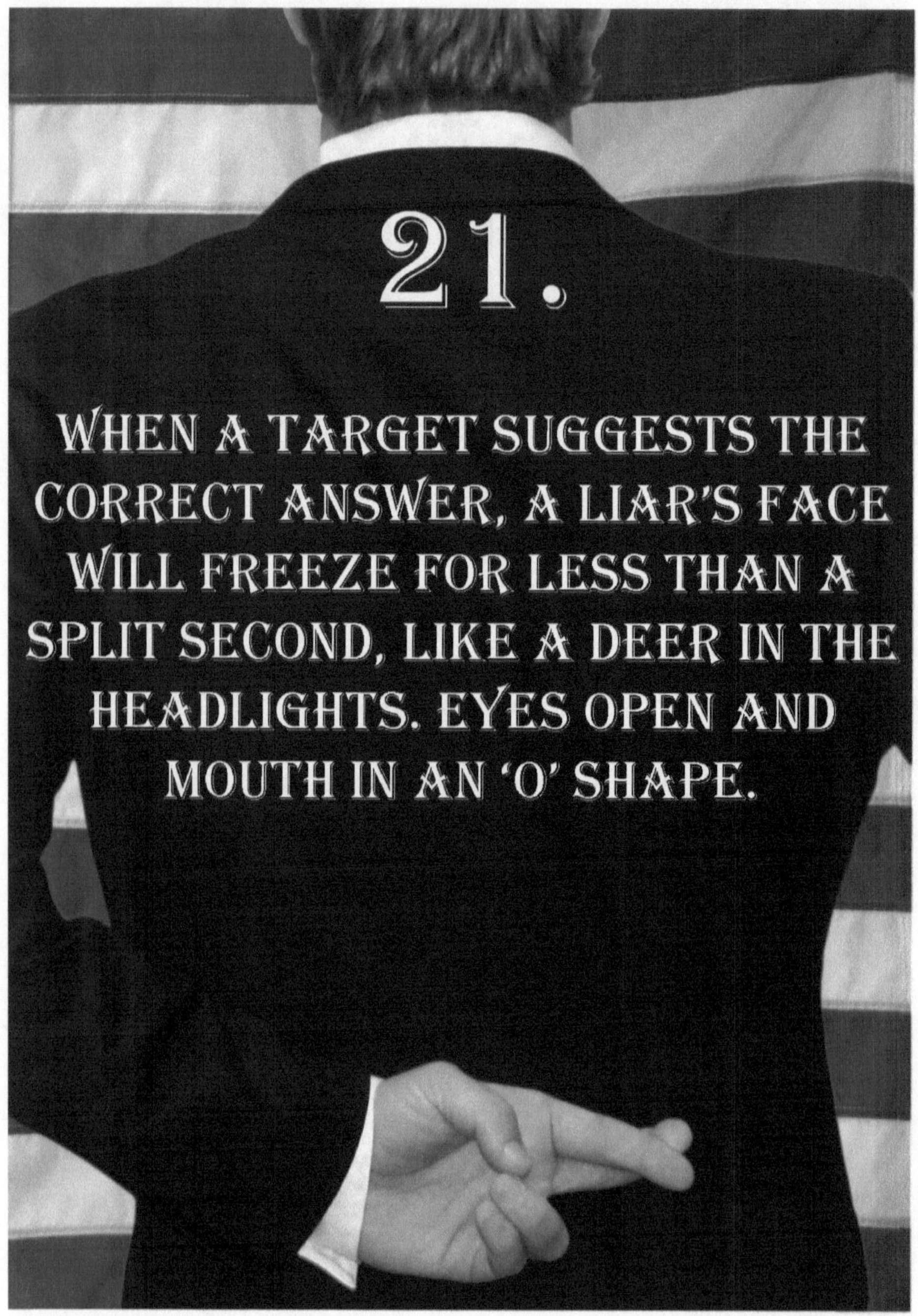
21.

WHEN A TARGET SUGGESTS THE
CORRECT ANSWER, A LIAR'S FACE
WILL FREEZE FOR LESS THAN A
SPLIT SECOND, LIKE A DEER IN THE
HEADLIGHTS. EYES OPEN AND
MOUTH IN AN 'O' SHAPE.

Deception Tip 21 – Suggesting Answers

When a target suggests the correct answer, a liar's face will freeze for less than a split second, like a deer in the headlights. Eyes open and mouth in an 'O' shape.

This is a great tactic that you can use when you know that someone is hiding something from you. It is more of a direct interrogation technique than a casual conversation. In addition, it also helps to know some of the possible truths that they might be hiding. Like where they hid your keys, for example.

At this point, you have already established that someone is being deceptive. You've caught them in their lie. Now you are working to reveal the truth. Chances are that the liar is being uncooperative so you have started to use guessing questions to find out what might be happening.

Pay close attention to his or her body language as you suggest possible answers. You may witness contempt if you start to get way off base. That can tell you that you need to change tactics. Once you start getting closer to the right answer you'll see the anxiety and nervousness start to show. Then, if you happen to guess the correct answer, the liar may freeze in a split second of shock and awe.

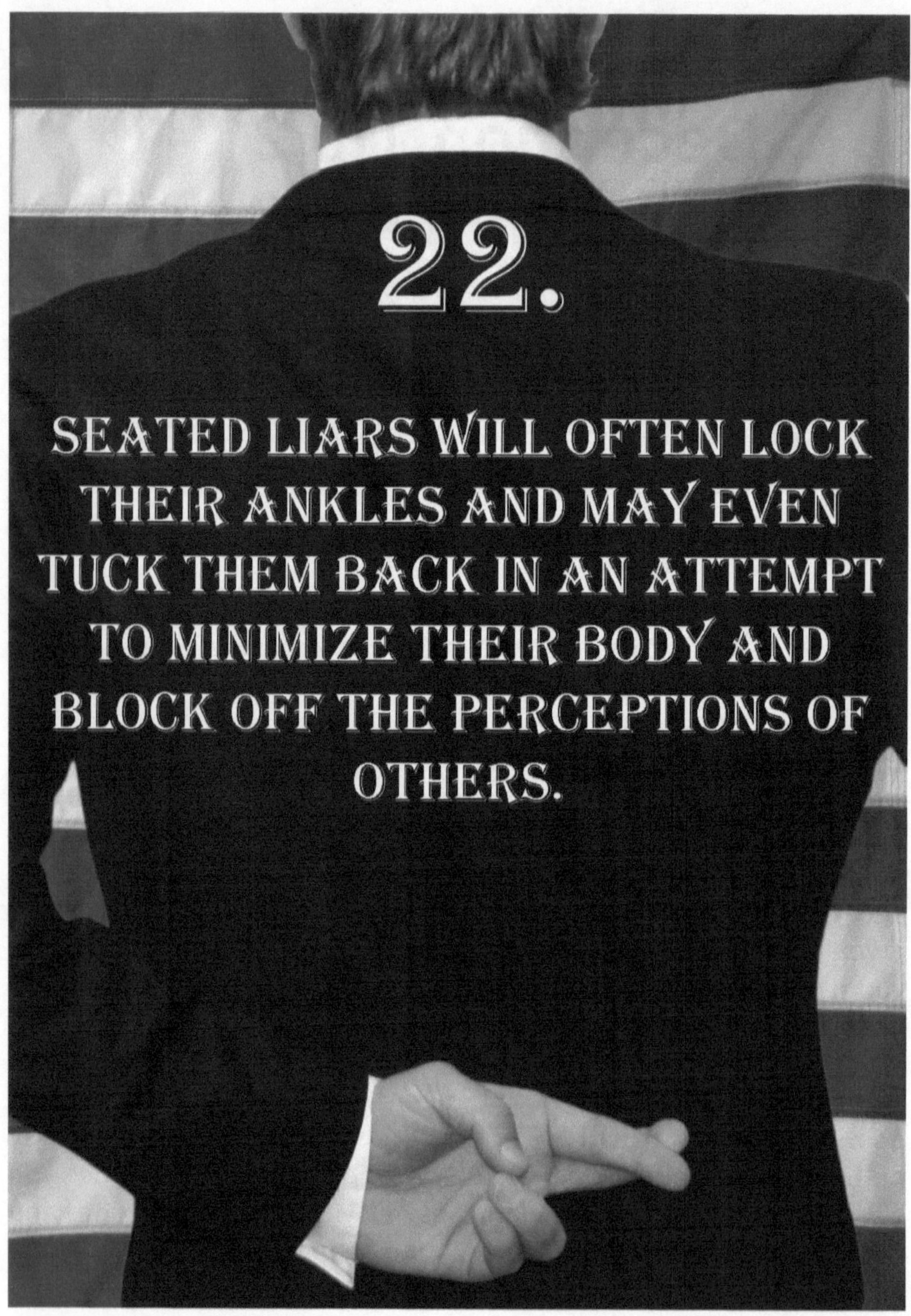
22.

SEATED LIARS WILL OFTEN LOCK
THEIR ANKLES AND MAY EVEN
TUCK THEM BACK IN AN ATTEMPT
TO MINIMIZE THEIR BODY AND
BLOCK OFF THE PERCEPTIONS OF
OTHERS.

Deception Tip 22 – Locked Ankles

Seated liars will often lock their ankles and may even tuck them back in an attempt to minimize their body and block off the perceptions of others.

This behavior is a variation of Deception Tip 1 Folding Arms. However, instead of folding the arms, the liar is folding his or her legs. This is a withholding gesture that signifies that a person is withdrawing from the conversation. It could also be that the person minimizing his or her body language to prevent people from seeing the leakage.

As stated in the tip, this happens with seated liars. A person will lock his or her ankles together almost to pull them apart. This is done to release some stress and tension. You'll usually see this behavior in college seminar classrooms or at business conferences. These are places where people are often frustrated that they have to be stuck there for the time period.

In addition, these people may tuck their feet back under the chair while keeping their ankles locked. This signifies withdrawing from the situation and shows that they are no longer engaged in whatever is going on. Watch for this behavior. If you are speaking then you may want to switch gears to re-engage your audience.

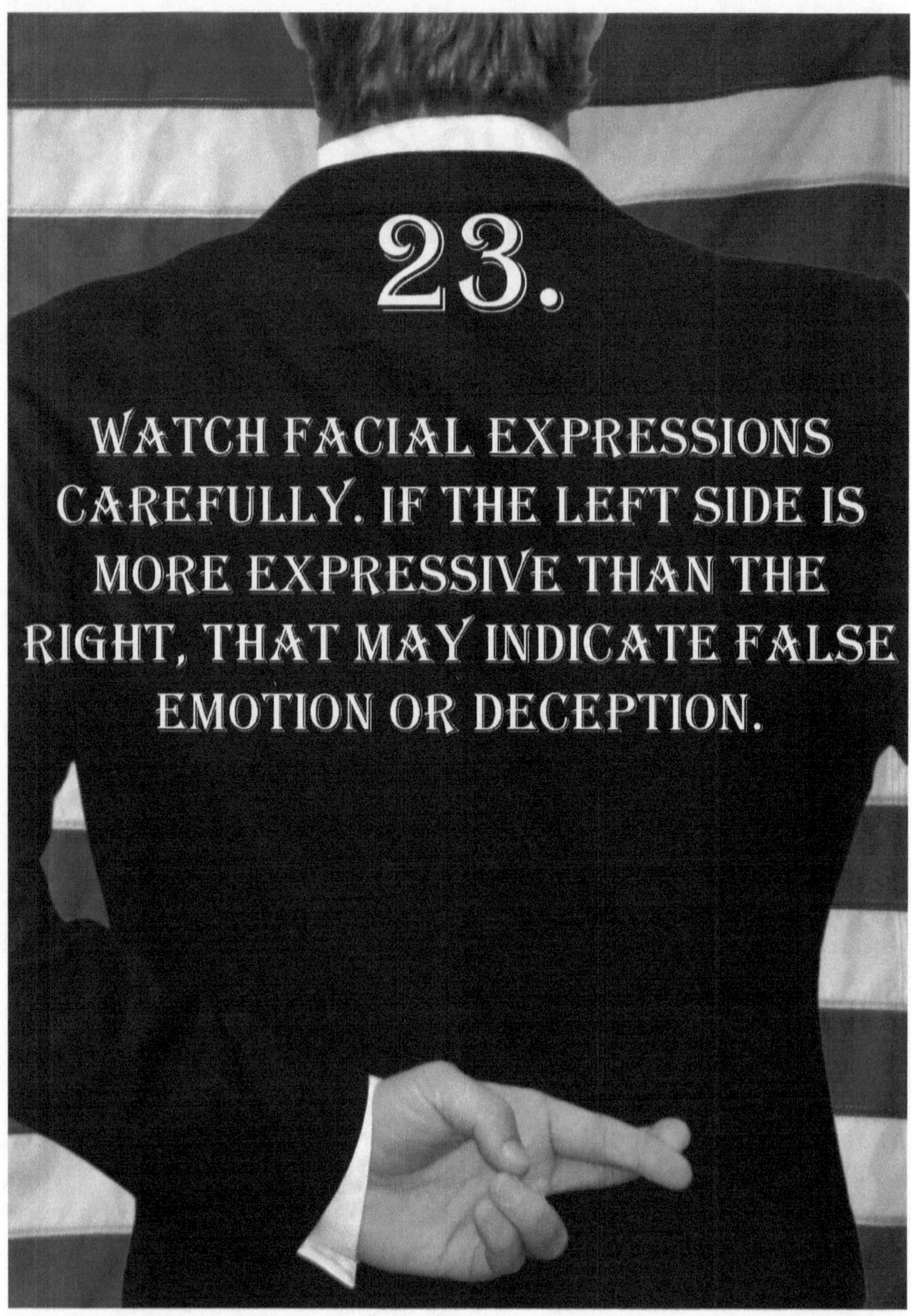
23.

WATCH FACIAL EXPRESSIONS CAREFULLY. IF THE LEFT SIDE IS MORE EXPRESSIVE THAN THE RIGHT, THAT MAY INDICATE FALSE EMOTION OR DECEPTION.

Deception Tip 23 – Left Side

Watch facial expressions carefully. If the left side is more expressive than the right, that may indicate false emotion or deception.

In Deception Tip 14 Symmetrical Expressions, I brought up that each side of the brain controls the opposite side of the body. This means that the cerebral hemispheres are contra-laterally related to the body. Therefore, the fact that the left side of the face is more expressive in false emotions means that the right side of the brain is more active in deception.

This makes sense if you reason with the popular belief that the right brain is more artistic and creative where the left brain is more logical and orderly. The right side of the brain has the creativity to come up with the lies, whereas the left side of the brain wouldn't like to tell lies because it wants to follow the rules.

Pay attention to the facial expressions when people are speaking. The most common one to watch for is smiling. Other expressions will happen so quickly that you may miss them entirely. Also, remember that contempt is asymmetrical and it will most likely happen more on the right side of the face than the left.

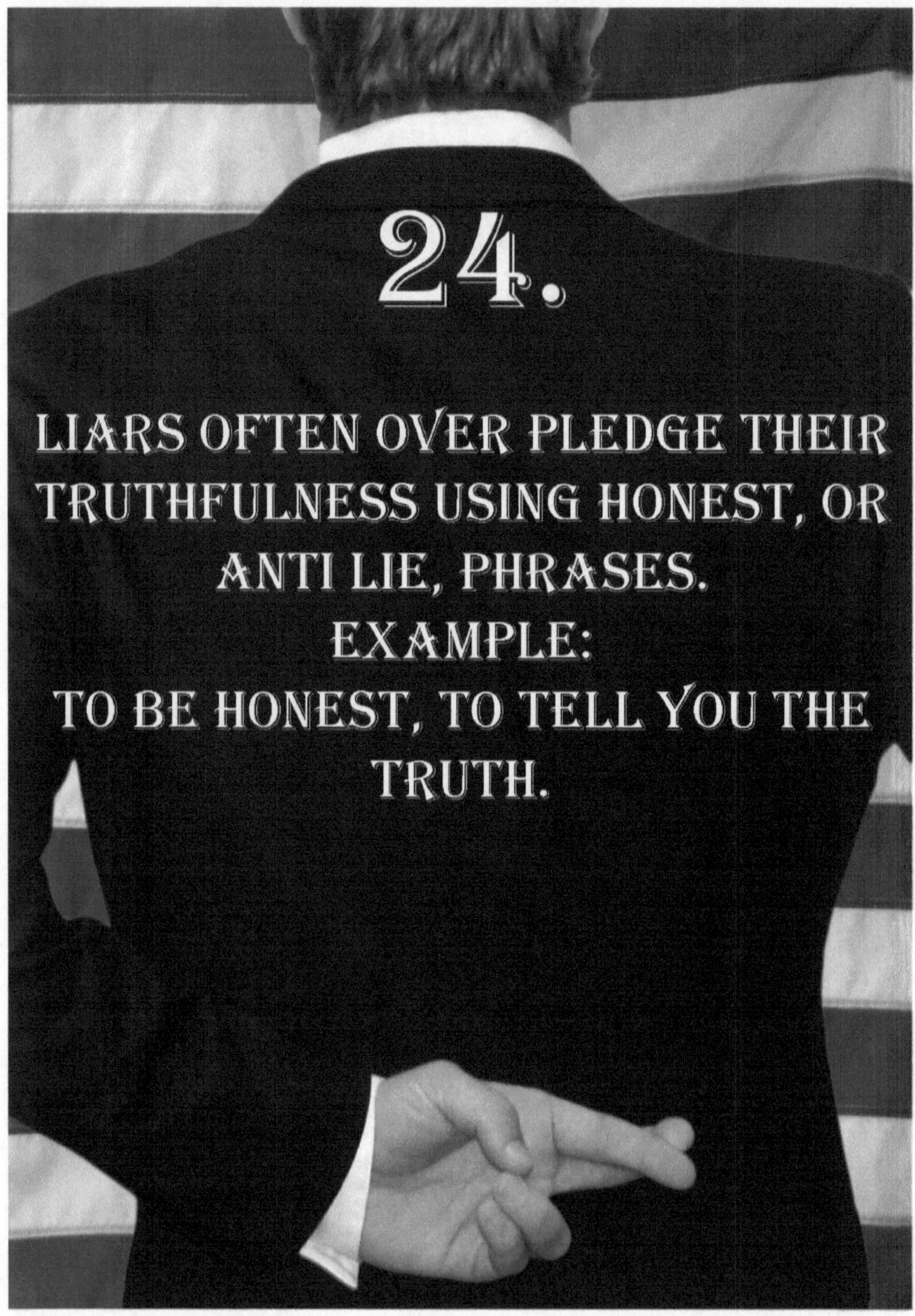
24.

LIARS OFTEN OVER PLEDGE THEIR
TRUTHFULNESS USING HONEST, OR
ANTI LIE, PHRASES.
EXAMPLE:
TO BE HONEST, TO TELL YOU THE
TRUTH.

Deception Tip 24 – Pledging Truthfulness

Liars often over pledge their truthfulness using honest, or anti lie, phrases. Example: To be honest, To tell you the truth.

Liars want to be believed and they love to say things that make them sound more truthful. These things can include separating contractions as mentioned in Deception Tip 5 and using lots of detail as mentioned in Deception Tip 17. In addition to that, they may also use anti-lie statements to sound more believable.

You hear these statements all the time. People typically use them before they are about to express their opinion on a matter. In addition, people like to use them before stating things that sound like facts. However, generally, it is merely their opinion once again.

Some examples of these statements are: "to be honest...", "to tell the truth...", and "I'm not gonna lie...". As you can see, they all sound like they start a sentence. Pay attention to the conversations you have with those around you. Odds are, you are going to start noticing these statements. When you do, listen for what comes next and use what you've learned to determine whether or not it's true.

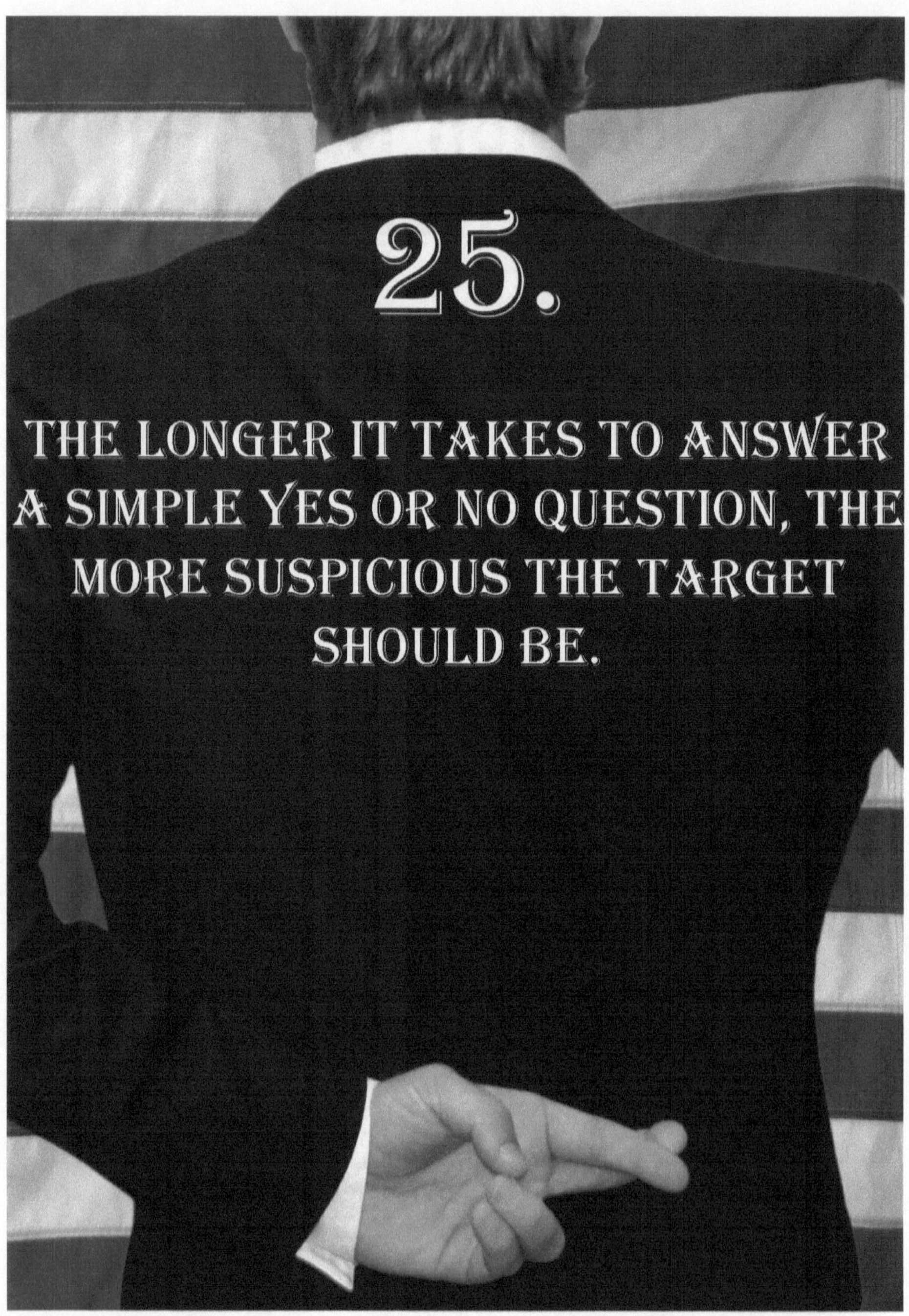
25.

THE LONGER IT TAKES TO ANSWER
A SIMPLE YES OR NO QUESTION, THE
MORE SUSPICIOUS THE TARGET
SHOULD BE.

Deception Tip 25 – Yes Or No

The longer it takes to answer a simple yes or no question, the more suspicious the target should be.

This is pretty straightforward. If I ask you a yes or no question then the best answer to that question is going to be "yes" or "no". That means it is very simple. It isn't an essay question. The answer is either "yes" or "no". Therefore, the next time you ask a yes or no question, keep that in mind when you listen for the answer.

In Deception Tip 10 Quick Answers, you learned about how people may answer quickly and then delay their explanation to give them a little more time to think about their response. This is pretty similar. However, generally, when someone asks a yes or no question, there shouldn't be an explanation. The answer should be either "yes" or "no", it's that simple.

With that in mind, the longer it takes for someone to answer a simple yes or no question, the more suspicious you should be. Remember, as long as the question was simple, then the answer should have been very easy. They only have two options: "Yes" or "No".

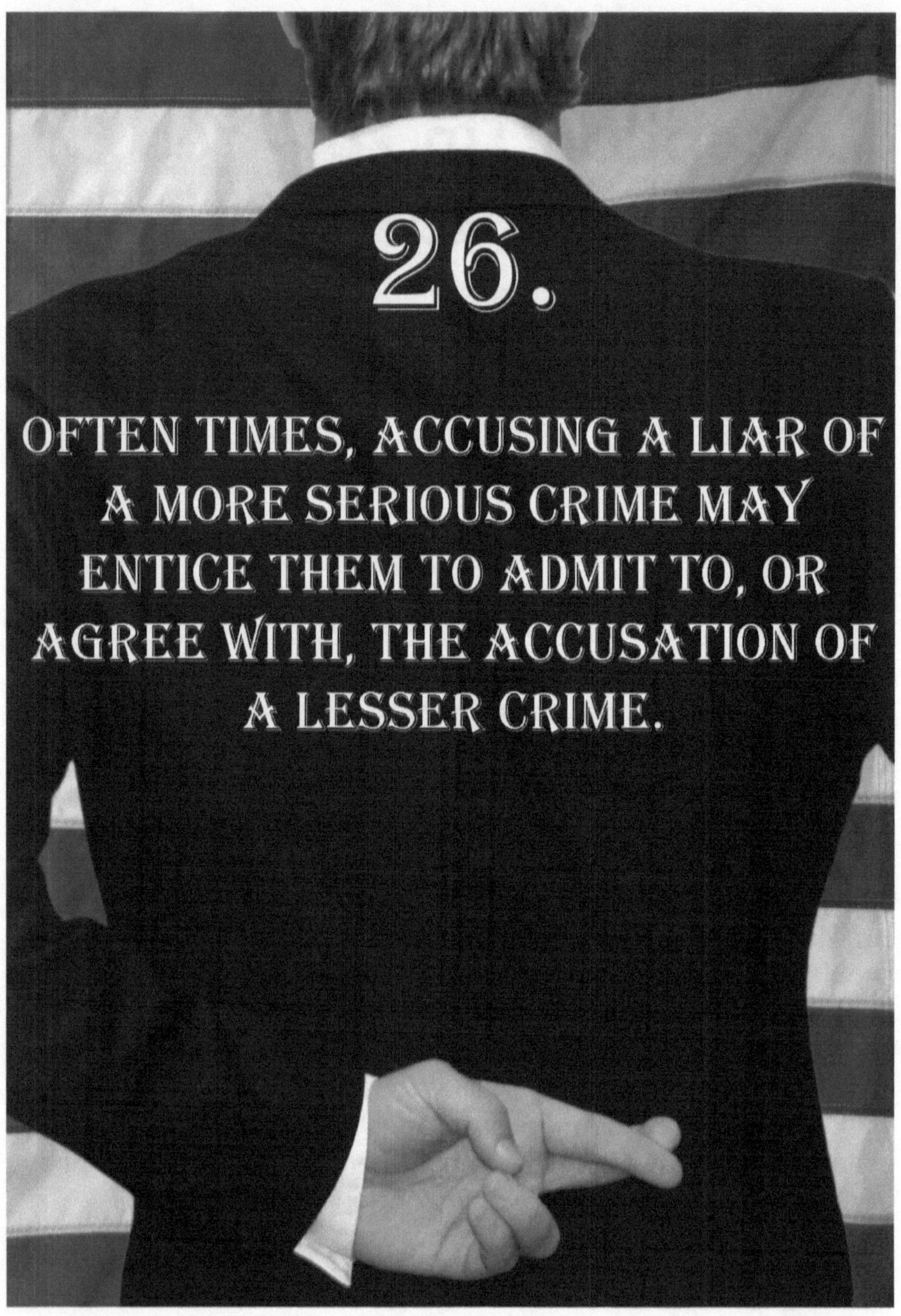
26.

OFTEN TIMES, ACCUSING A LIAR OF
A MORE SERIOUS CRIME MAY
ENTICE THEM TO ADMIT TO, OR
AGREE WITH, THE ACCUSATION OF
A LESSER CRIME.

Deception Tip 26 – Accusing Liars

Often times, accusing a liar of a more serious crime may entice them to admit to, or agree with, the accusation of a lesser crime.

One of the main reasons people tell a lie is to get out of something. They do not want to suffer the consequence of whatever they were involved in so they lie to get out of it. They want to avoid blame. If this is the case with whomever you are speaking with, then you have a huge advantage.

If that person is motivated to avoid the consequence then the best way to get him or her to fess up and accept the consequence is to accuse them of something with a greater consequence. Bluff. If you convince him or her that you are convinced that they did something worse then you will inspire fear in them.

Play it off like you no longer care about whatever it is they were lying about. You're way beyond that petty offense. Now you're throwing the book at them for the larger crime. Chances are that the liar will realize what's about to happen and they will stop you by fessing up to the smaller consequence so that they avoid the larger penalty.

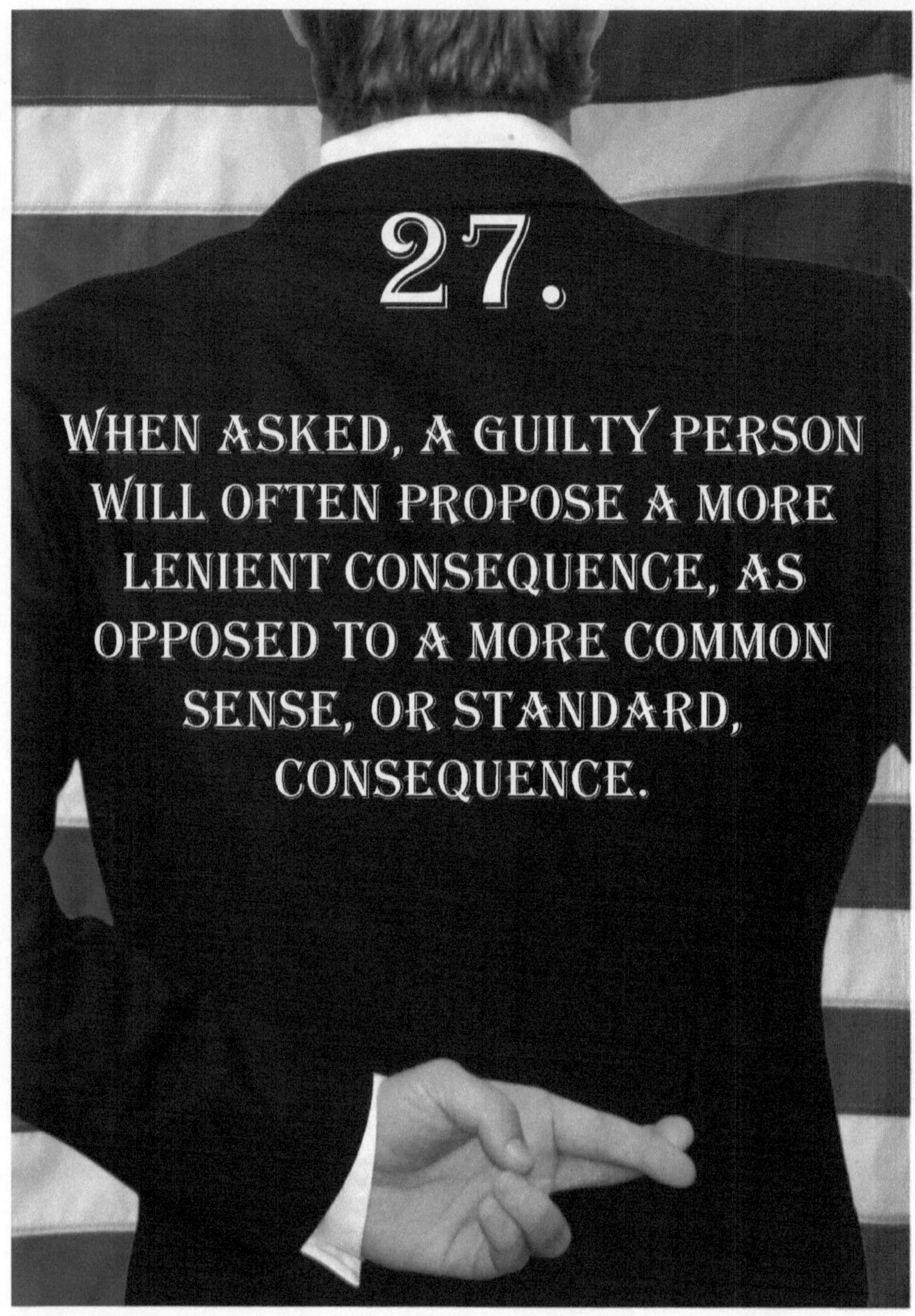
27.
WHEN ASKED, A GUILTY PERSON WILL OFTEN PROPOSE A MORE LENIENT CONSEQUENCE, AS OPPOSED TO A MORE COMMON SENSE, OR STANDARD, CONSEQUENCE.

Deception Tip 27 – Suggesting Consequences

When asked, a guilty person will often propose a more lenient consequence, as opposed to a more common sense, or standard, consequence.

People who are guilty want to experience the least possible consequence if they happen to be caught. After all, one of the main reasons that motivated him or her to tell a lie was to avoid consequences. Therefore, a guilty person would hardly ever suggest a reasonable consequence. This is because they unconsciously know that they might have to endure it.

Use this to your advantage when trying to find the truth. If you've already tried accusing them of a larger crime as mentioned in Deception Tip 26 then you can move on to asking them what type of consequences go with those crimes. You could also use this technique before you start accusing them of larger crimes so that they understand the consequences.

Either way, liars are motivated to avoid consequences. Therefore, once they know they have been caught in their lie, they will want to get out with as little damage as possible. Thus, if you ask them what they think, guilty people will often propose more lenient consequences, whereas truthful people will generally propose reasonable consequences.

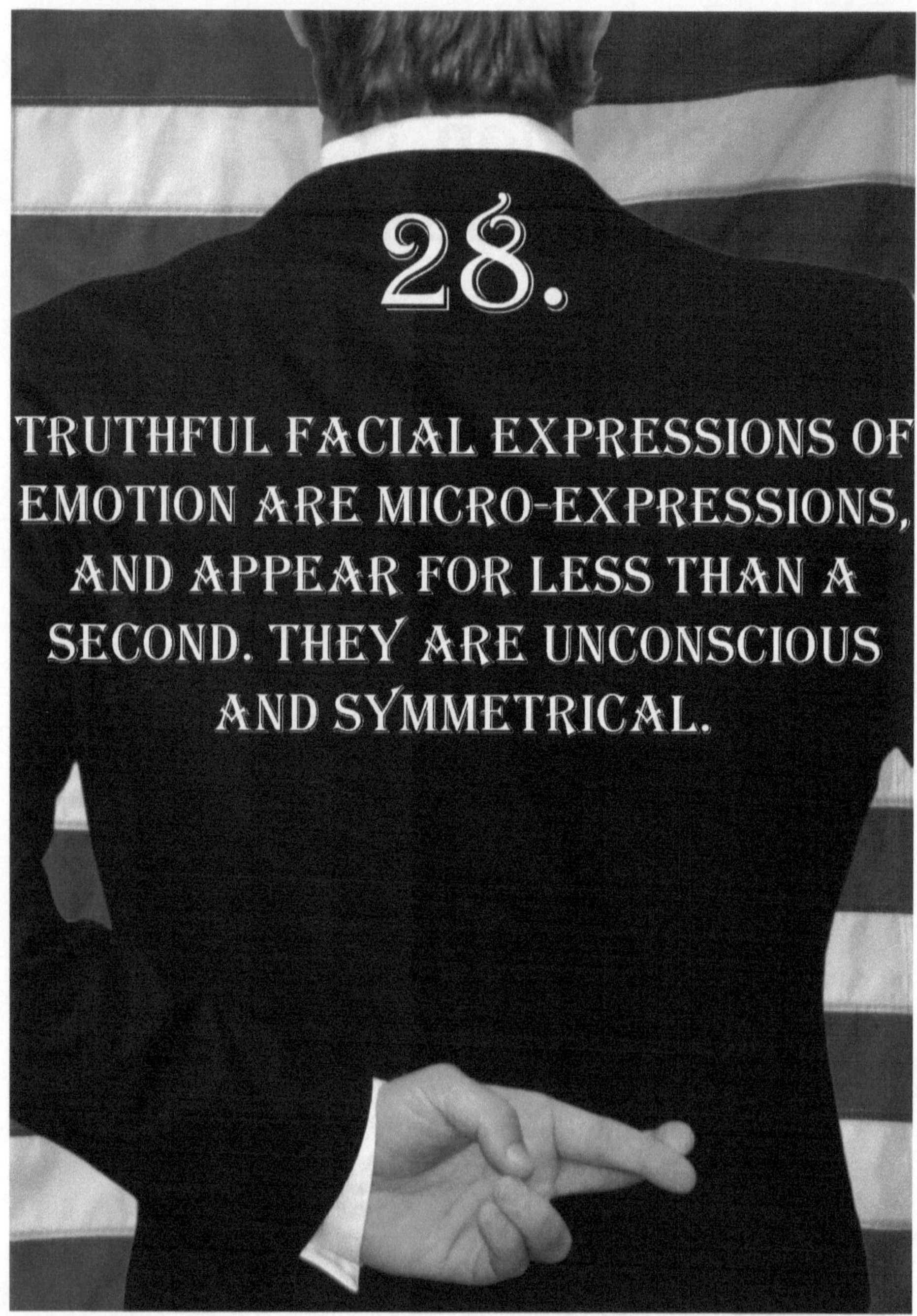
28.
TRUTHFUL FACIAL EXPRESSIONS OF
EMOTION ARE MICRO-EXPRESSIONS,
AND APPEAR FOR LESS THAN A
SECOND. THEY ARE UNCONSCIOUS
AND SYMMETRICAL.

Deception Tip 28 – Micro Expressions

Truthful facial expressions of emotion are micro-expressions, and appear for less than a second. They are unconscious and symmetrical.

Micro expressions can be very difficult for people to understand let alone notice. They happen in a fraction of a second and are usually masked with some other facial expression. Remember that genuine facial expression is symmetrical, with the exception of contempt. Thus, micro expressions are also symmetrical.

Learning how to accurately see and understand micro expressions can take time. However, with training, you can begin to improve your skills in a matter of hours. If you continue to practice, then you'll be able to accurately detect micro expressions and read people's emotions in no time at all.

When a facial expression is truthful, it often appears on the face for less than a second. Smiles, however, can last up to four seconds. In any case, if you see expressions that tend to last more than a second or an extended smile, then there is a good chance that that person is faking it.

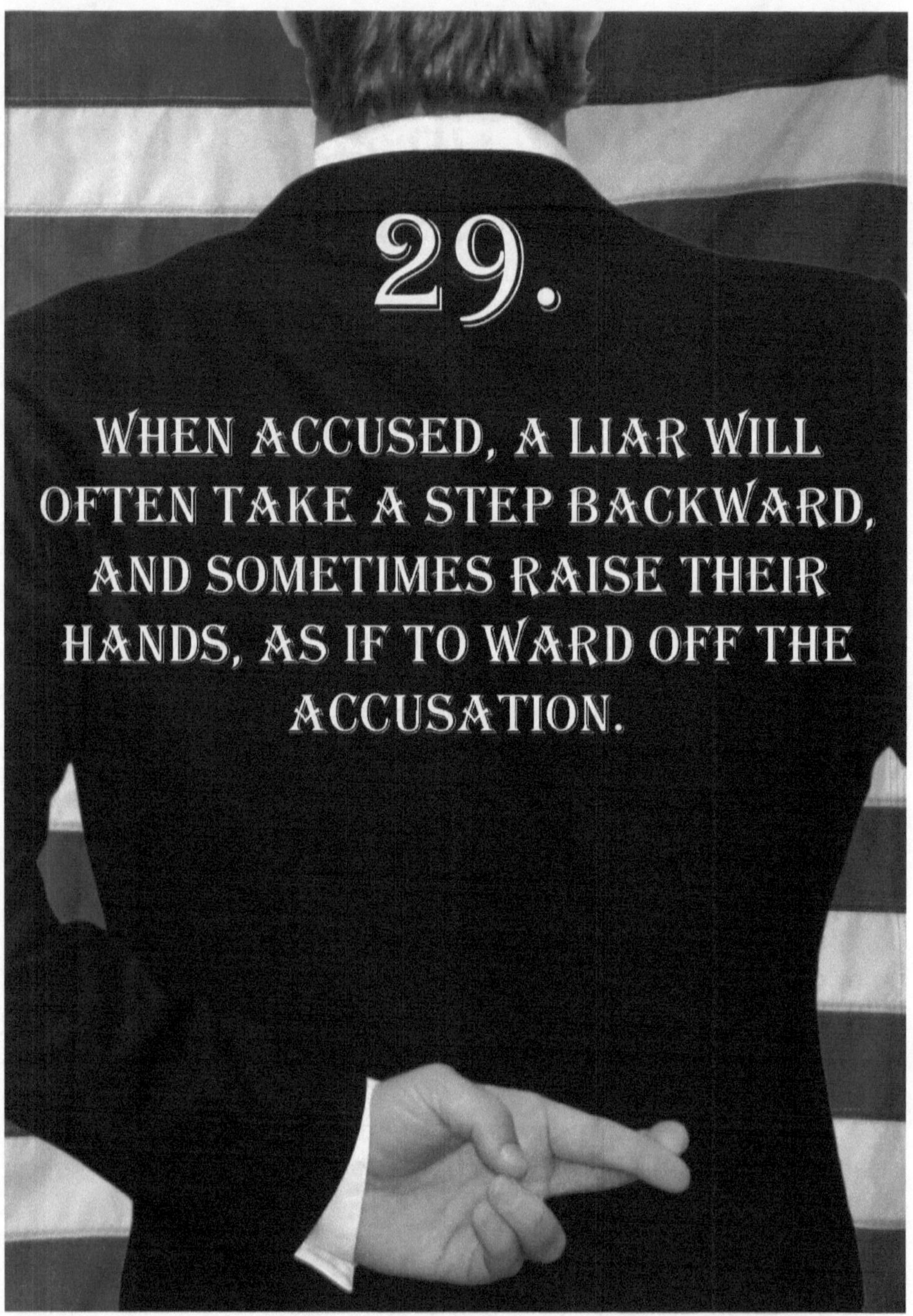

29.

WHEN ACCUSED, A LIAR WILL
OFTEN TAKE A STEP BACKWARD,
AND SOMETIMES RAISE THEIR
HANDS, AS IF TO WARD OFF THE
ACCUSATION.

Deception Tip 29 – Step Backward

When accused, a liar will often take a step backward, and sometimes raise their hands, as if to ward off the accusation.

When someone is lying, he or she can often be very defensive. This can be displayed through any number of forms of bodily leakage such as folding the arms, locking the ankles, tucking back the feet, et cetera. Another behavior that is indicative of defensiveness is stepping backward. The liar may raise his or her hands in accompaniment to this gesture as well.

If you suspect someone of lying and directly accuse them of their lie, then he or she might step backward. Although this seems like a natural response to an accusation, it isn't. If someone was innocently accused, then he or she would most likely engage in the conversation to fight for his or her innocence. However, guilty people often withdraw by stepping back.

In addition, this person may also raise his or her hands to ward off the accusation you threw at them. It is a gesture of innocence. After all, when someone comes in with a gun you put your hands up to show them that you are innocent and not a threat. Therefore, watch for this because I assure you, if you wrongly accuse an innocent person then they will most likely fight back.

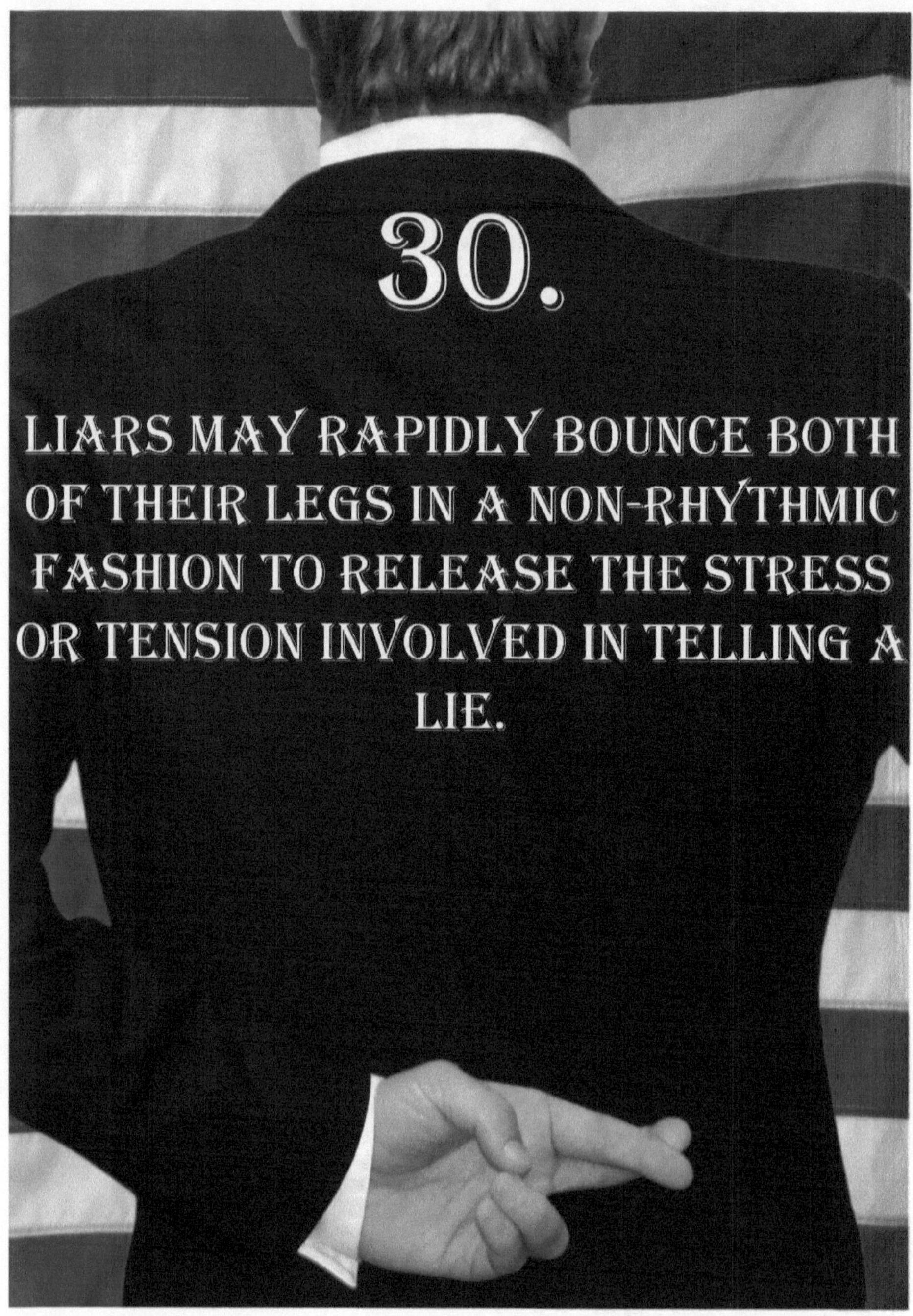
30.

LIARS MAY RAPIDLY BOUNCE BOTH OF THEIR LEGS IN A NON-RHYTHMIC FASHION TO RELEASE THE STRESS OR TENSION INVOLVED IN TELLING A LIE.

Deception Tip 30 – Bounce Both Legs

Liars may rapidly bounce both of their legs in a non-rhythmic fashion to release the stress or tension involved in telling a lie.

As mentioned earlier, when people lie they are under a huge amount of stress and tension. Not only are they worried about telling the lie, but they are also worried about whether or not you will believe the lie. In addition, they are worried about the consequence of whatever they are lying about and the consequence of getting caught lying.

All of this stress and tension can exit the body in a variety of ways. One of these ways is by bouncing the legs up and down. This is more than a normal bounce. It is like a car piston going up and down at a hundred miles an hour. Bing bing bing bing. Often times, you'll see someone bouncing one leg. Then, when things get really serious, both legs will start bouncing.

It is important to note that this behavior is a display of stress and tension. The person is trying to release stress and tension. This doesn't mean that the person is lying. Look around a college classroom on exam day and you'll see several students bouncing their legs beneath the desks.

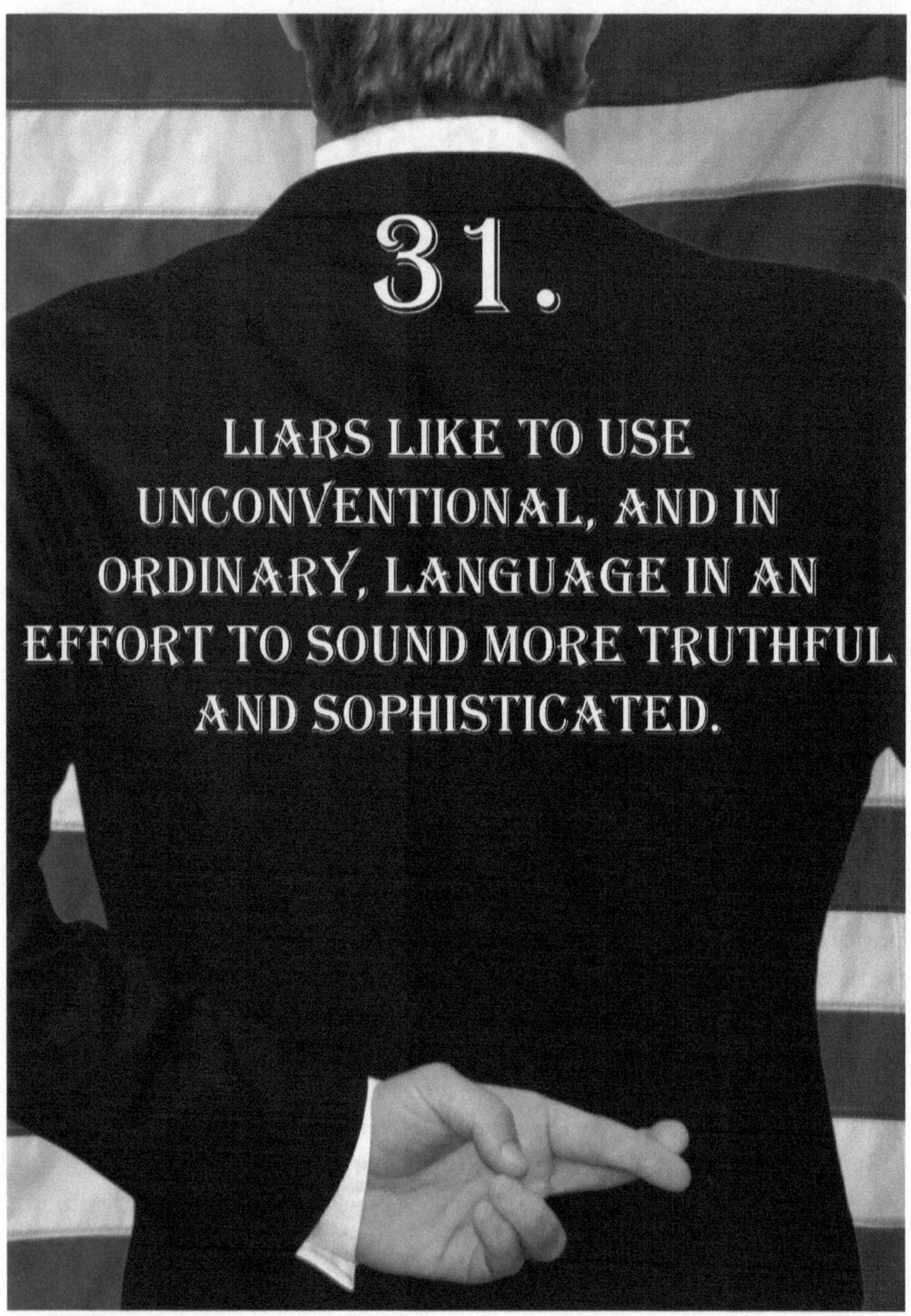
31.

LIARS LIKE TO USE
UNCONVENTIONAL, AND IN
ORDINARY, LANGUAGE IN AN
EFFORT TO SOUND MORE TRUTHFUL
AND SOPHISTICATED.

Deception Tip 31 – Unconventional Language

Liars like to use unconventional, and in ordinary, language in an effort to sound more truthful and sophisticated.

Liars love to sound more educated than they are. That is a lie within the lie they are telling. They believe that if they sound more educated, then that means they are more believable. While this theory may have some merit, it often ends up hurting them more than helping. The reason is because they cannot keep up with the facade.

Remember in Deception Tip 17 Detailed Stories, you learned that liars like to add extra detail and sometimes some statistics in an effort to sound more believable. The trouble is, that once they are questioned about that knowledge they can rarely keep up. This unravels the lie very quickly and is a great way for you to catch liars.

Keep in mind that when people start using inordinacy language that doesn't seem to fit their personality or the context of the situation, that he or she might be lying. Confirm this by pushing a little deeper into the conversation and see how they react. If they can maintain, then maybe they really do know what they are talking about. If not, then you may have caught a liar.

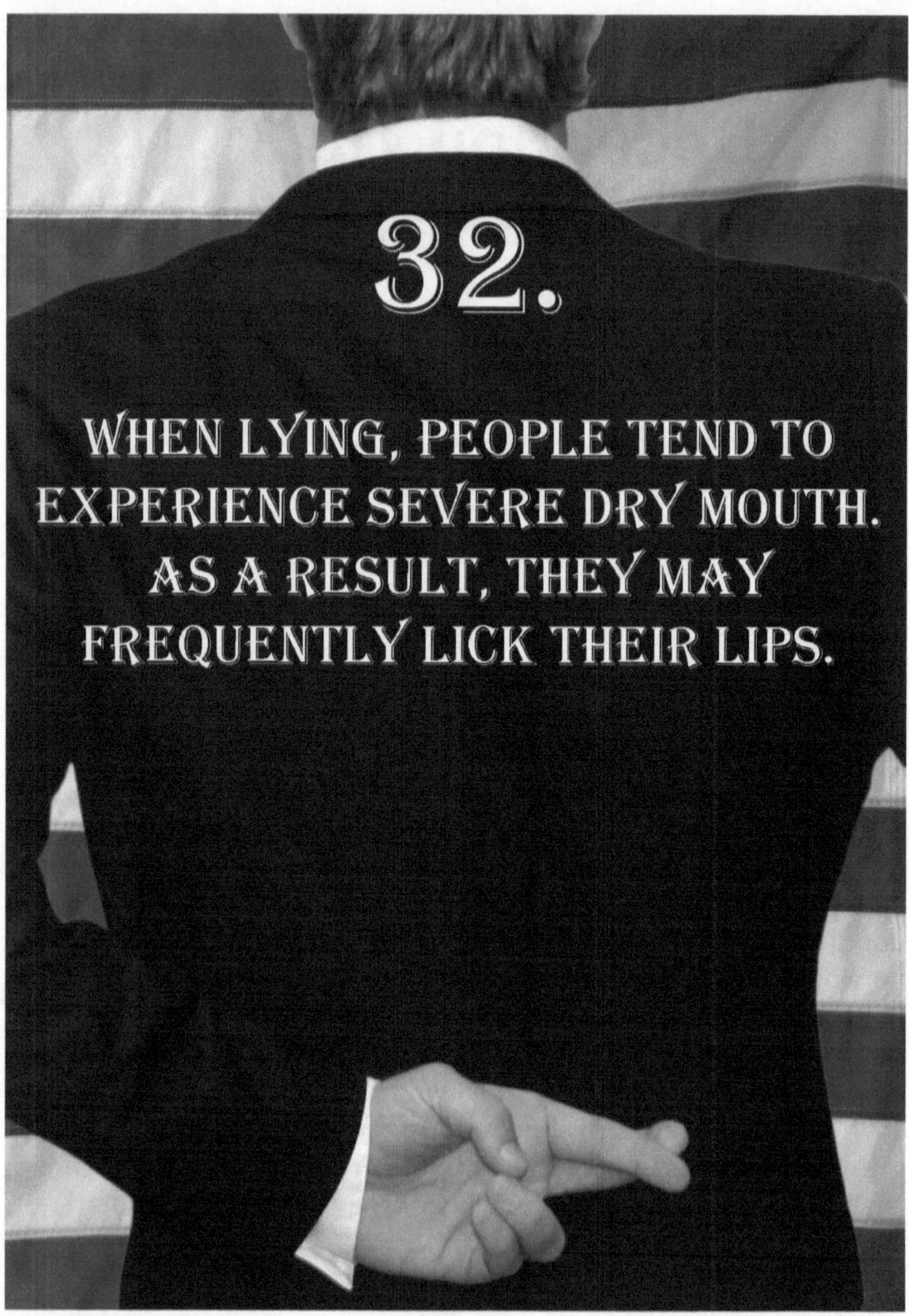
32.
WHEN LYING, PEOPLE TEND TO
EXPERIENCE SEVERE DRY MOUTH.
AS A RESULT, THEY MAY
FREQUENTLY LICK THEIR LIPS.

Deception Tip 32 – Lick Lips

When lying, people tend to experience severe dry mouth. As a result, they may frequently lick their lips.

Dry mouth has many different causes, one of which is stress. As mentioned before, when people lie they are under a tremendous amount of stress. Therefore, it is reasonable to say that his or her mouth may become very dry when telling a lie. This is something for you to watch for and use to help you find the truth.

There are many outward signs of dry mouth. One of the most common is that a person continually sips the glass of water that you may or may not have provided for them. However, this tip is about how liars will continually lick their lips in an effort to combat the dry mouth feeling that they are experiencing.

Keep in mind that there are many different reasons that someone may choose to lick his or her lips. Maybe the lips are very chapped and they need to keep them moist. Therefore, if you see this behavior, take a look at the lips and note their condition. If they appear fine, then look for other potential signs of deception.

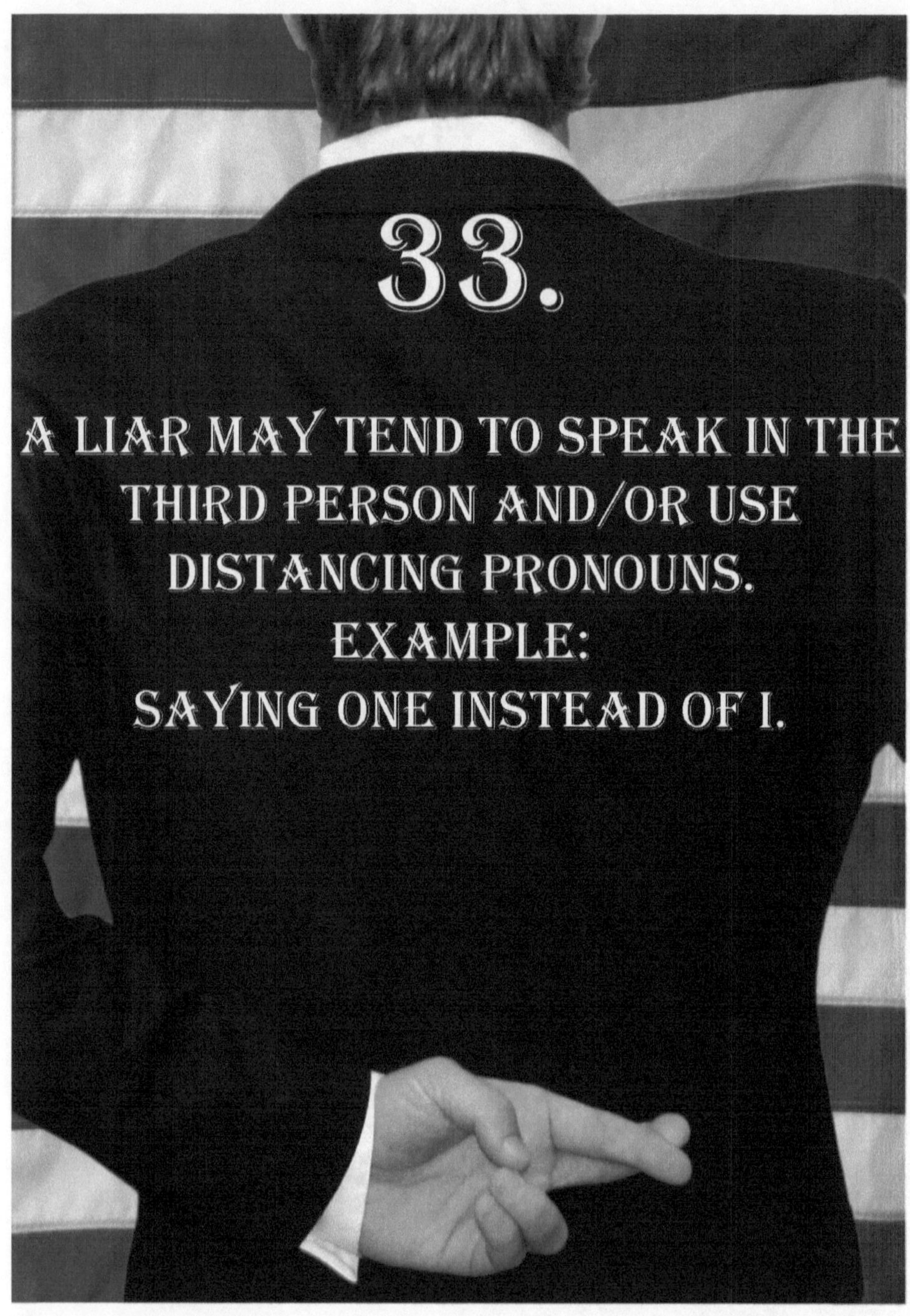
33.
A LIAR MAY TEND TO SPEAK IN THE
THIRD PERSON AND/OR USE
DISTANCING PRONOUNS.
EXAMPLE:
SAYING ONE INSTEAD OF I.

Deception Tip 33 – Third Person

A liar may tend to speak in the third person and/or use distancing pronouns. Example: Saying one instead of I.

When people lie, they do not wish to be associated with whatever it is that might tie them to getting caught. They want to make sure people believe that they are far from that. Therefore, as mentioned in Deception Tip 18, they may use distancing language.

In addition, liars may also speak in the third person as another means of separating themselves from whatever it is they are discussing. They want the target to believe that they are in no way associated with the topic at hand. Using the third person helps accomplish this.

However, when people speak in the third person about themselves, it sounds a little strange. Instead of saying "I would think…" they say "one would think…". It is a little off. Pay attention to this because if the person is using a lot of third person pronouns when it would make more sense to use first person pronouns then something may be going on.

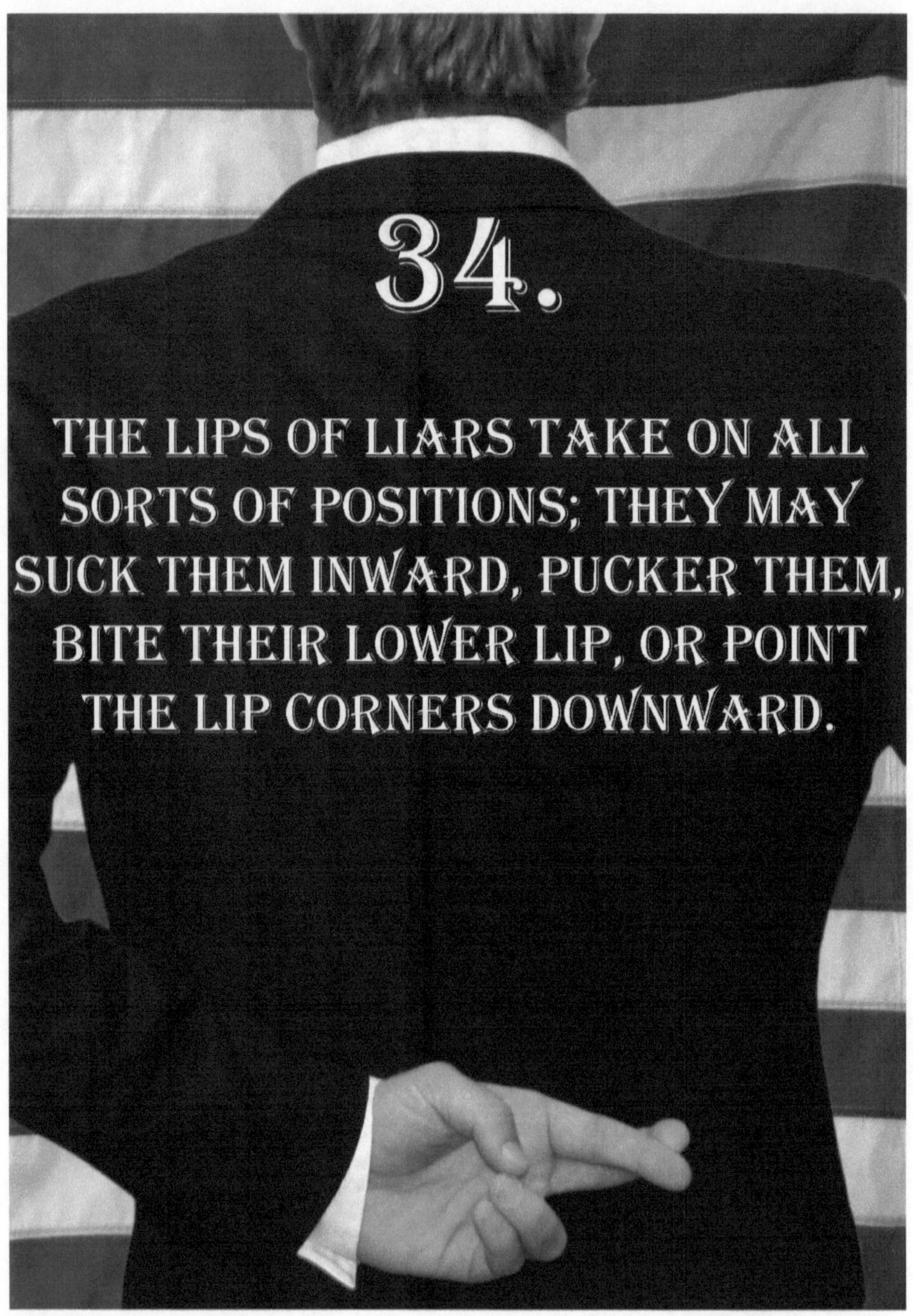

34.

THE LIPS OF LIARS TAKE ON ALL
SORTS OF POSITIONS; THEY MAY
SUCK THEM INWARD, PUCKER THEM,
BITE THEIR LOWER LIP, OR POINT
THE LIP CORNERS DOWNWARD.

Deception Tip 34 – Liar's Lips

The lips of liars take on all sorts of positions; they may suck them inward, pucker them, bite their lower lip, or point the lip corners downward.

When people move their lips like crazy it is usually because they are releasing tension. In addition, toying with the lips can also be a behavior that indicates deep thought. As you know, when people lie they are under a lot of stress and tension. They may also be in some deep thought while they come up with what to say.

As a result, liars may often move their lips into some strange positions. They may suck them inward to try and release some stress or pacify their desire to talk. In addition, they may pucker them in an attempt to think of something more enjoyable. Often times, liars may bite their lower lip while they think of what to say. Another thing they may do is point the lip corners downward, which is almost a micro expression, so watch closely.

There are also several micro expressions that can occur around the lips so pay close attention. If you see anything going on with the lips then start looking for other signs of deceptive behavior. Use your skills to see if you can figure out what's really going on.

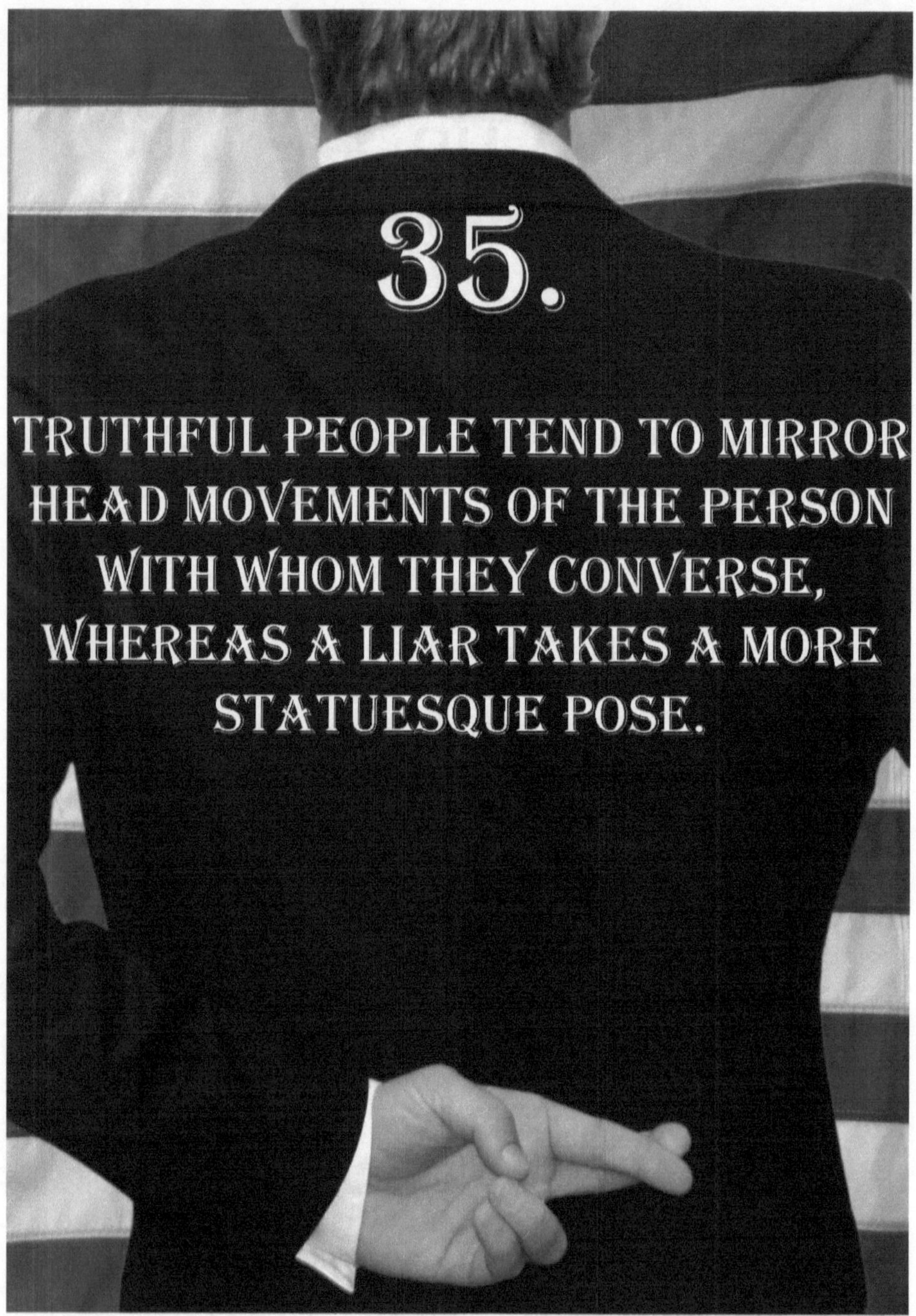
35.

TRUTHFUL PEOPLE TEND TO MIRROR
HEAD MOVEMENTS OF THE PERSON
WITH WHOM THEY CONVERSE,
WHEREAS A LIAR TAKES A MORE
STATUESQUE POSE.

Deception Tip 35 – Mirror Movements

Truthful people tend to mirror head movements of the person with whom they converse, whereas a liar takes a more statuesque pose.

Humans are social creatures. We like to fit in with the people around us. It is something that we are made to do. People always want to make sure they fit in and are not left out. One of the best ways to do that is by copying those around you, by "blending in". It is an honest and natural behavior.

When people are telling the truth, they generally mirror the behaviors of the person leading the conversation. This is especially true with hand to face gestures. Things like touching your nose, rubbing your eye, wiping your lip corners, scratching your whiskers, et cetera. These behaviors are unconscious and copied as a means of unconsciously connecting with one another.

On the other hand, when people are being deceptive, they are thinking about their lie. They are worried and stressed about whether or not they are going to get away with the lie. Therefore, their unconscious mind is occupied with trying to leak the truth. As a result, the natural unconscious mirroring gestures do not occur.

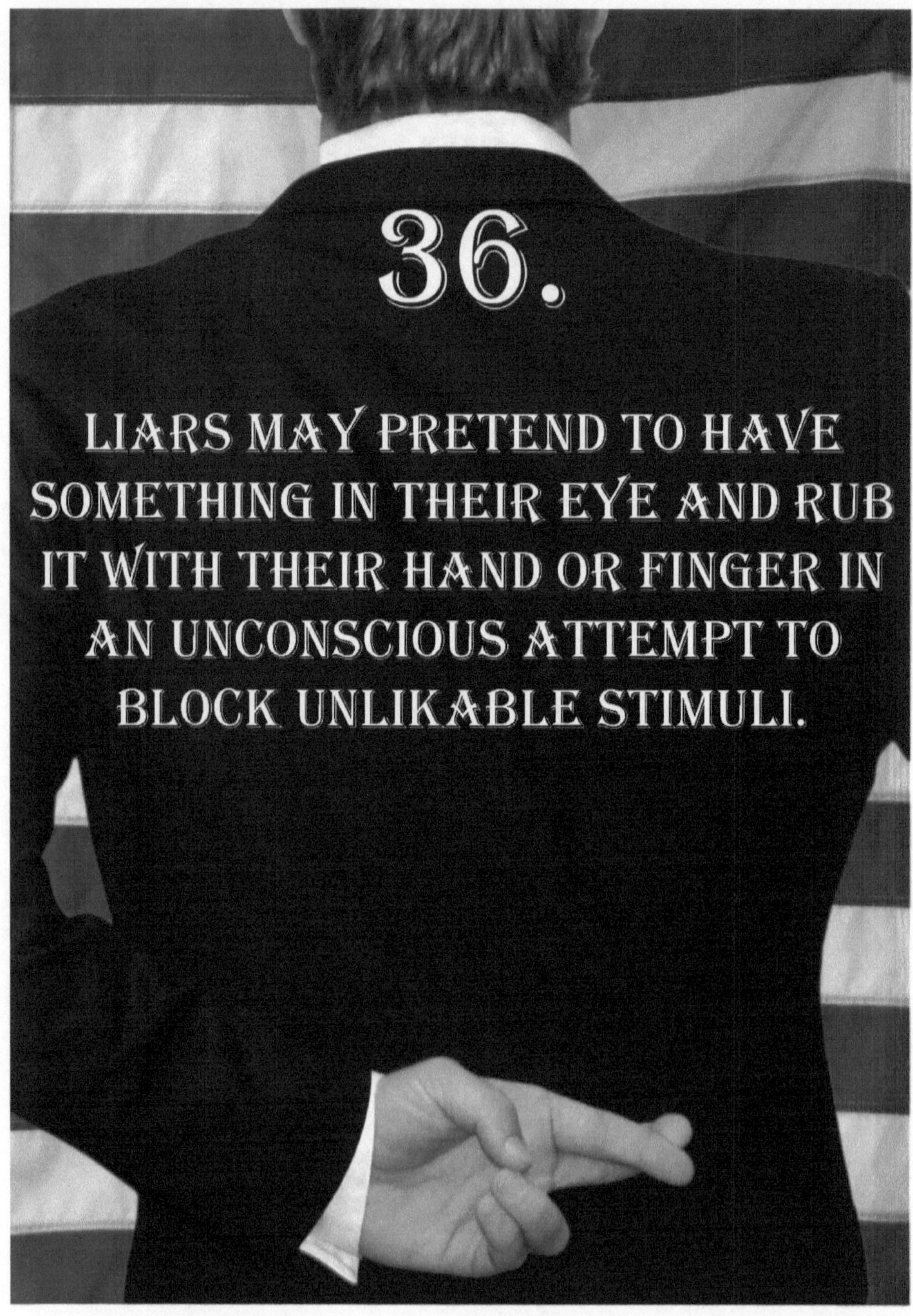

36.
LIARS MAY PRETEND TO HAVE SOMETHING IN THEIR EYE AND RUB IT WITH THEIR HAND OR FINGER IN AN UNCONSCIOUS ATTEMPT TO BLOCK UNLIKABLE STIMULI.

Deception Tip 36 – Rubbing Eyes

Liars may pretend to have something in their eye and rub it with their hand or finger in an unconscious attempt to block unlikable stimuli.

This is a very natural reaction. Anytime you don't like something you look away. You'll see this in children. They haven't learned how to be polite about these things yet and are pretty blunt. When a child sees something awful, he or she will most likely state it and blatantly look away or close their eyes. However, once people get older, and learn how to politely lie, they block these unlikable stimuli in a different way.

A very popular method is when someone pretends to have something in his or her eye. They may rub their eye with a hand or finger while closing the eye to prevent seeing whatever it is they don't want to see. It is important to note that this behavior can also occur with non-visual stimuli. Meaning that someone may do this if they hear something they don't like.

Therefore, pay attention when people start putting things in front of their eyes. Take notice and see if they really have something in their eye or if they may be doing it as a means of blocking out something.

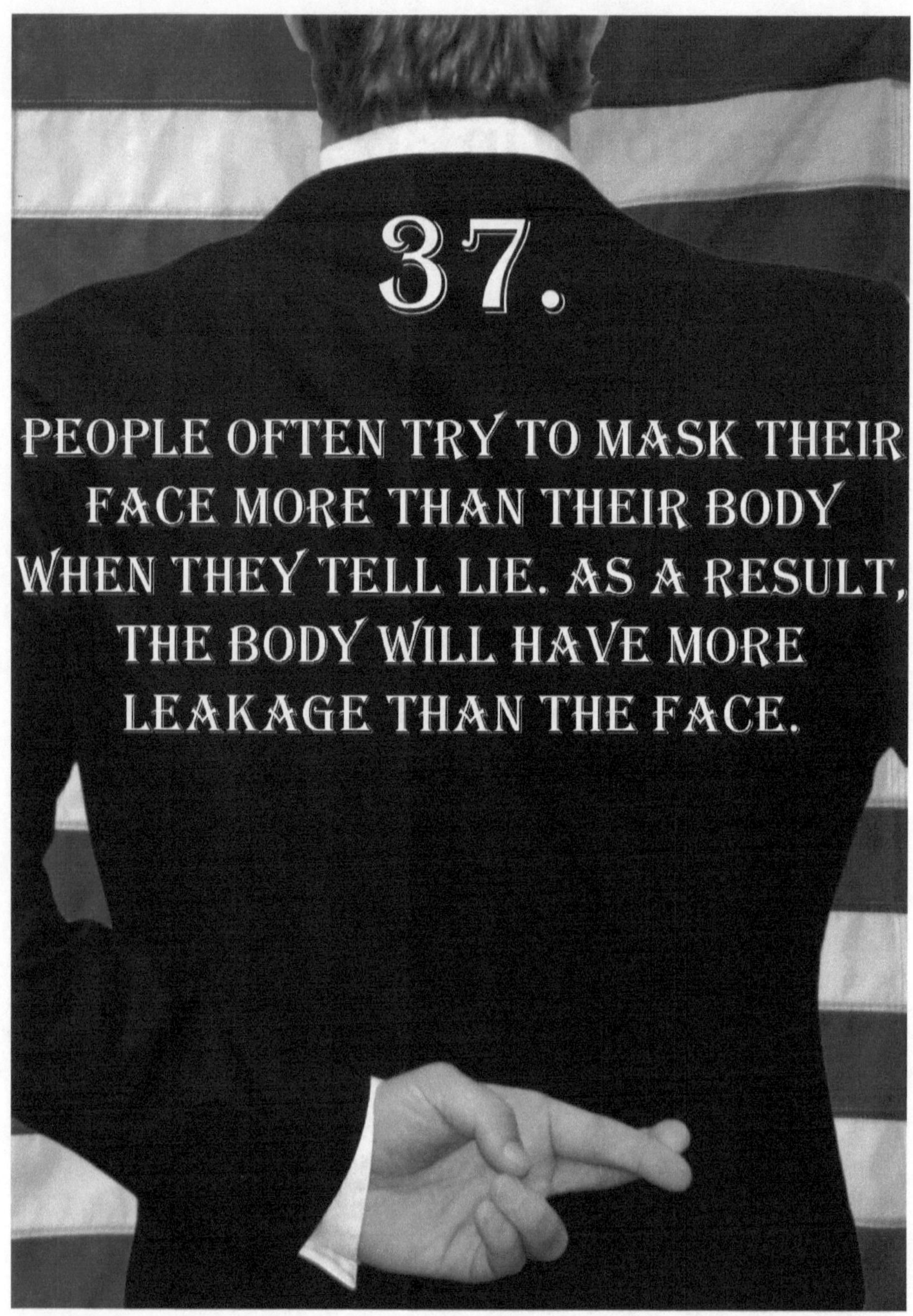

37.

PEOPLE OFTEN TRY TO MASK THEIR
FACE MORE THAN THEIR BODY
WHEN THEY TELL LIE. AS A RESULT,
THE BODY WILL HAVE MORE
LEAKAGE THAN THE FACE.

Deception Tip 37 – Mask The Face

People often try to mask their face more than their body when they tell lie. As a result, the body will have more leakage than the face.

During conversation, people look at the face more than the body. It is part of the polite rules of society that we are all taught to follow while growing up. Have good manners, be respectful, look people in the eye when speaking with them. These behaviors are ingrained in us throughout all of life.

Due to this teaching, many people know that others will be watching their faces when they speak. Therefore, when people lie, they will try to mask the face so that they don't get caught. They will work hard to make sure they have fewer expressions. In addition, they may even cover up some expressions.

Since people concentrate so hard on hiding the emotional expressions on their faces, the body is a better source of leakage. In addition, the body is also larger than the face so there are a lot more behaviors and signs that can occur there. Therefore, be sure to watch the entire body when speaking with others.

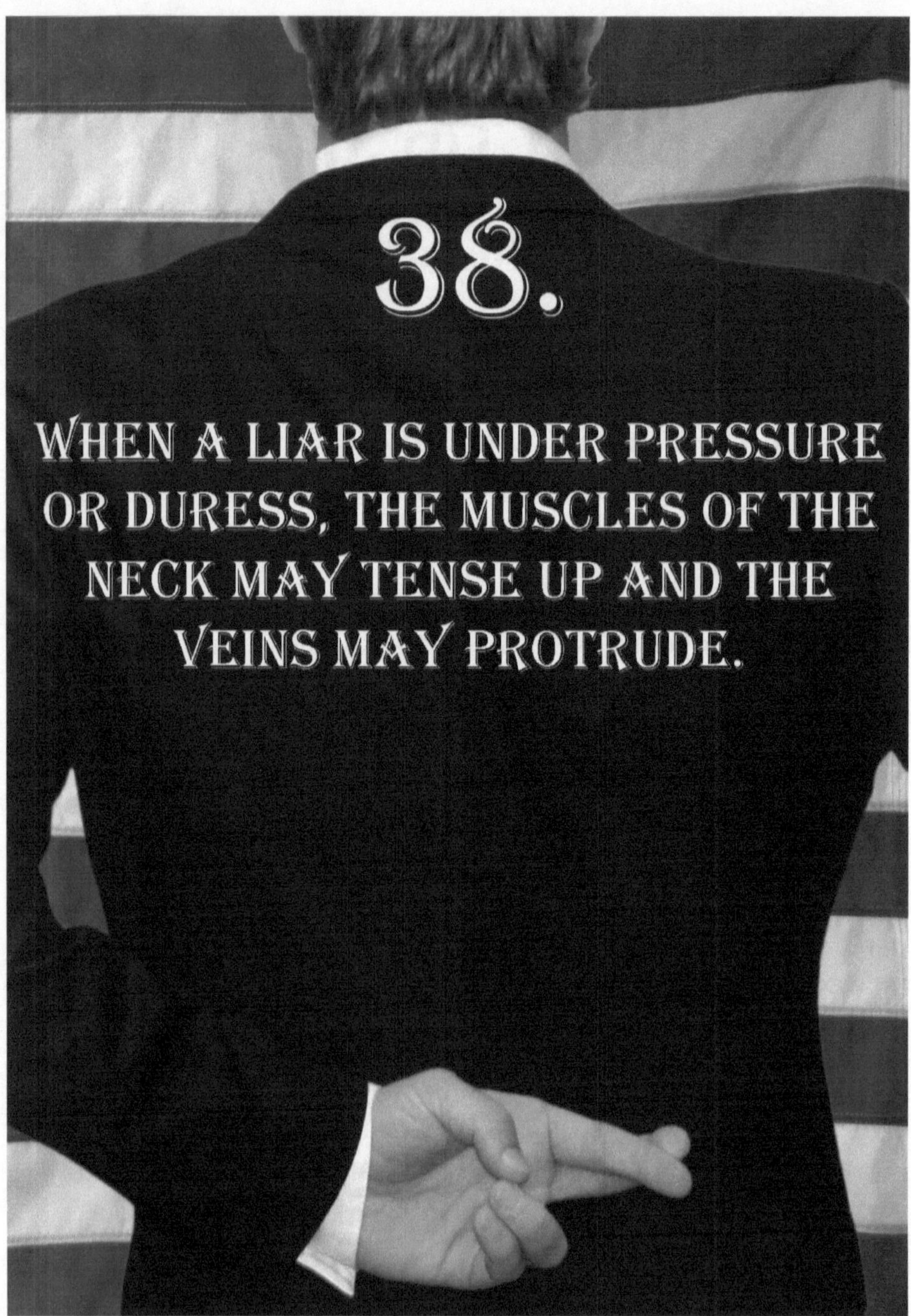
38.
WHEN A LIAR IS UNDER PRESSURE
OR DURESS, THE MUSCLES OF THE
NECK MAY TENSE UP AND THE
VEINS MAY PROTRUDE.

Deception Tip 38 – Tense Neck

When a liar is under pressure or duress, the muscles of the neck may tense up and the veins may protrude.

Liars are under a lot of stress. This is something that I have said again and again and will continue to say again and again. When people are under stress it shows in a variety of different ways. This type of stress is a little more serious though. This is more of aggravation or frustration and is a precursor to anger.

When the veins in the neck start to protrude you can tell that people are feeling stressed. They are feeling like they are not being heard. Therefore, this behavior could be seen in both liars and sometimes in truth tellers if they are not being believed.

When you see it in lying individuals it will most likely be only with protruded veins. When you see it in truth tellers then you will start to see the anger show up. This is because they are innocent and are not being believed. Therefore, liars may display tense muscles and protruding veins. When people are telling the truth, this may turn into signs of anger.

39.
LIARS MAY YAWN REPEATEDLY AS IF TO CONVEY BOREDOM OR RELAXATION.

Deception Tip 39 – Liars Yawn

Liars may yawn repeatedly as if to convey boredom or relaxation.

When someone is trying to get away with telling a lie, they want to play it cool. Obviously, he or she wants others to believe the story. Therefore, in an effort to seem more relaxed and calm, they may fake yawns. This could also be done in an attempt to control the behavior of the situation.

Remember in Deception Tip 35 that truthful people tend to mirror the behaviors of others in the conversation. Yawns are very contagious. Therefore, if a liar yawns then the other people in the conversation may also yawn. This may help the liar sound more believable.

The reason is that when people mirror other people's behaviors, they feel connected to them on an unconscious level. Of course, the liar may or may not know this when he or she fakes a yawn. However, it's worth considering. In addition, yawning also makes them seem, board, which could convey innocence. Therefore, beware of multiple yawns in a conversation.

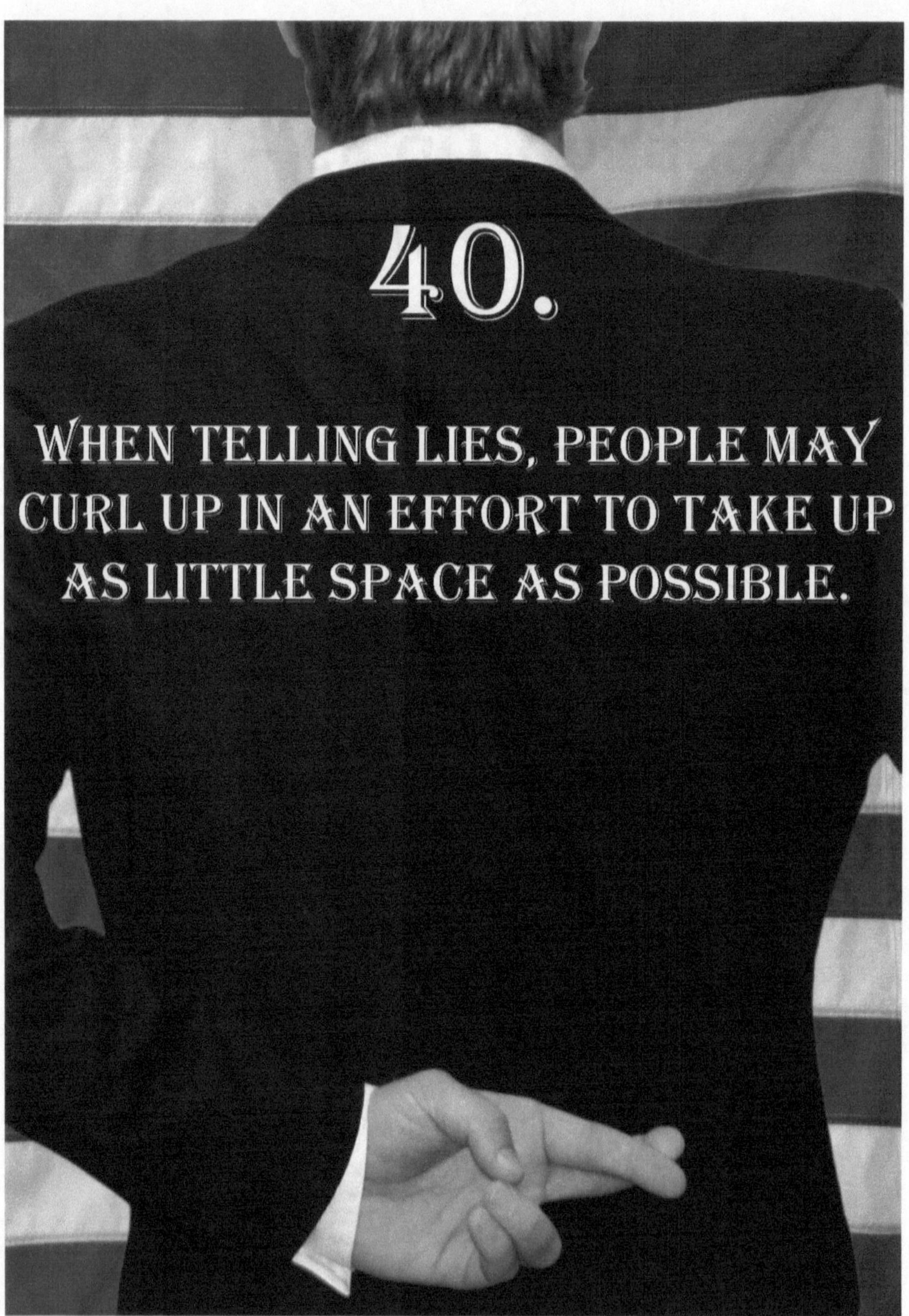
40.

WHEN TELLING LIES, PEOPLE MAY CURL UP IN AN EFFORT TO TAKE UP AS LITTLE SPACE AS POSSIBLE.

Deception Tip 40 – Take Up Space

When telling lies, people may curl up in an effort to take up as little space as possible.

Remember that when people lie, they do not want others to notice the different signs of deception that may be displayed on their bodies. There is a huge battle happening between the conscious and the unconscious. The unconscious is constantly trying to leak truthful body language. However, the conscious is trying to get away with the lie.

One of the ways that a liar will attempt to hide the many different signs of deception is by reducing the amount of their body that other people will be able to see. Therefore, he or she may curl up so that there is less chance that the others in the conversation will notice the different signs of deception.

Therefore, pay attention to how people position themselves when they are in conversation. If they start reducing their bodily visibility, especially when questioned, then you may wish to push them a little further with your questions to see if you can find any other signs of deception.

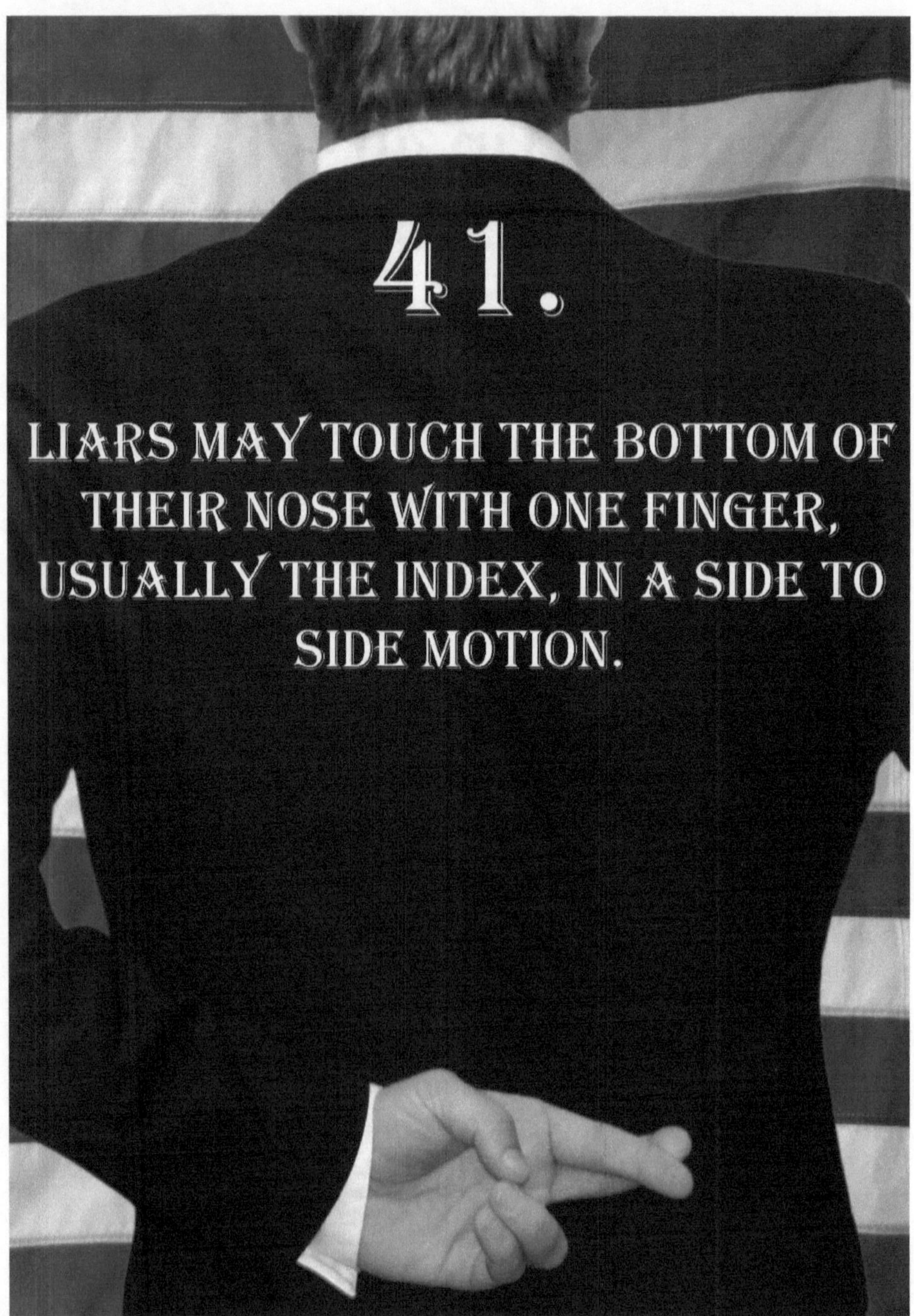
41.

LIARS MAY TOUCH THE BOTTOM OF
THEIR NOSE WITH ONE FINGER,
USUALLY THE INDEX, IN A SIDE TO
SIDE MOTION.

Deception Tip 41 – Touch The Nose

Liars may touch the bottom of their nose with one finger, usually the index, in a side-to-side motion.

Fidgeting is a common behavior that people display when they would like to release tension. Deception Tip 30 Bounce Both Legs was another example of this. When people lie, there are certain areas of the body that feel different than when people tell the truth.

One of these areas is the nose. When people lie, their nose tends to itch. There is sensitive tissue between the nostrils on the bridge of the nose. It is the skin that covers the cartilage. Therefore, a person may use his or her finger to scratch the itch that occurs when he or she lies.

It is important to note that this behavior more commonly occurs with men than with women. This is because the tissue there is more sensitive for men than women. Therefore, anytime you see someone rubbing the bottom of their nose you should definitely look for other signs of deception.

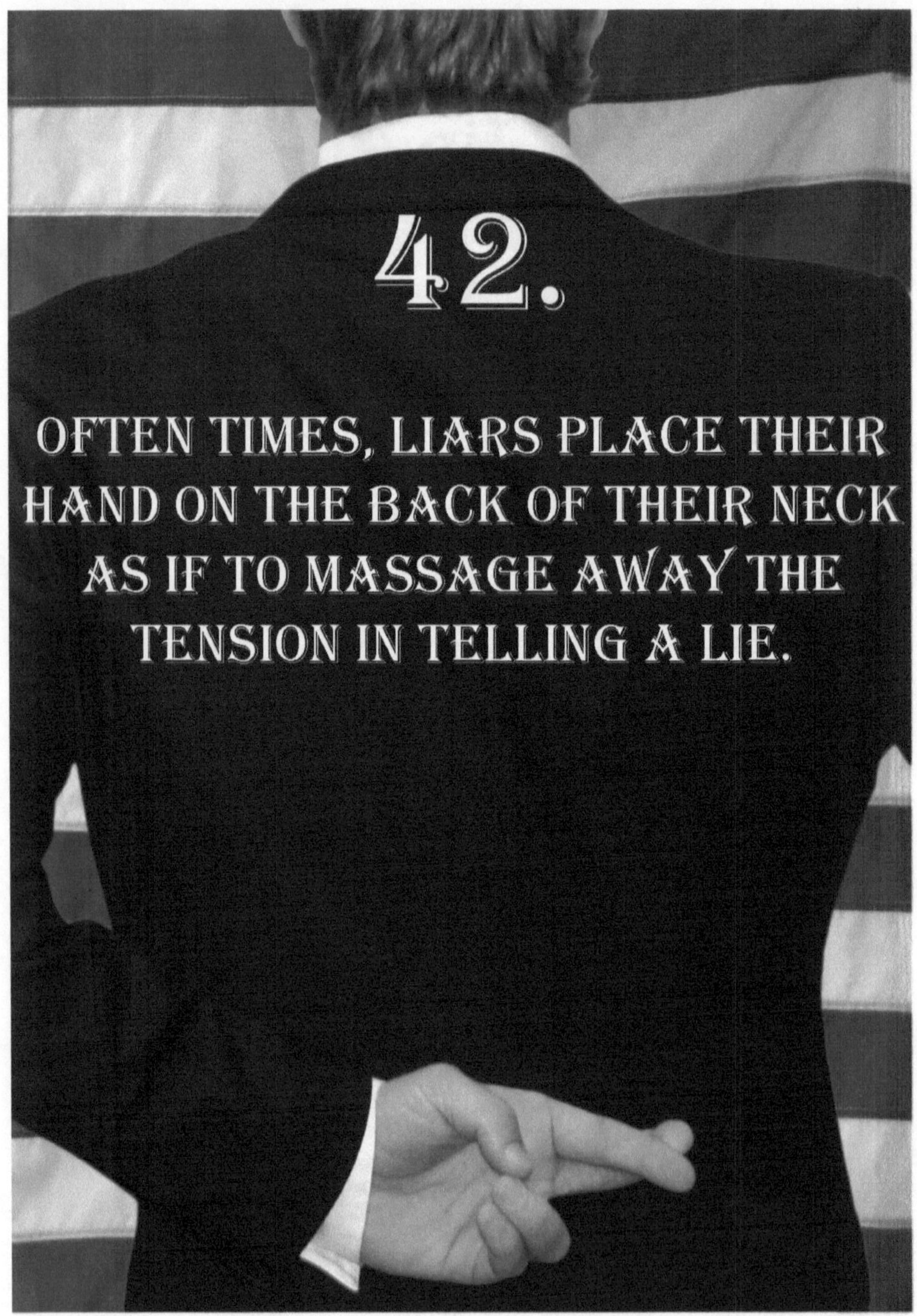
42.
OFTEN TIMES, LIARS PLACE THEIR HAND ON THE BACK OF THEIR NECK AS IF TO MASSAGE AWAY THE TENSION IN TELLING A LIE.

Deception Tip 42 – Back Of Neck

Often times, liars place their hand on the back of their neck as if to massage away the tension in telling a lie.

When people lie they are under an immense amount of stress and tension. Liars may sometimes try to massage away this tension by rubbing the back of their neck. This behavior is often witnessed almost immediately after a lie is told. It is an unconscious behavior that is done to massage away the tension before it occurs.

It is something that will happen very quickly and may not be that noticeable. In addition, there can be any number of reasons for this behavior. Remember that there will always be more than one sign of deception if someone is lying. Therefore, when you see this behavior, start looking for other signs.

The neck can get very tense when people tell lies and liars may massage it away by putting their hand on the back of their neck. In addition, you may not see this during the lie. It may be an instant behavior that may go unnoticed. Therefore, watch for it and pay attention to other signs of tension release.

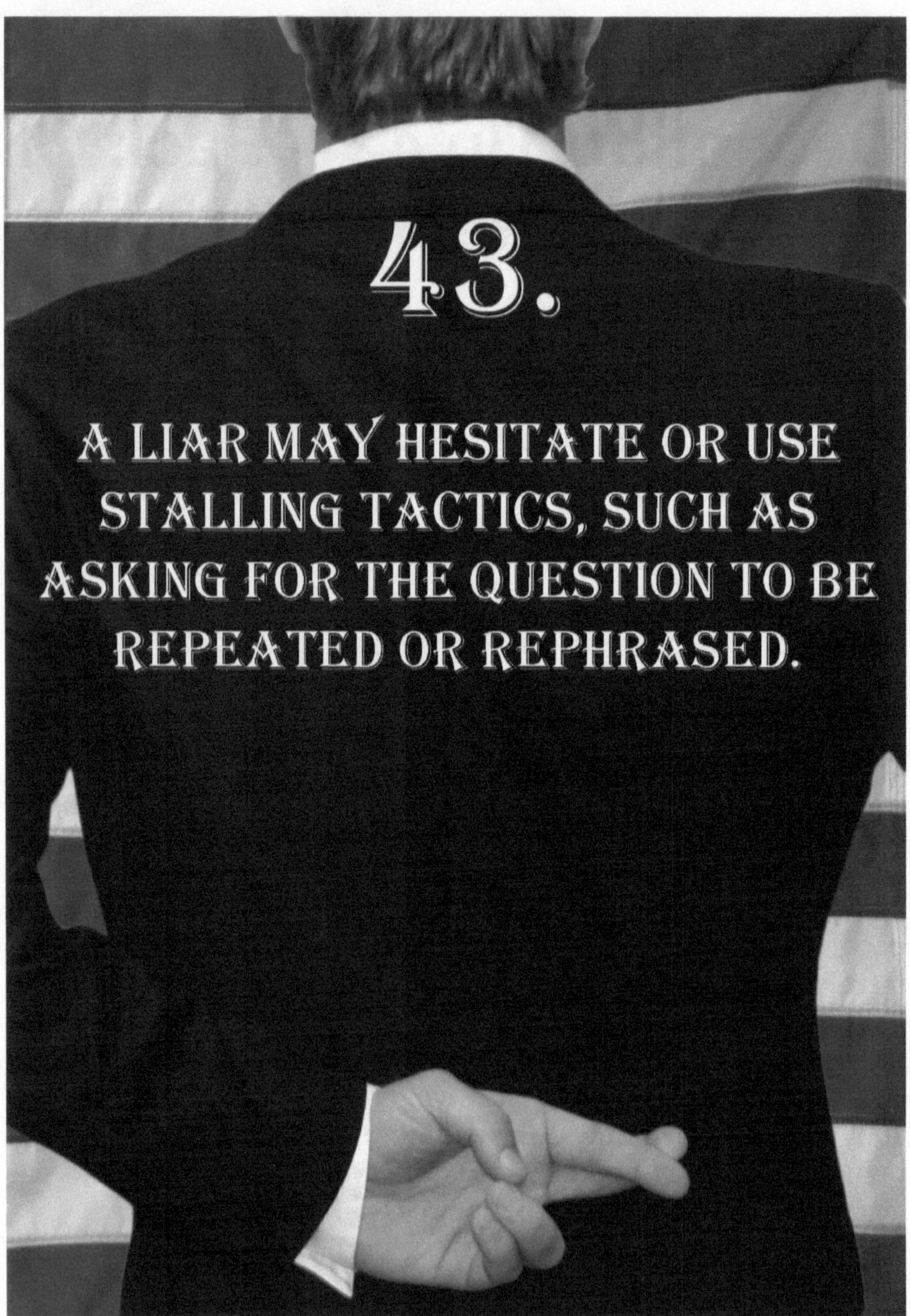
43.
A LIAR MAY HESITATE OR USE STALLING TACTICS, SUCH AS ASKING FOR THE QUESTION TO BE REPEATED OR REPHRASED.

Deception Tip 43 – Repeat The Question

A liar may hesitate or use stalling tactics, such as asking for the question to be repeated or rephrased.

There is a lot of mental activity that goes on when people lie. They are thinking of so many different things and are worrying about all of them. In addition, they are trying to keep the different points of their lie straight and thinking about how not to get caught. In short, they are stressed.

When you question a liar, he or she may not be ready to honestly answer the question. Therefore, they may ask for the question to be repeated in an effort to have a little more time to think. Not only that, but they may also ask for the question to be rephrased for the same reason.

Yes, this doesn't give the liar a lot of time to think. However, it is more of a mental break than time to think. They are not using the few seconds to come up with the lie. They are using it as a means of taking a mental breath and getting ready to deliver the lie in the most believable way possible.

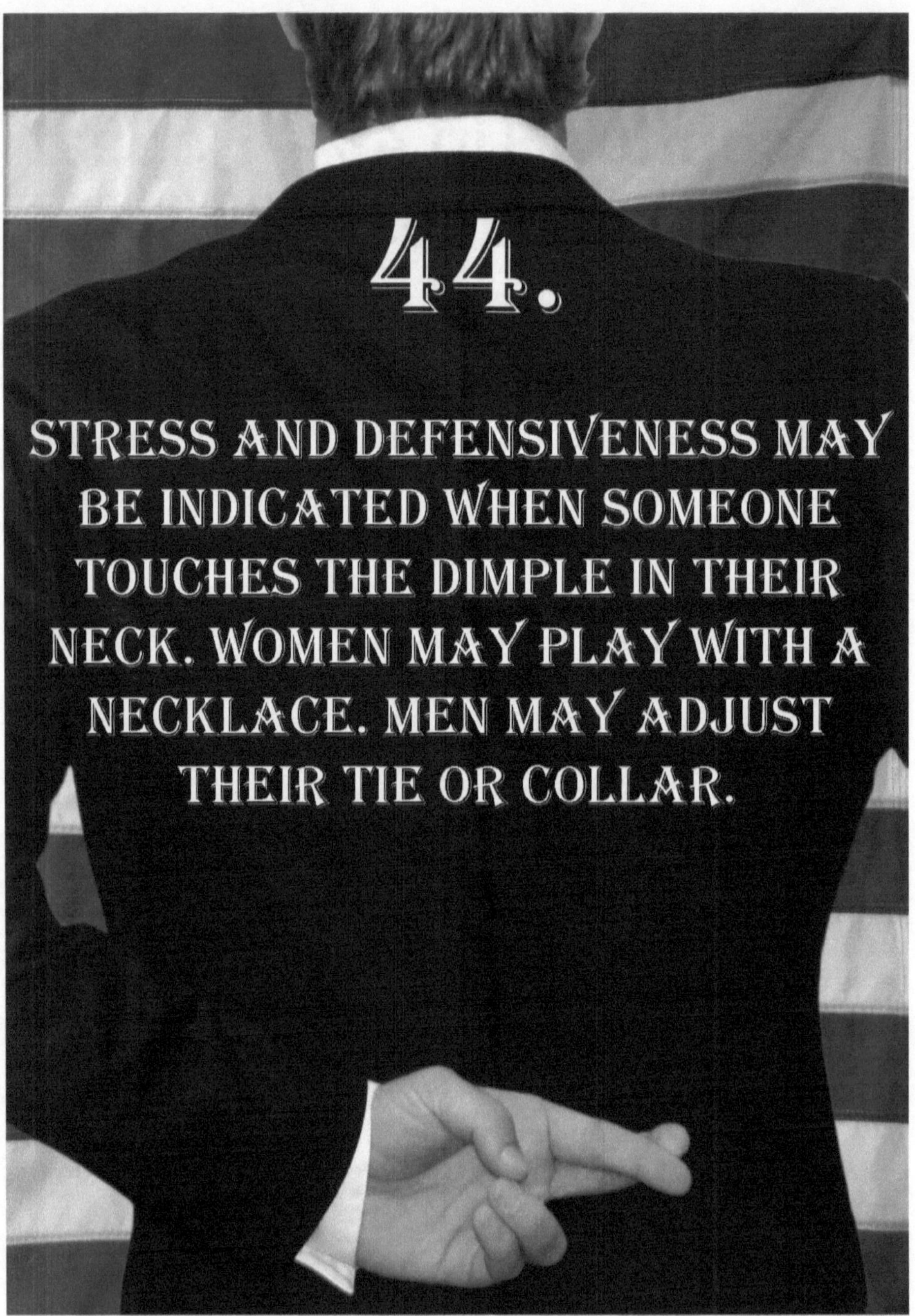
44.
STRESS AND DEFENSIVENESS MAY
BE INDICATED WHEN SOMEONE
TOUCHES THE DIMPLE IN THEIR
NECK. WOMEN MAY PLAY WITH A
NECKLACE. MEN MAY ADJUST
THEIR TIE OR COLLAR.

Deception Tip 44 – Neck Dimple

Stress and defensiveness may be indicated when someone touches the dimple in their neck. Women may play with a necklace. Men may adjust their tie or collar.

Defensiveness is a popular behavior when people are questioned or are accused of lying. In Deception Tip 1, we discussed arm folding and how it may be a sign of defensive behavior. This is similar in that it is sort of half an arm fold. The person is reaching one arm across to the other side of the body.

This can be displayed in a number of different ways. A liar may touch, or fidget with, the neck dimple. This is located at the top of the sternum right beneath the throat. If you feel the front of your collarbone you'll feel where it turns into a "V". This is the neck dimple.

There are variations of this that you may see with men and women. A man may adjust his tie and a woman may fidget, or play with, her necklace. Of course, a man could also fidget with a necklace. The point is, anytime you see someone touching the area above the sternum you should be on the lookout for deception.

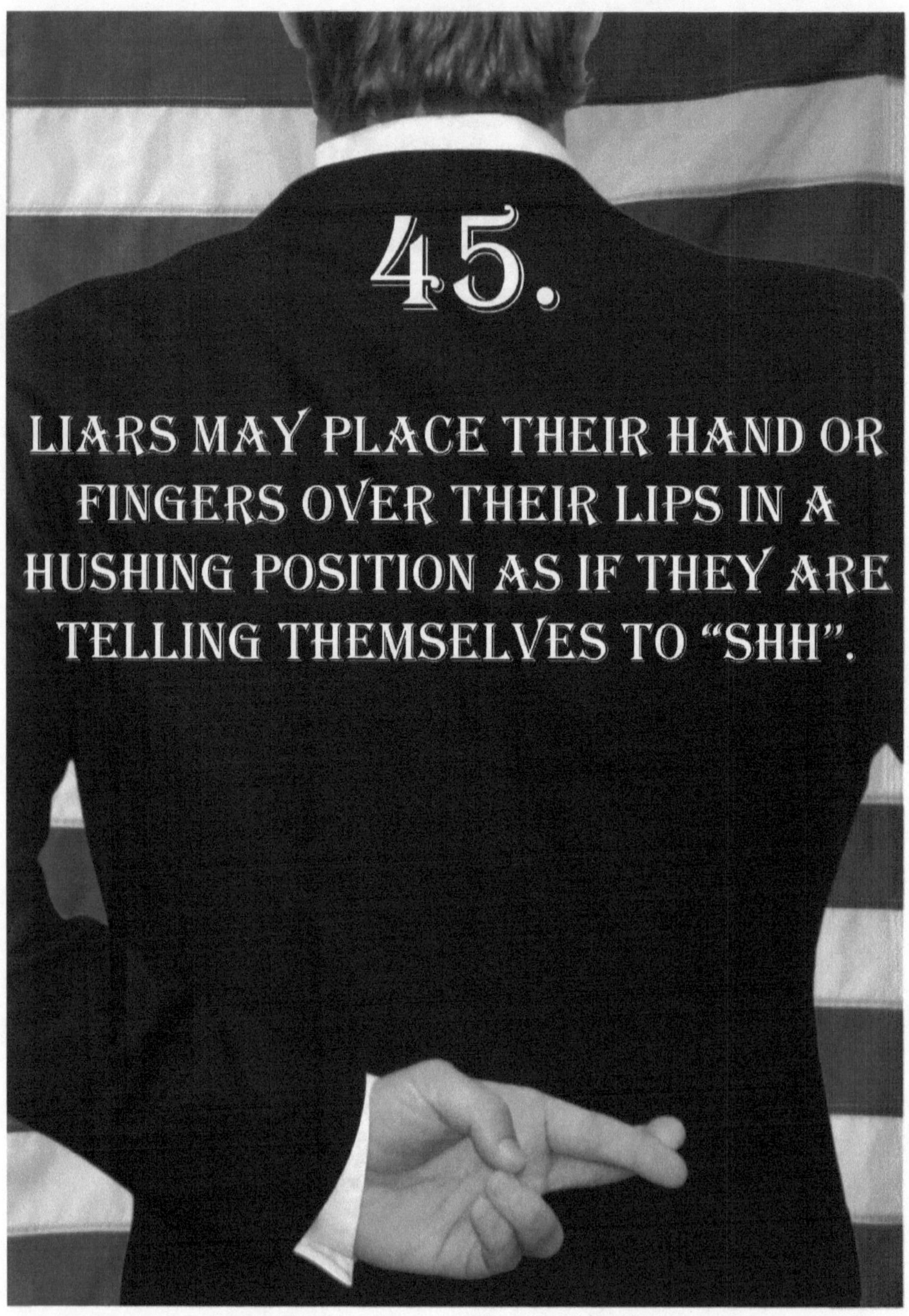
45.

LIARS MAY PLACE THEIR HAND OR
FINGERS OVER THEIR LIPS IN A
HUSHING POSITION AS IF THEY ARE
TELLING THEMSELVES TO "SHH".

Deception Tip 45 – Hushing Lips

Liars may place their hand or fingers over their lips in a hushing position as if they are telling themselves to "shh".

There is a huge battle going on between the conscious and the unconscious. The conscious wants to get away with telling a lie and the unconscious wants people to know the truth. Therefore, when the conscious is lying the unconscious is always leaking signs of truthful behavior. Remember, there will always be more than one sign.

One of these behaviors is when liars may unconsciously hush themselves. They are telling themselves to be quiet. This is often demonstrated when someone places his or her fingers over their lips. The unconscious is trying to silence the conscious and prevent the lie from being told.

It is important to note that this is most likely done with the index finger. That means, that in any instance in which you see it, you must consider it as a potential sign of deception. Even if it looks like someone is only thinking. It could still be a potential sign. Therefore, watch for additional signs that may confirm whether or not they are telling the truth.

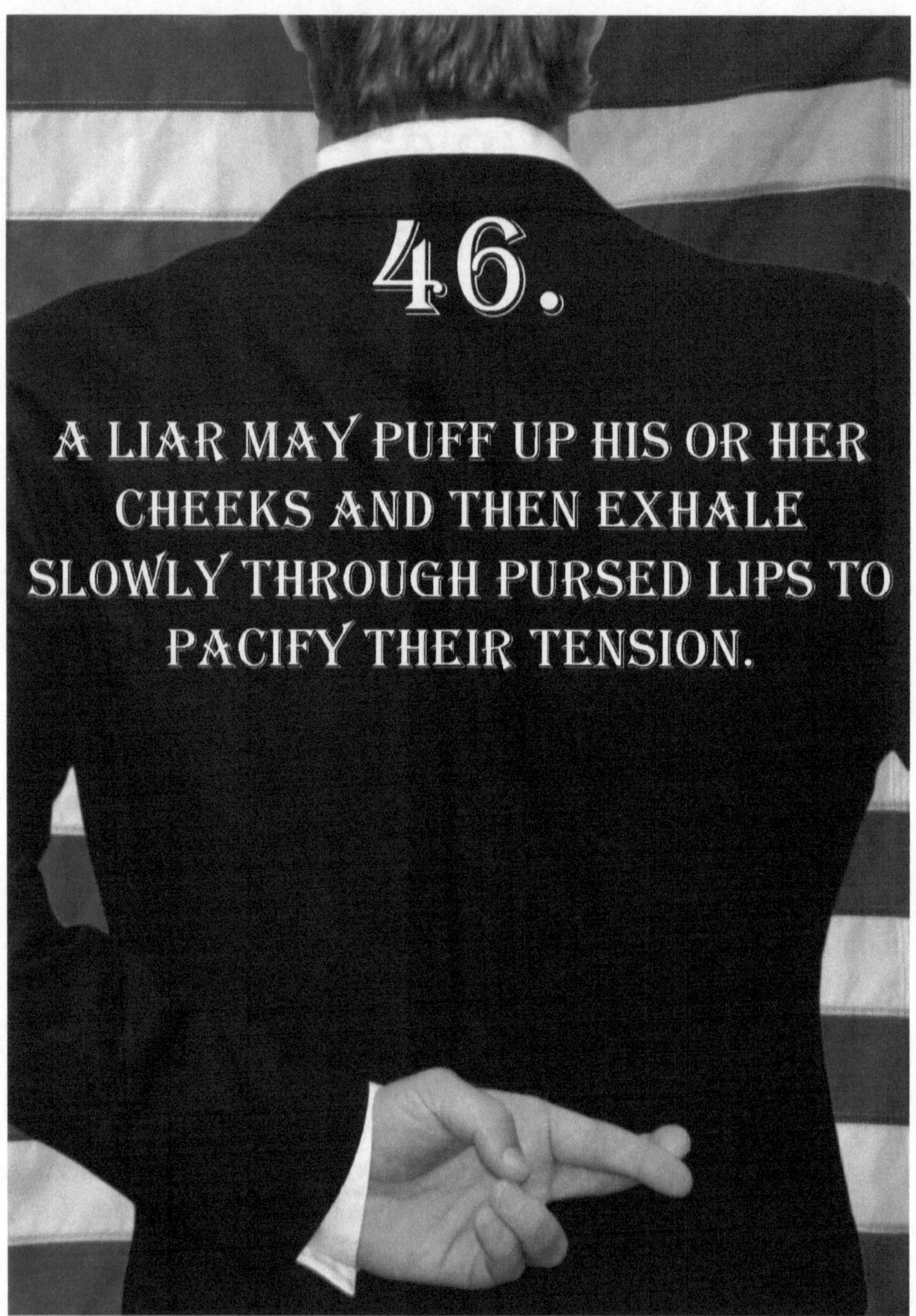
46.
A LIAR MAY PUFF UP HIS OR HER
CHEEKS AND THEN EXHALE
SLOWLY THROUGH PURSED LIPS TO
PACIFY THEIR TENSION.

Deception Tip 46 – Pursed Lips

A liar may puff up his or her cheeks and then exhale slowly through pursed lips to pacify their tension.

Pacification gestures are very popular when people lie. They are done in an attempt to cope, or deal, with the stress and tension involved in telling a lie. You'll see them all the time when people are feeling overwhelmed and like they need a little breather.

This behavior is when someone puffs up his or her cheeks, kind of like a blowfish. Then, they exhale slowly to help pacify the tension involved in telling that lie. This is a slow exhale sort of like when they are taking a deep breath. It is a means of gathering their thoughts so that they can continue the lie.

Watch for this, because pacification gestures are very prominent when people tell lies. In addition, you'll see those gestures as well as the other signs of deception that you've learned about. Remember, that these signs can always have more than one meaning so you must look for clusters and patterns of behavior.

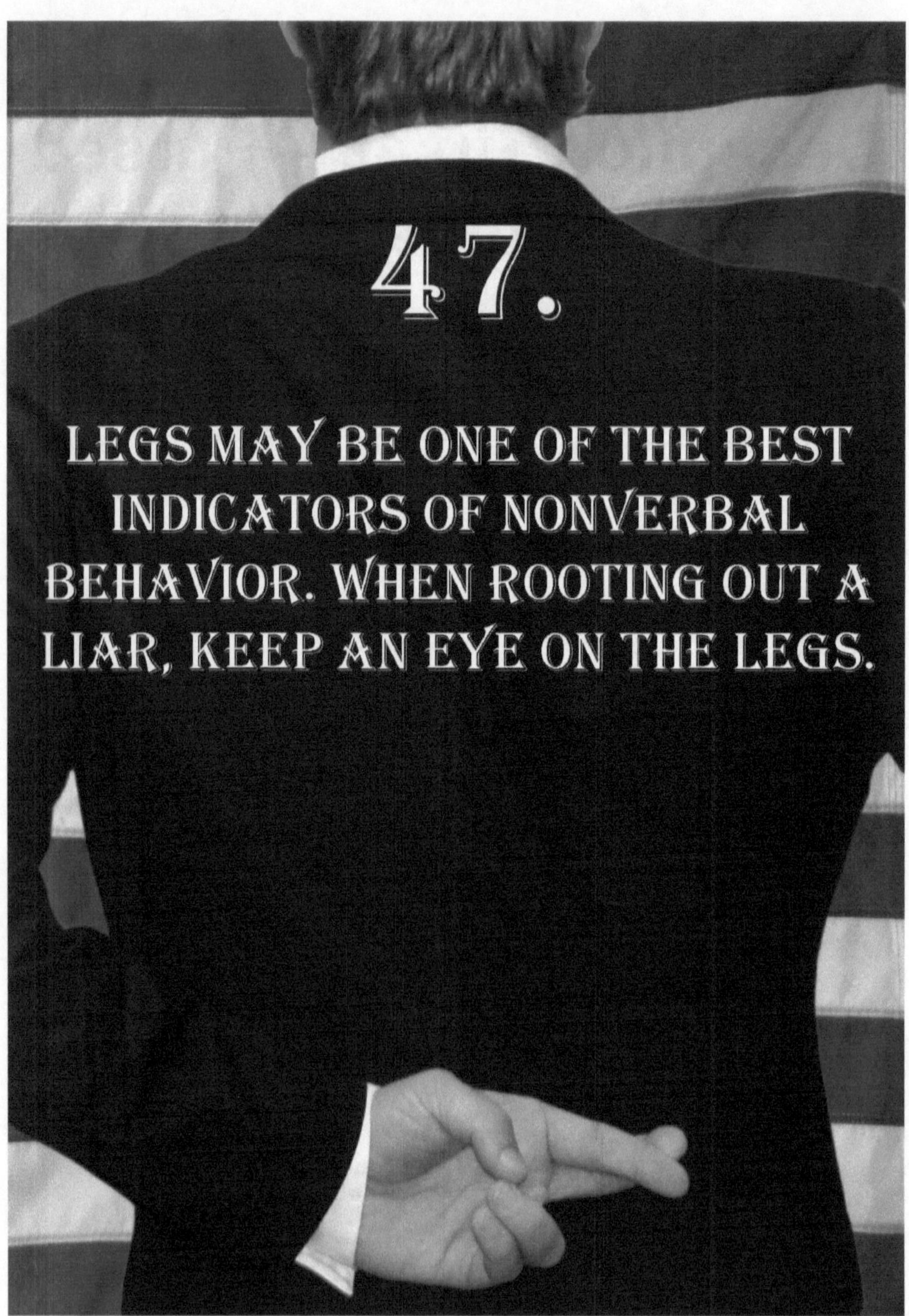
47.

LEGS MAY BE ONE OF THE BEST
INDICATORS OF NONVERBAL
BEHAVIOR. WHEN ROOTING OUT A
LIAR, KEEP AN EYE ON THE LEGS.

Deception Tip 47 – Watch The Legs

Legs may be one of the best indicators of nonverbal behavior. When rooting out a liar, keep an eye on the legs.

In Deception Tip 37 Mask The Face, you learned how liars attempt to mask their faces more so than the rest of the body. This is because most people watch the face more than the rest of the body. Therefore, it makes sense that people will try to hide the signs on their faces more than their bodies.

Due to this fact, you may have better luck watching the legs over other parts of the body. This is because the legs are extremely expressive. In Deception Tip 30, you learned about how liars may bounce their legs in an effort to pacify the tension involved in lying.

Therefore, pay attention to the legs. They can be very expressive because most people know that the legs are not watched. Thus, they will be a little less cautious about letting signs of leakage show up. This can be a huge advantage for you when you are trying to find the truth and detect deception.

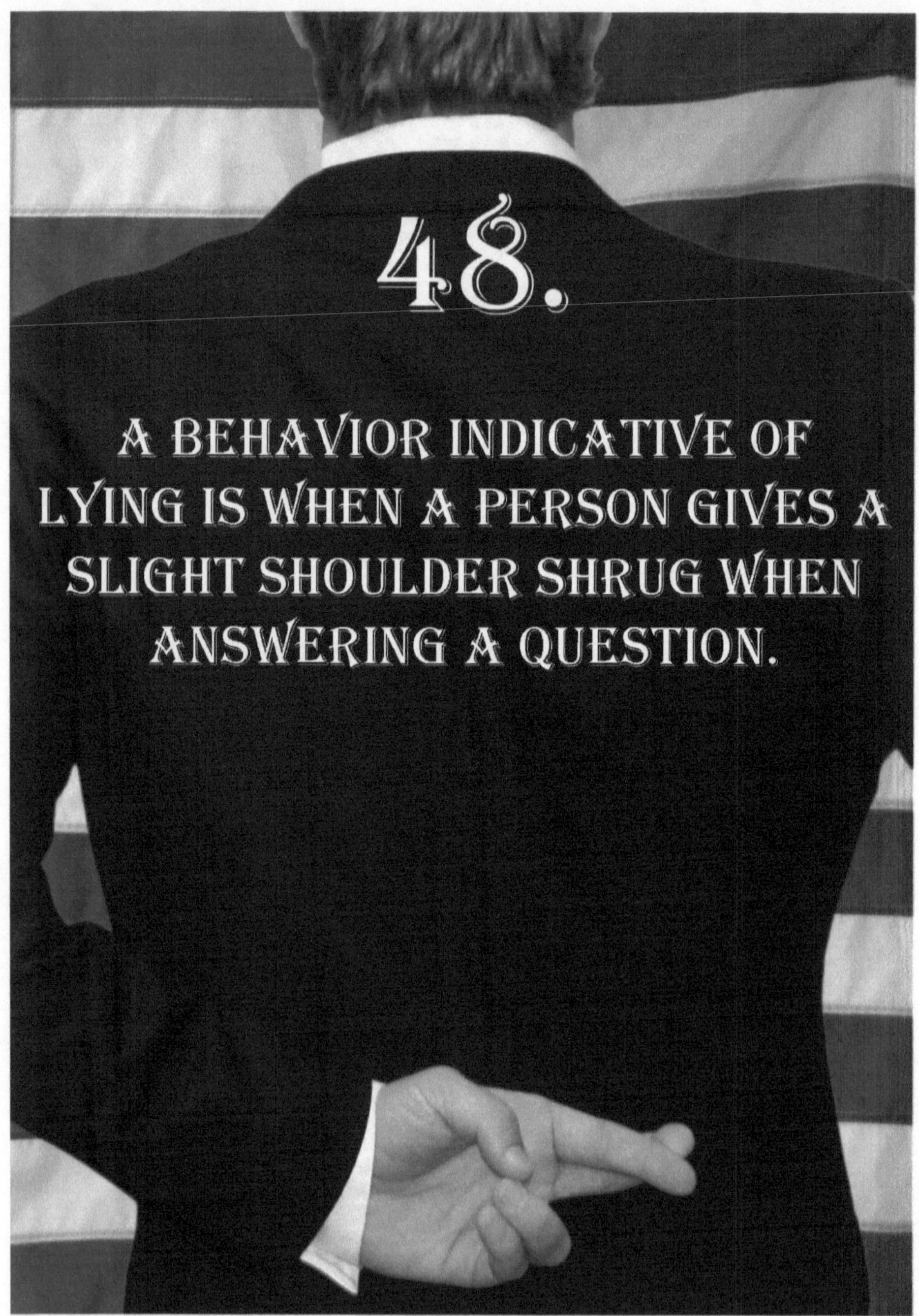

48.

A BEHAVIOR INDICATIVE OF
LYING IS WHEN A PERSON GIVES A
SLIGHT SHOULDER SHRUG WHEN
ANSWERING A QUESTION.

Deception Tip 48 – Slight Shoulder Shrug

A behavior indicative of lying is when a person gives a slight shoulder shrug when answering a question.

When behaviors are asymmetrical they are usually untrue. It is only when they are symmetrical that they are true. We've discussed this several times before how gestures and expressions must be symmetrical. Deception Tip 16 showed you that when something happens on one side of the body it should also happen on the other.

Therefore, watch body language and keep watching if you don't see it on both sides of the body. It must occur on both sides of the body. If it doesn't then there is a good chance that the person is lying. A typical shoulder shrug happens with both shoulders.

When you see someone answer a question and only shrug one shoulder it means that they really don't know what they are saying. They don't have confidence in their answer. Keep in mind that this behavior can be truthful if they are telling you that they don't know. However, if you see it with a direct answer, the person doesn't have a lot of confidence in their response.

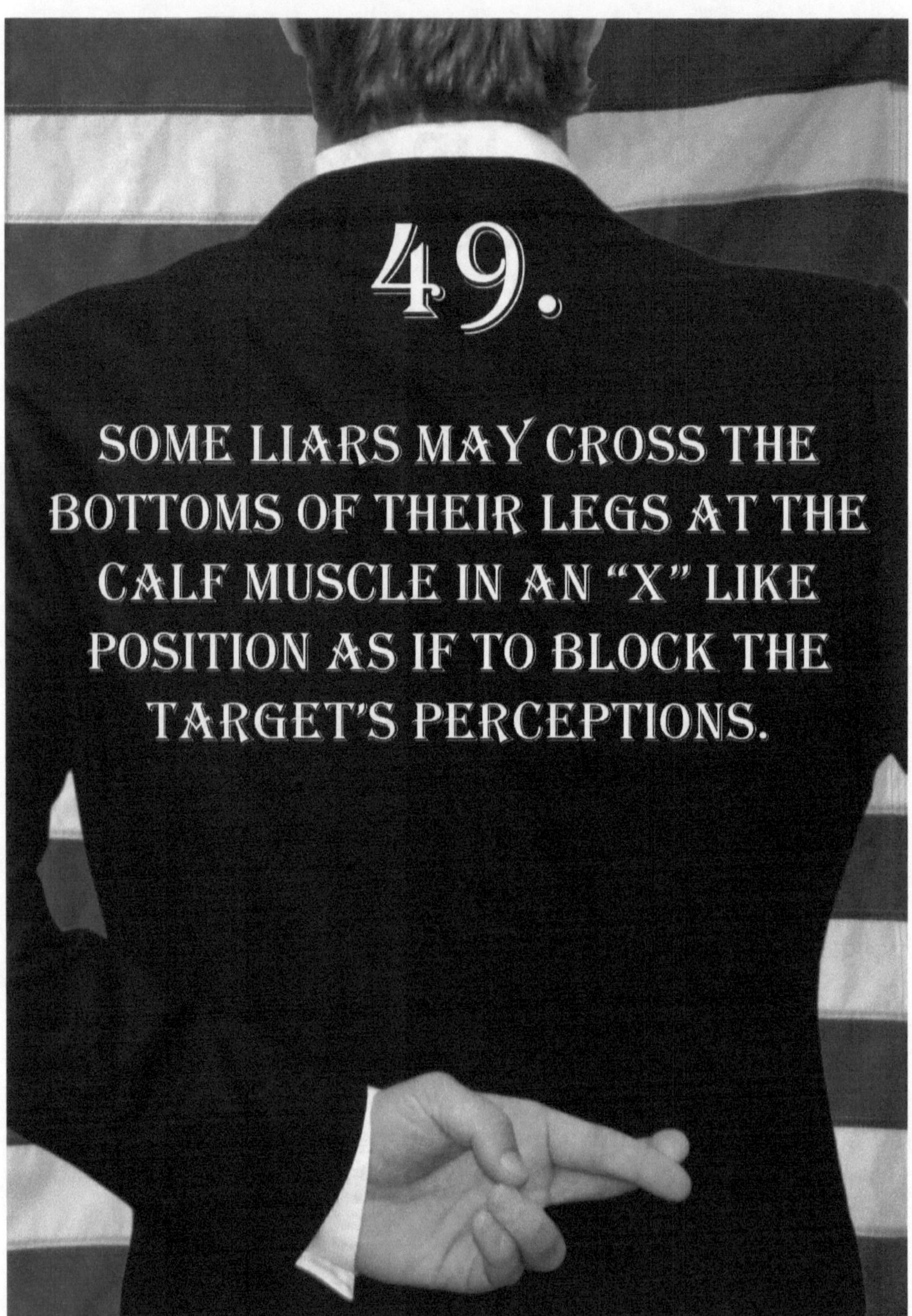
49.

SOME LIARS MAY CROSS THE
BOTTOMS OF THEIR LEGS AT THE
CALF MUSCLE IN AN "X" LIKE
POSITION AS IF TO BLOCK THE
TARGET'S PERCEPTIONS.

Deception Tip 49 – Calf Muscle

Some liars may cross the bottoms of their legs at the calf muscle in an "X" like position as if to block the target's perceptions.

Liars don't want targets to spot their lies. They will try whatever they can to hide the different signs of leakage. Whether they reduce their visible body language or try to hide it, they are always looking to get away with a lie. This tip is similar to Deception Tip 22 Locked Ankles.

When a liar crosses the bottom of his or her legs at the calf muscle it is similar to locking the ankles. When the legs are in an "X" like position it is almost as if they are being folded. This is also similar to Deception Tip 1 Folding Arms. It is a sign of defensiveness and withholding.

Pay attention to this behavior. When you see it, you must ask yourself what the liar doesn't want to share with you. The liar is being withholding and defensive. Look for a cluster of behaviors to go along with this. Some examples might be folding the arms, locking the ankles, and tucking the legs back. When you see these, continue asking questions.

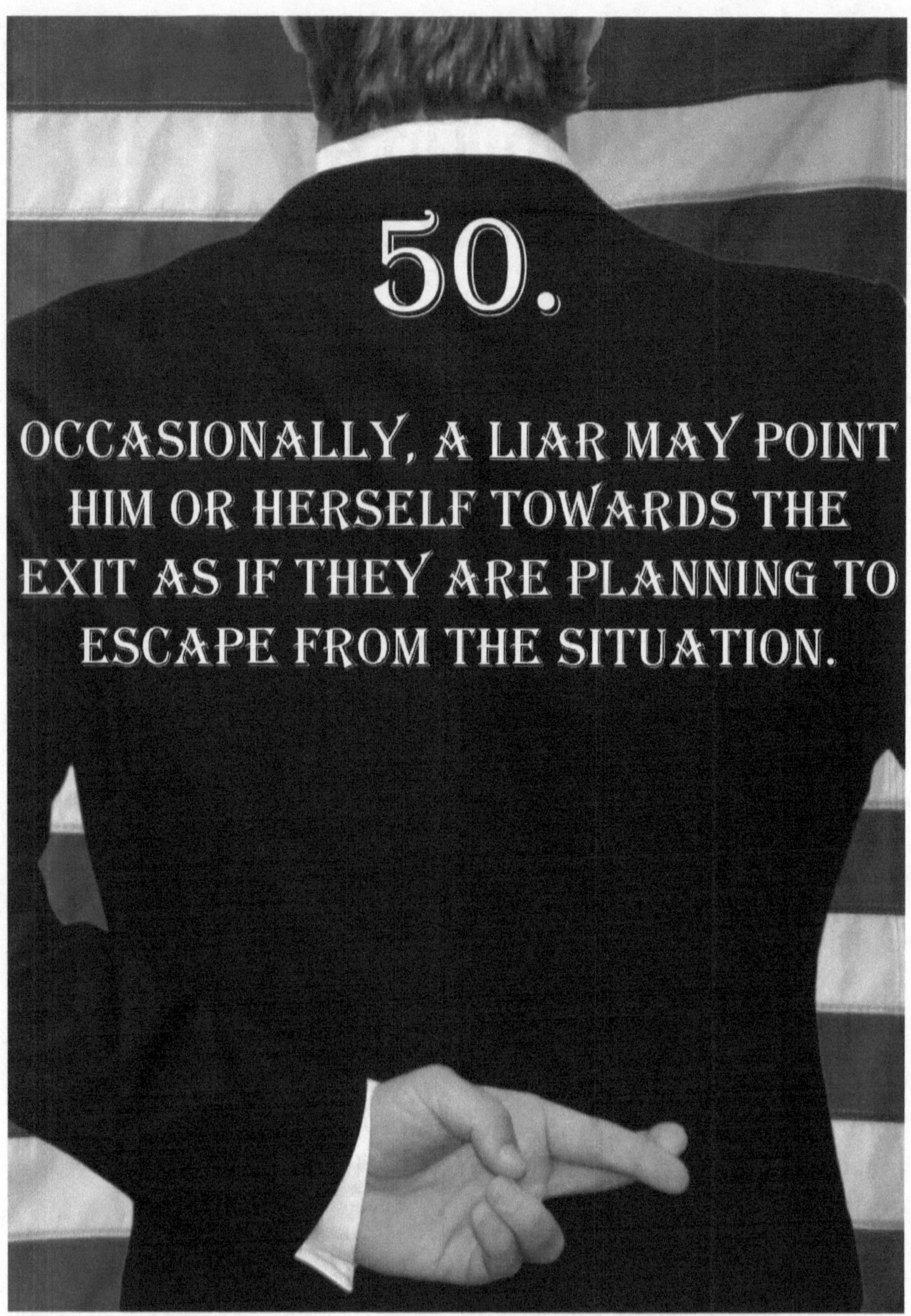
50.
OCCASIONALLY, A LIAR MAY POINT
HIM OR HERSELF TOWARDS THE
EXIT AS IF THEY ARE PLANNING TO
ESCAPE FROM THE SITUATION.

Deception Tip 50 – Towards The Exit

Occasionally, a liar may point him or herself towards the exit as if they are planning to escape from the situation.

As you know, people are under a lot of stress and tension when they lie. They are really hoping to get away with the lie so that they don't have to face the consequences of whatever the truth would present. This tip is one that you will most likely see when people are starting to feel like they are about to get caught in the lie.

If people feel like the situation is about to turn against them, then they will think about leaving. This is true for any person. It doesn't matter whether they are liars or truth tellers everyone wants to leave when the situation gets worse. You can watch for this as a sign of deception because it is especially so when people feel like they are about to get caught.

When a liar feels like their lie is about to be discovered, they may point themselves toward the exit in preparation to flee the situation. Of course, they may not actually flee. However, you'll see that they unconsciously want to. This can be observed in both standing and seated liars.

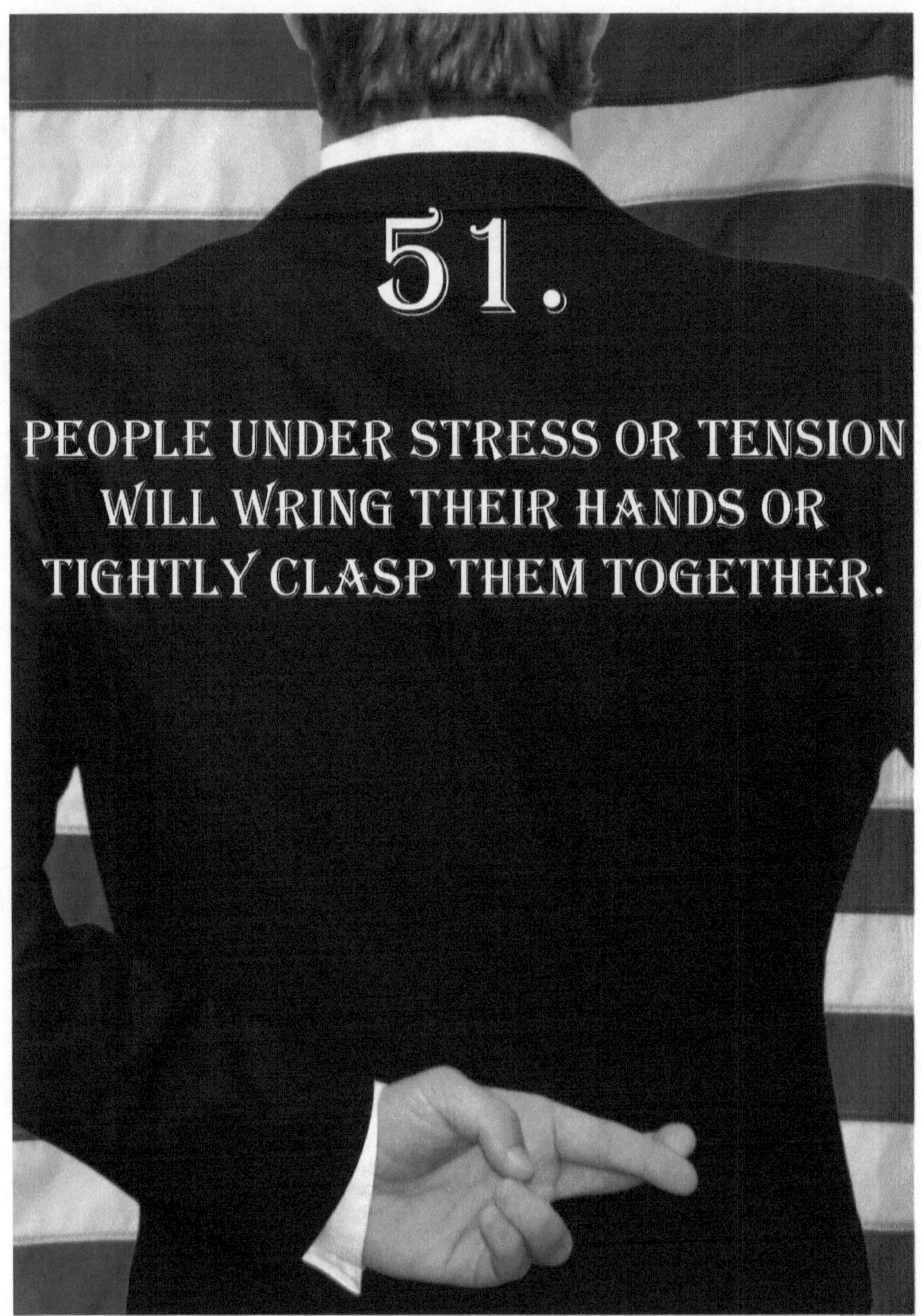

51.

PEOPLE UNDER STRESS OR TENSION
WILL WRING THEIR HANDS OR
TIGHTLY CLASP THEM TOGETHER.

Deception Tip 51 – Wringing Hands

People under stress or tension will wring their hands or tightly clasp them together.

Pacification and stress releasing gestures are very common with liars. We've discussed several different types of them already. Hopefully, you remember most of them and know what to look for. Basically, any type of behavior that makes people feel better is a pacification gesture and anything that exerts energy is a stress release gesture.

Things, like bouncing the legs, licking the lips, puffing the cheeks, breathing deeply, et cetera, are some examples we've covered. If those words don't jog your memory then I encourage you to go back and study them once more so that you have a good understanding of them.

When people are stressed they may tightly clasp their hands and wring them together as if they were wringing out a wet cloth. This provides a massage-like feeling of relief. It also serves to pacify the stress and tension they are feeling. If you notice this behavior, ask yourself why they may be stressed and tense. If there isn't a valid reason, then they may be lying about something.

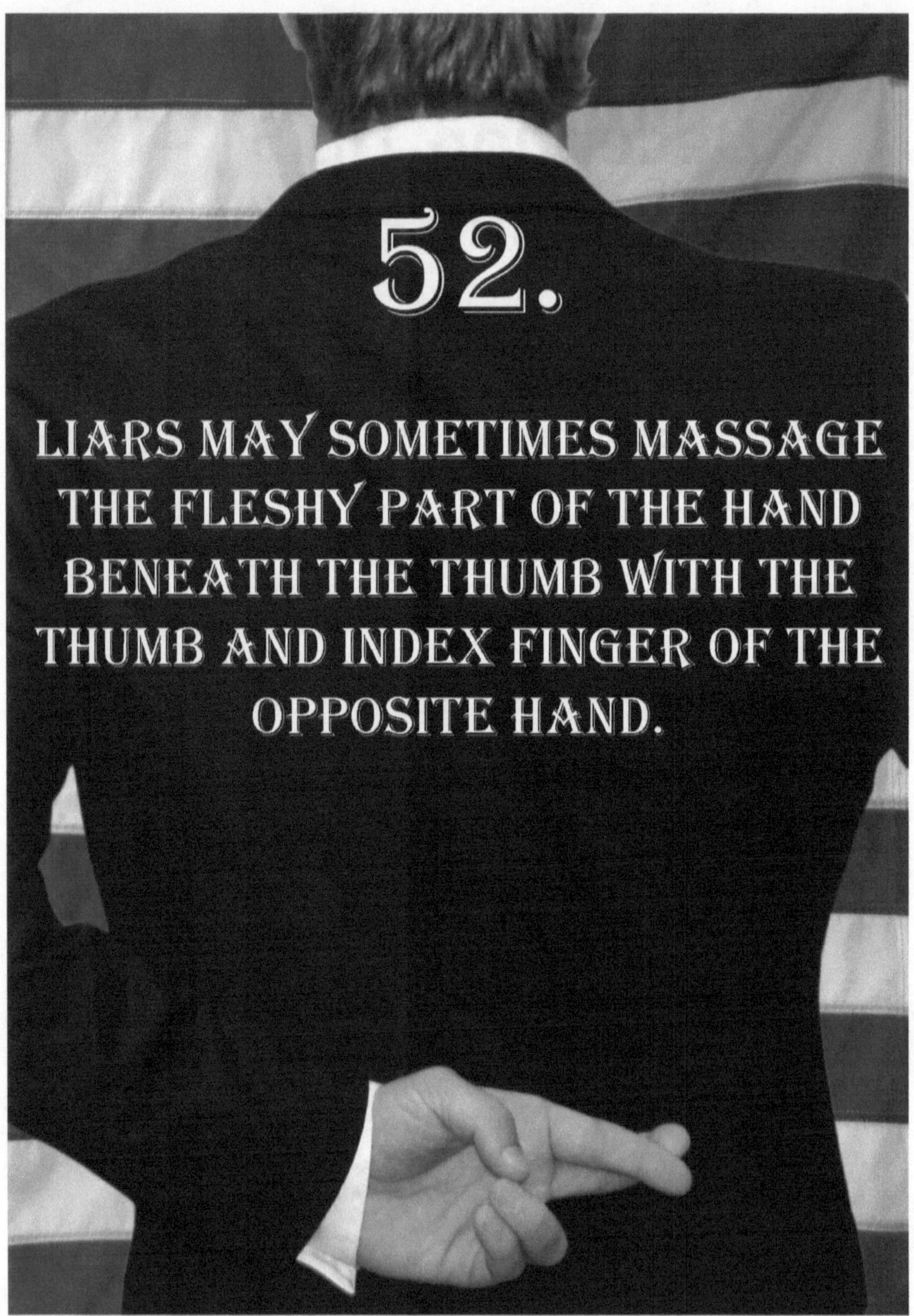

52.

LIARS MAY SOMETIMES MASSAGE THE FLESHY PART OF THE HAND BENEATH THE THUMB WITH THE THUMB AND INDEX FINGER OF THE OPPOSITE HAND.

Deception Tip 52 – Massage Hand

Liars may sometimes massage the fleshy part of the hand beneath the thumb with the thumb and index finger of the opposite hand.

In Deception Tip 51, you learned of how people who are stressed may tightly clasp and wring their hands. This is a form of stress relief and a pacification gesture. They are trying to cope with the tension that they are feeling. Whether it is due to telling a lie or something else.

This is another similar tip. People who feel stressed and anxious may massage the area between their thumb and index finger. This is a great example of a pacification gesture because the person is doing something that makes them feel better and relieves feelings of stress and anxiety. Anytime someone massages any muscle it feels good. Therefore, remember that it may not always indicate lying.

When you notice this happening, you need to be on the lookout for additional signs of deception. Remember, that there will always be more than one sign and you must look for patterns and clusters of behavior. No single behavior is conclusive enough to tell you that someone is telling a lie.

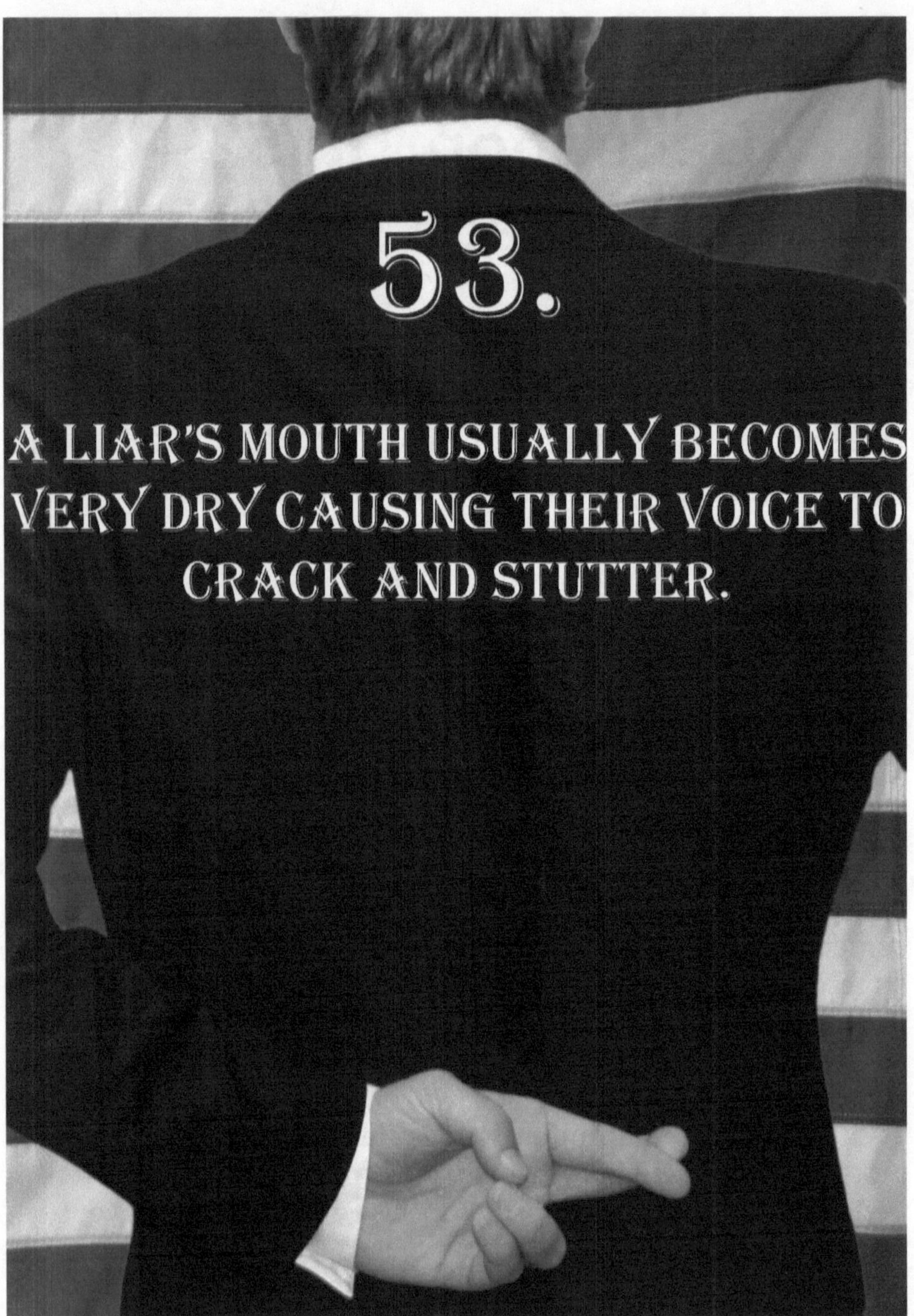
53.
A LIAR'S MOUTH USUALLY BECOMES
VERY DRY CAUSING THEIR VOICE TO
CRACK AND STUTTER.

Deception Tip 53 – Voice Crack

A liar's mouth usually becomes very dry causing their voice to crack and stutter.

In Deception Tip 32 Lick Lips, you learned about how when people lie they may experience dry mouth and lick their lips in an effort to combat this feeling. They experience the feeling of dry mouth due to the stress and tension involved in lying.

Of course, dry mouth can occur due to any stress or tension, the person doesn't have to be lying. Therefore, make sure you look for other signs of deception to form a pattern or cluster of behaviors. The cracking of someone's voice is a great additional sign to look for. Or should I say listen?

Another side effect of dry mouth is the cracking of one's voice. When people lie, they may experience this. Of course, the person might simply be thirsty. However, if you see them licking their lips a lot and then hear the voice start cracking like their throat has dried up, then you have reason to be suspicious. Therefore, pay attention to the sound of their voice and the additional signs that may occur.

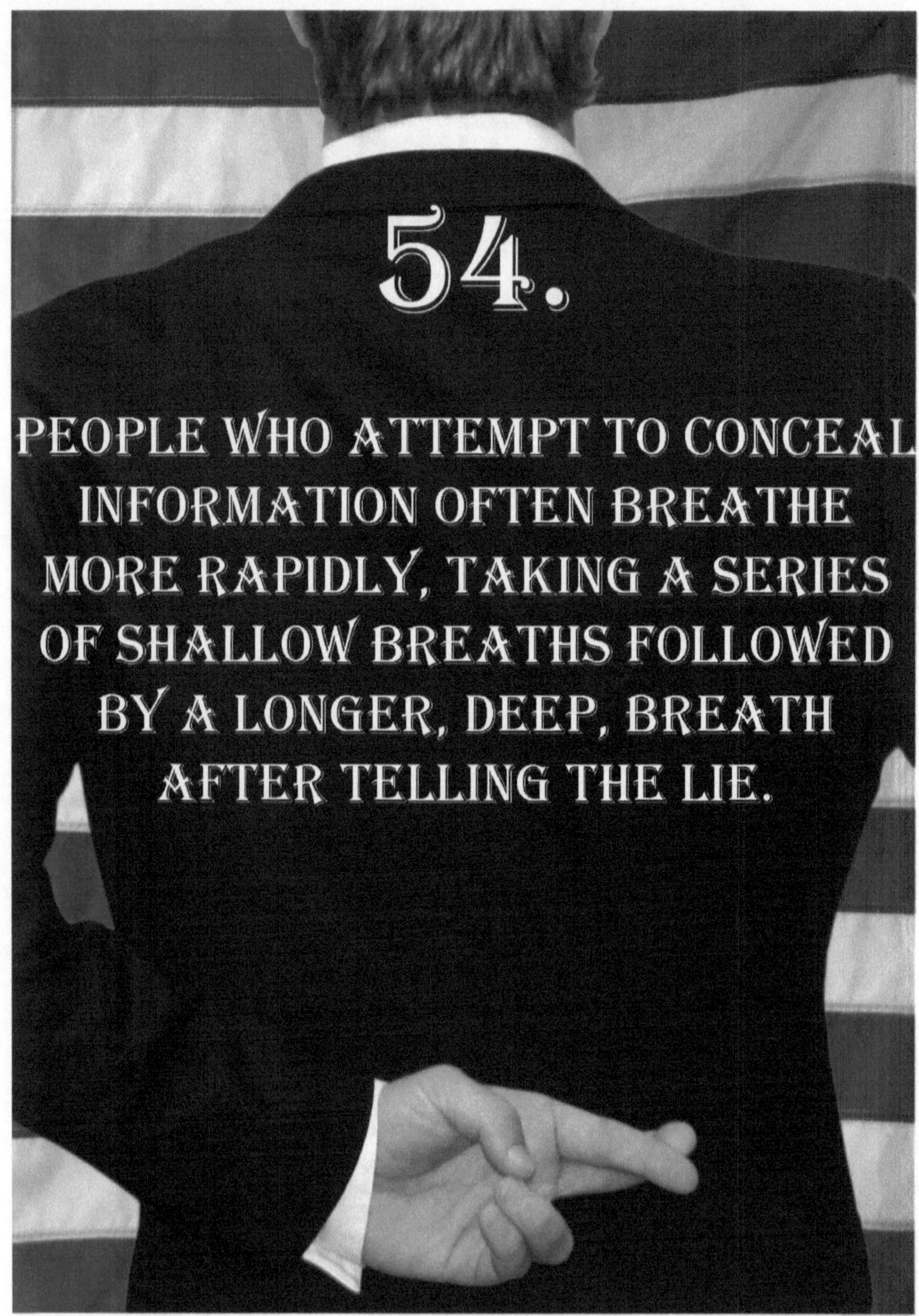
54.

PEOPLE WHO ATTEMPT TO CONCEAL
INFORMATION OFTEN BREATHE
MORE RAPIDLY, TAKING A SERIES
OF SHALLOW BREATHS FOLLOWED
BY A LONGER, DEEP, BREATH
AFTER TELLING THE LIE.

Deception Tip 54 – Breathe Rapidly

People who attempt to conceal information often breathe more rapidly, taking a series of shallow breaths followed by a longer, deep, breath after telling the lie.

Breathing is something that everyone must do. If they don't breathe now, then they will have to sooner or later. If not, they won't be around much longer. Since everyone must breathe, this is a great sign on which to focus your attention. You should be able to recognize normal breathing and abnormal breathing pretty easily.

When people breathe abnormally, there is a reason. If it's some form of medical reason then you can dismiss it as a sign of deception. Often times, you may not know the reason. This is why it is essential to look for other signs of deception and find clusters of behavior. However, this form of breathing is a little more than abnormal.

It involves breathing with short shallow breaths, almost like the person is panting or hyperventilating. This will occur when the person is telling the lie. It may also happen before they tell the lie and shortly after they tell the lie. Then, once the lie has been told, the person may take a long, deep breath. This is almost like a sigh of relief that the lie is over.

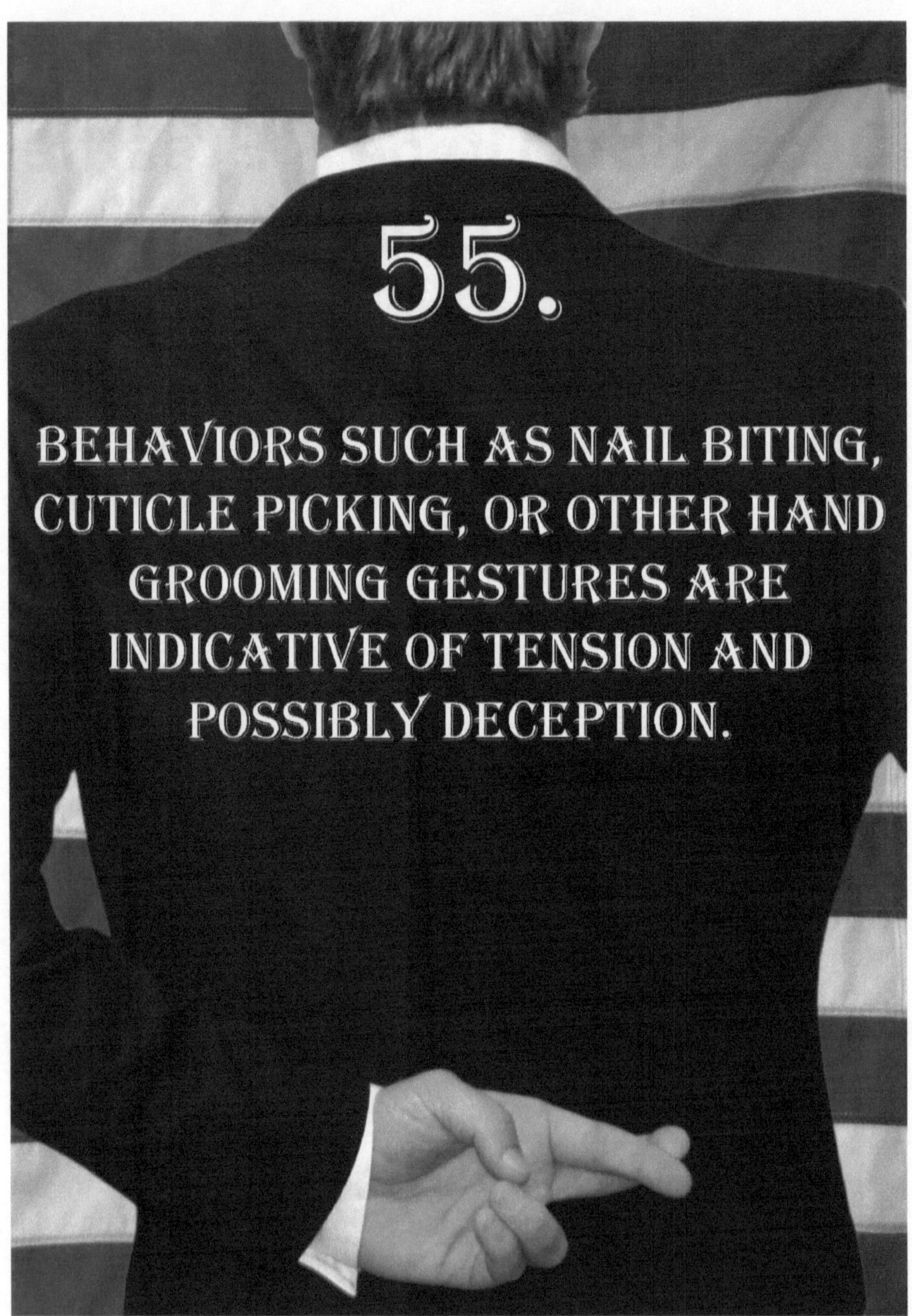
55.

BEHAVIORS SUCH AS NAIL BITING, CUTICLE PICKING, OR OTHER HAND GROOMING GESTURES ARE INDICATIVE OF TENSION AND POSSIBLY DECEPTION.

Deception Tip 55 – Grooming Hands

Behaviors such as nail biting, cuticle picking, or other hand grooming gestures are indicative of tension and possibly deception.

People like to pacify the time, especially when they are being questioned or interrogated. Often, when there is nothing else to do, people will engage in self-grooming gestures. This is often because when there is nothing else to notice they start taking notice of themselves. They have time to be critical.

In addition to improving appearance, self-grooming gestures can also promote peace of mind and release tension. This is because the person can now feel a little better and more confident in his or her appearance. As you know, when people are being deceptive they experience a lot of tension. Since self-grooming is a form of tension release it could also be a sign of deception.

Be on the lookout for self-grooming, and when you see it, ask yourself why the person may be engaging in that behavior. Do they have an important meeting? Are they trying to impress someone? There is often a reasonable explanation. However, if there isn't, then watch for other signs of deception to appear.

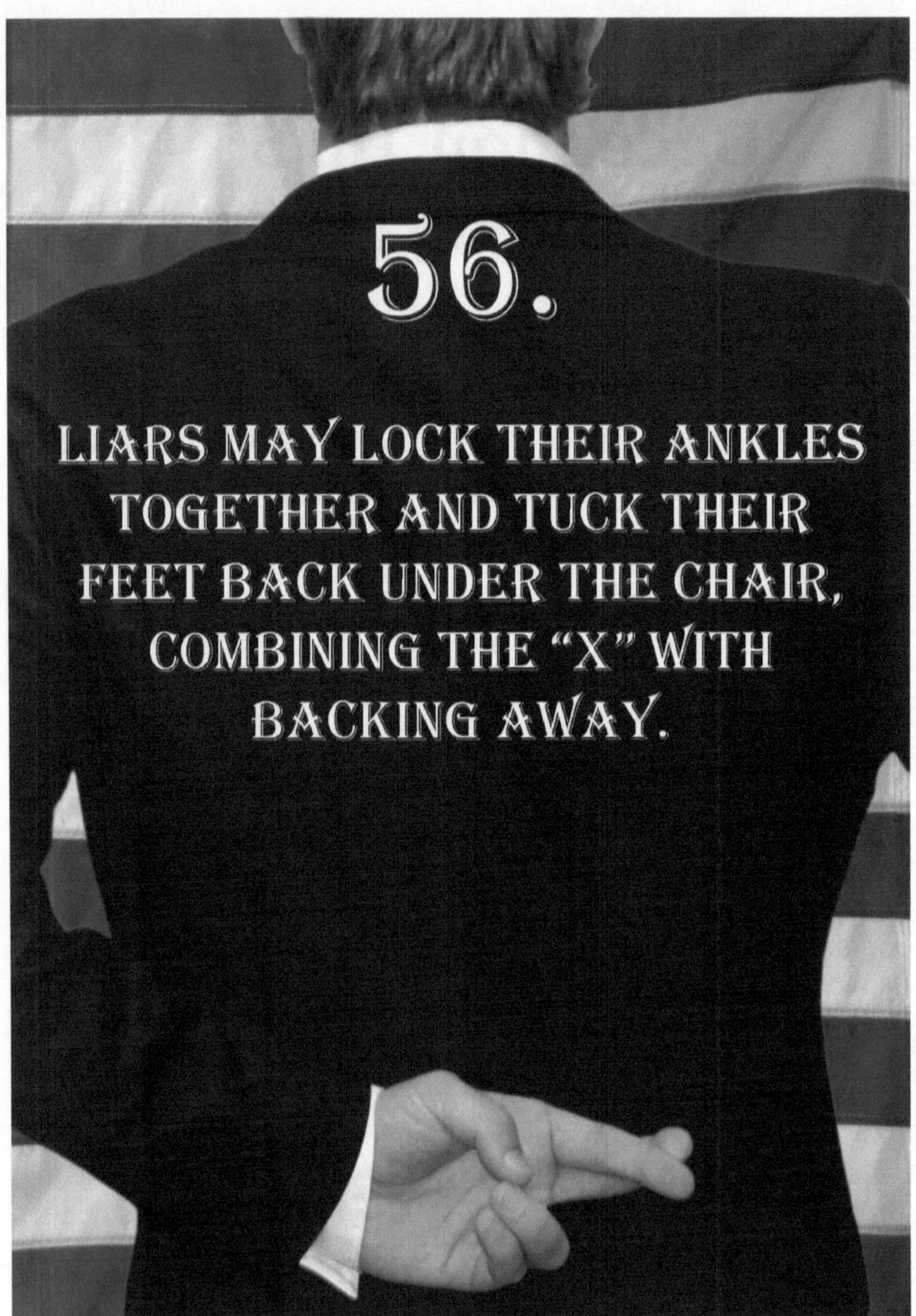
56.

LIARS MAY LOCK THEIR ANKLES TOGETHER AND TUCK THEIR FEET BACK UNDER THE CHAIR, COMBINING THE "X" WITH BACKING AWAY.

Deception Tip 56 – Ankles Backing Away

Liars may lock their ankles together and tuck their feet back under the chair, combining the "X" with backing away.

This tip is one that you should already be familiar with and hopefully, understand. Therefore, if you don't understand it fully, I encourage you to go back and check out Deception Tip 22 Locked Ankles, Deception Tip 29 Step Backward, and Deception Tip 49 Calf Muscle.

Each of these tips has similar components that all make up the current tip. Liars may lock their ankles together. You learned this in Deception Tip 22. It is a form of stress release and tension. In addition, liars may tuck their feet back. This is a variation of backing away from the situation, which you learned about in Deception Tip 29. Finally, they may cross their legs in an "X" to block the perceptions of the target. This was mentioned in Deception Tip 49.

All of these tips can be combined into the common behavior of locked ankles, crossed legs, and tucked back feet. Although this is somewhat of a cluster of behaviors, due to the fact that it all occurs within one area of the body it isn't considered a defining cluster. Therefore, you must watch for additional signs of deception before making any conclusions.

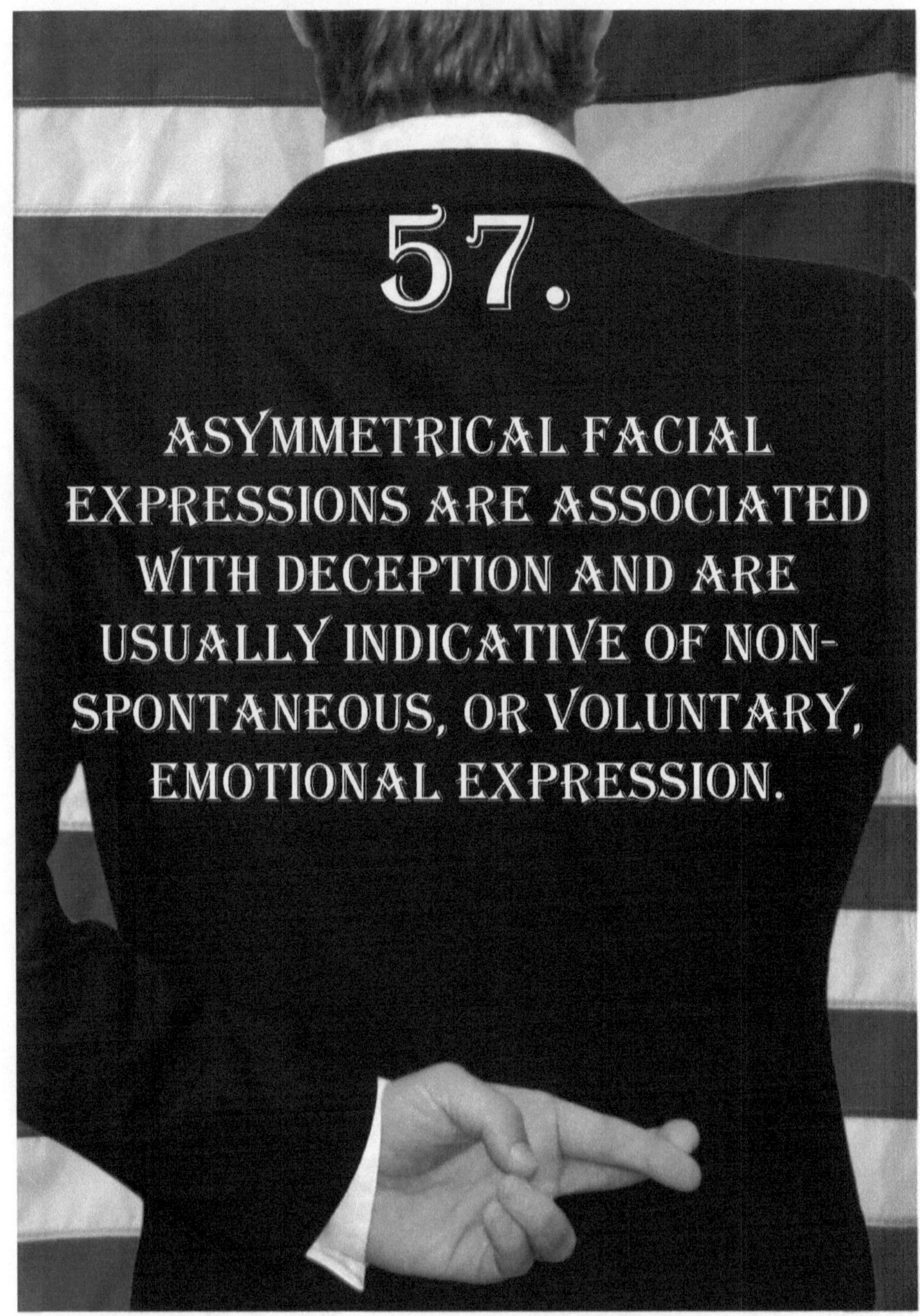
57.

ASYMMETRICAL FACIAL
EXPRESSIONS ARE ASSOCIATED
WITH DECEPTION AND ARE
USUALLY INDICATIVE OF NON-
SPONTANEOUS, OR VOLUNTARY,
EMOTIONAL EXPRESSION.

Deception Tip 57 – Asymmetrical Expressions

Asymmetrical facial expressions are associated with deception and are usually indicative of non-spontaneous, or voluntary, emotional expression.

You know from Deception Tip 14 Symmetrical Expressions that the facial expressions people display must be symmetrical. If they are asymmetrical, then there is a pretty good chance that the person is being deceptive. Of course, contempt is the exception to this rule because it is the only truthful asymmetrical expression.

Remember that the brain has two hemispheres and each one controls the opposite side of the body. The right hemisphere controls the left side of the body and the left hemisphere controls the right side of the body. In addition, do you remember which side of the brain is more active in false emotions or lying? If not, check out Deception Tip 23 once more.

It is the right side of the brain. This means that false emotions will be more prominent on the left side of the face. Therefore, if you notice that people are more expressive on the left side of the face, then there is a good chance they are being deceptive. Of course, the expression may be displayed on both sides of the face. However, it will be the left that is more expressive.

58.

WHEN DETECTING DECEPTION,
WATCH THE ADAM'S APPLE.
IT MAY JUMP OR MOVE
IRREGULARLY WHEN
SOMEONE IS LYING.

Deception Tip 58 – Adam's Apple

When detecting deception, watch the Adam's apple. It may jump or move irregularly when someone is lying.

There are so many different signs that may indicate that someone is being deceptive. In addition, many of these signs are only potential signs in that they have more than one meaning. This is why your biggest friends when detecting deception are patterns and clusters of behavior. You must always look for more than one sign because if someone is lying there will definitely be more than one sign.

While speaking with someone, pay attention to the Adam's apple. Of course, on some people, this will be more difficult than others. Some people, especially women, don't have much of an Adam's apple. Therefore, this is merely something to keep in mind when detecting deception. It's an item to check off your list. If they have an Adam's apple then watch it when they speak.

Sometimes, when people are telling lies, their Adam's apple may jump, or suddenly move. It will look a little strange and be very sudden and unnatural. You may also hear voice cracking, which we discussed in Deception Tip 53. Now you are on your way to building a cluster of deceptive behavior.

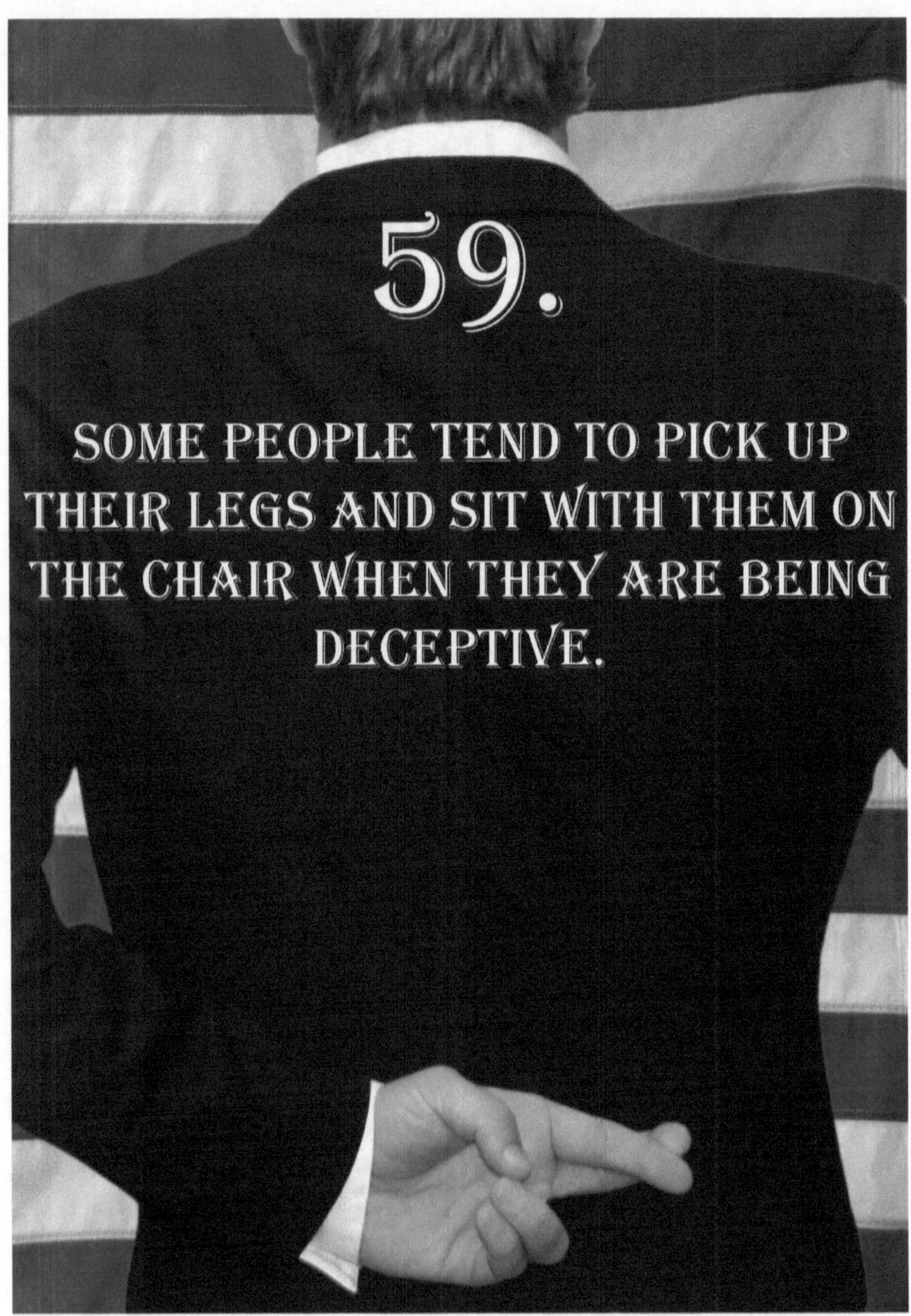
59.

SOME PEOPLE TEND TO PICK UP
THEIR LEGS AND SIT WITH THEM ON
THE CHAIR WHEN THEY ARE BEING
DECEPTIVE.

Deception Tip 59 – Pick Up Legs

Some people tend to pick up their legs and sit with them on the chair when they are being deceptive.

When people are lying, there is a huge battle happening in their mind. This is a war waging between the conscious and the unconscious minds. The conscious is trying to tell, and get away with, the lie. The unconscious is trying to reveal the truth. Due to the fact that the conscious has the voice, and is in the front, so to speak, the unconscious must use other methods.

To put it simply, the conscious is by definition conscious. The unconscious is by definition unconscious. The conscious uses outward communication whereas the unconscious must use hidden signs. They are both speaking a different language and your goal is to learn the unconscious language and make it conscious.

Remember in Deception Tip 40 Take Up Space, that liars tend to reduce the amount of space they occupy so that people will be unable to see the unconscious truthful signs that are being leaked. People may also sit with their legs on the chair for the same reason. Therefore, if you see this, watch for additional signs of deception.

60.

CONFIDENT PEOPLE TEND TO
DOMINATE THE SPACE THEY
OCCUPY, WHEREAS LIARS TAKE
UP THE LEAST AMOUNT OF
SPACE POSSIBLE.

Deception Tip 60 – Dominate Space

Confident people tend to dominate the space they occupy, whereas liars take up the least amount of space possible.

This is a tip that you should already understand. Liars tend to shrink and take up less space. They like to curl up so that other people will not be able to notice the different signs of deception that may be leaked as a result of telling a lie. You learned about this is Deception Tip 40 Take Up Space and Deception Tip 59 Pick Up Legs.

This tip is the opposite. When someone is confident, he or she will dominate the space they occupy. This is usually pretty obvious. Look at any business meeting or conference. There are certain people who put their papers all over the table and lean back in their chair with extended feet. They are confident. They occupy the most real estate. People listen to them.

This is a great way to see how things will play out. Watch people and if they spread out then you know they are confident. However, if they curl up and cower then you know they are shy. Seems like common sense. However, it will really help you realize what is going on, or what is about to go on, in a situation.

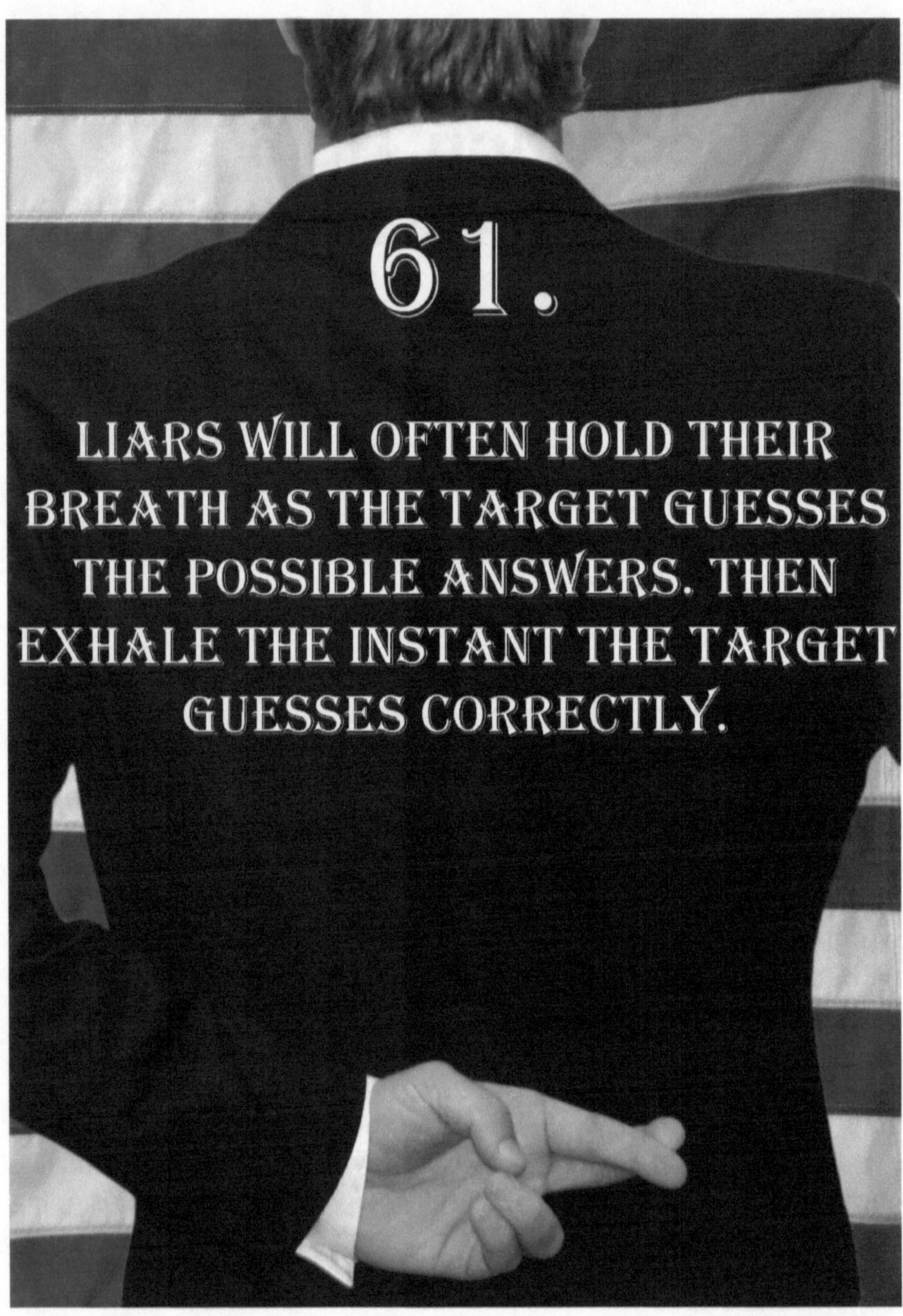
61.

LIARS WILL OFTEN HOLD THEIR
BREATH AS THE TARGET GUESSES
THE POSSIBLE ANSWERS. THEN
EXHALE THE INSTANT THE TARGET
GUESSES CORRECTLY.

Deception Tip 61 – Guessing Answers

Liars will often hold their breath as the target guesses the possible answers. Then exhale the instant the target guesses correctly.

In Deception Tip 21 Suggesting Answers, we discussed how when the target guesses the correct answer a liar may freeze for a split second. It is almost as if they are in shock that the target found the correct answer. This is a very similar tip. In addition to potentially freezing like a deer in the headlights, a liar may exhale.

This might sound a little confusing so I'll break it down for you. When a target is going through the possible answers and guessing the possibilities. A liar may be holding his or her breath in fear and anticipation. Then, the instant the target guesses correctly, the liar will freeze with surprise and then exhale in relief.

This relief is the unconscious relief that appears because the truth came out. All of this will happen in a matter of seconds. The good news is that if you miss the freezing and mouth in an "O" shape that you may still be able to notice the exhale of relief.

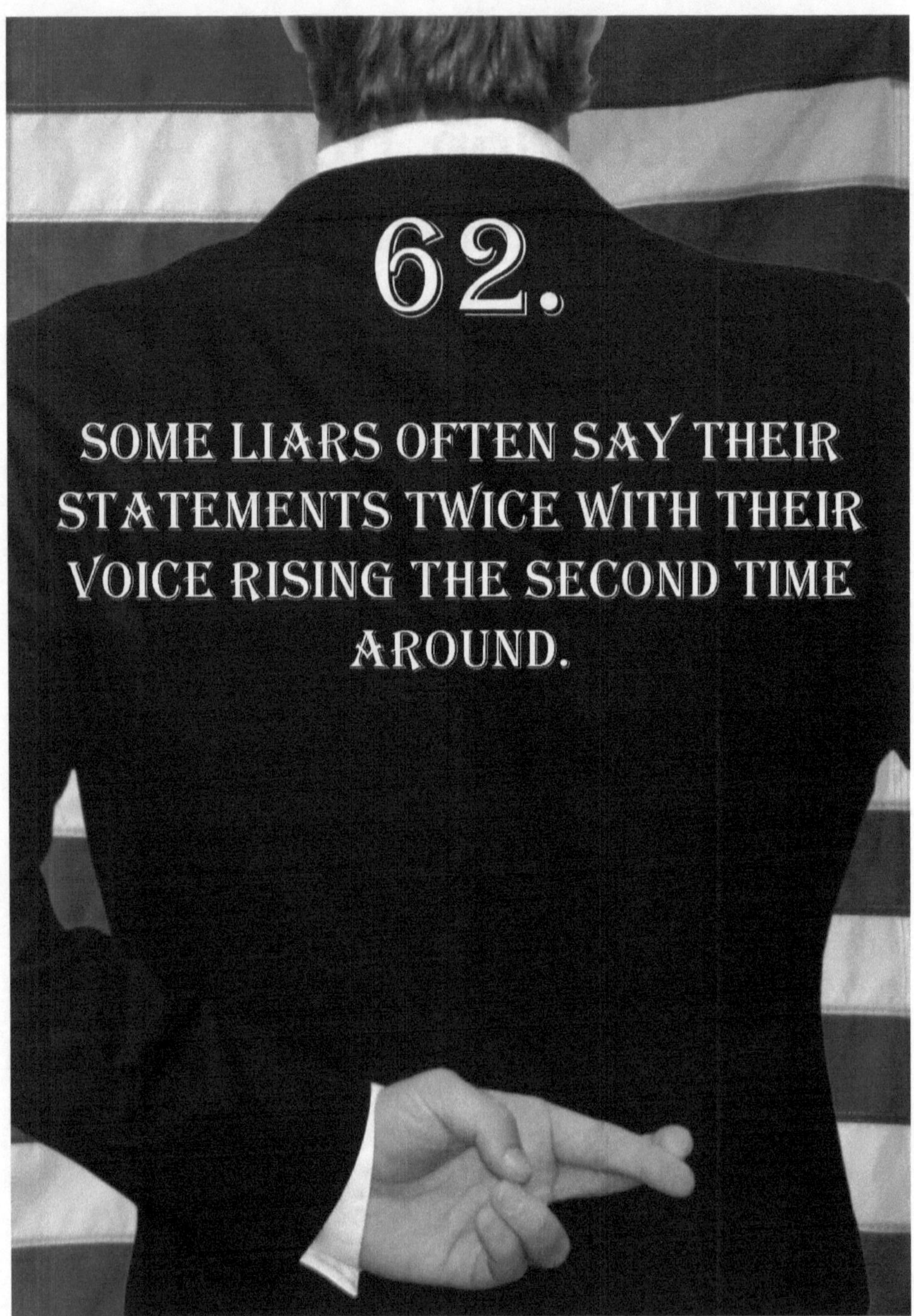

62.

SOME LIARS OFTEN SAY THEIR
STATEMENTS TWICE WITH THEIR
VOICE RISING THE SECOND TIME
AROUND.

Deception Tip 62 – Statements Twice

Some liars often say their statements twice with their voice rising the second time around.

When people lie, they want other people to believe them. This is one of the primary goals when lying. They want people to believe the lie as if it were true. Of course, they also want to get away with the lie so that they don't have to experience the potential consequences presented by the truth. Therefore, they will often emphasize what they are saying.

You have learned about this several times already in a few different tips. Deception Tips 5 Contractions, 24 Pledging Truthfulness, and 31 Unconventional Language are great examples of this. Therefore, if you don't remember them entirely it may be wise to go back and review them. In all of these examples, liars emphasized what they were saying.

This tip is very similar. Some liars may repeat what they say to further emphasize what they are saying. This is done so that people will think it is important and then potentially believe it. However, the liar's voice may get higher the second time they say the statement.

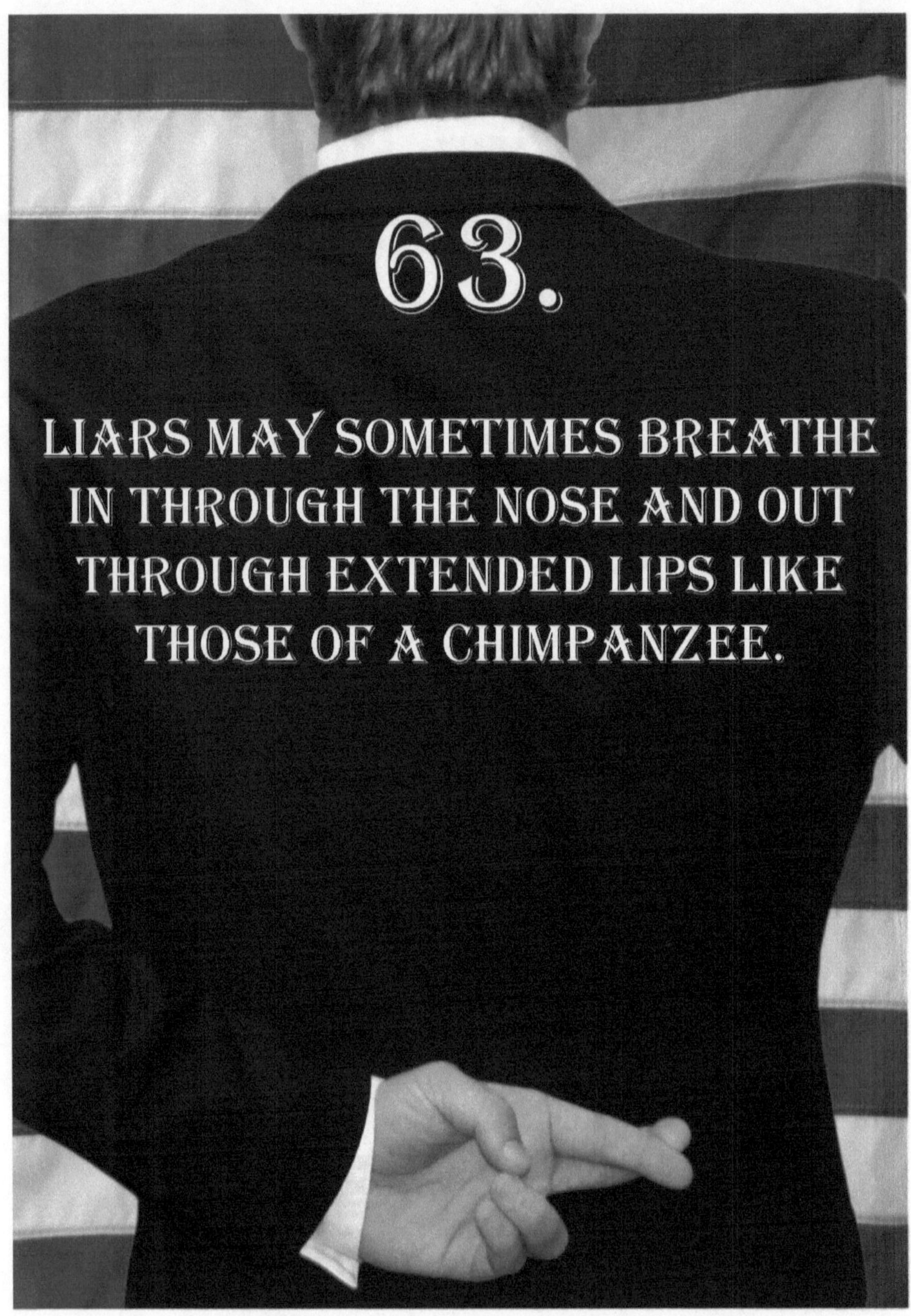
63.
LIARS MAY SOMETIMES BREATHE
IN THROUGH THE NOSE AND OUT
THROUGH EXTENDED LIPS LIKE
THOSE OF A CHIMPANZEE.

Deception Tip 63 – Chimpanzee Lips

Liars may sometimes breathe in through the nose and out through extended lips like those of a chimpanzee.

Controlled breathing is a wonderful way to release stress and tension. As you know, when people lie they are under a lot of stress and tension. There is not only the stress of telling the lie, but there also is the stress of getting caught, potential consequences of the truth, consequences of getting caught lying, what others will think, and more.

In Deception Tip 46 Pursed Lips, you learned that liars might sometimes exhale slowly through pursed lips. The liar might puff up his or her cheeks like a blowfish to pacify the stress and tension involved in telling a lie. This tip is very similar in that it is a breathing exercise that involves exhaling through extended lips like a chimpanzee.

Remember that the lips of liars take on all sorts of different positions so anytime you see something strange going on with someone's lips then pay attention. There may be other signs of deception. In addition, if people start doing funny things with their breathing then pay attention as well. Either there is a medical problem or they are being deceptive.

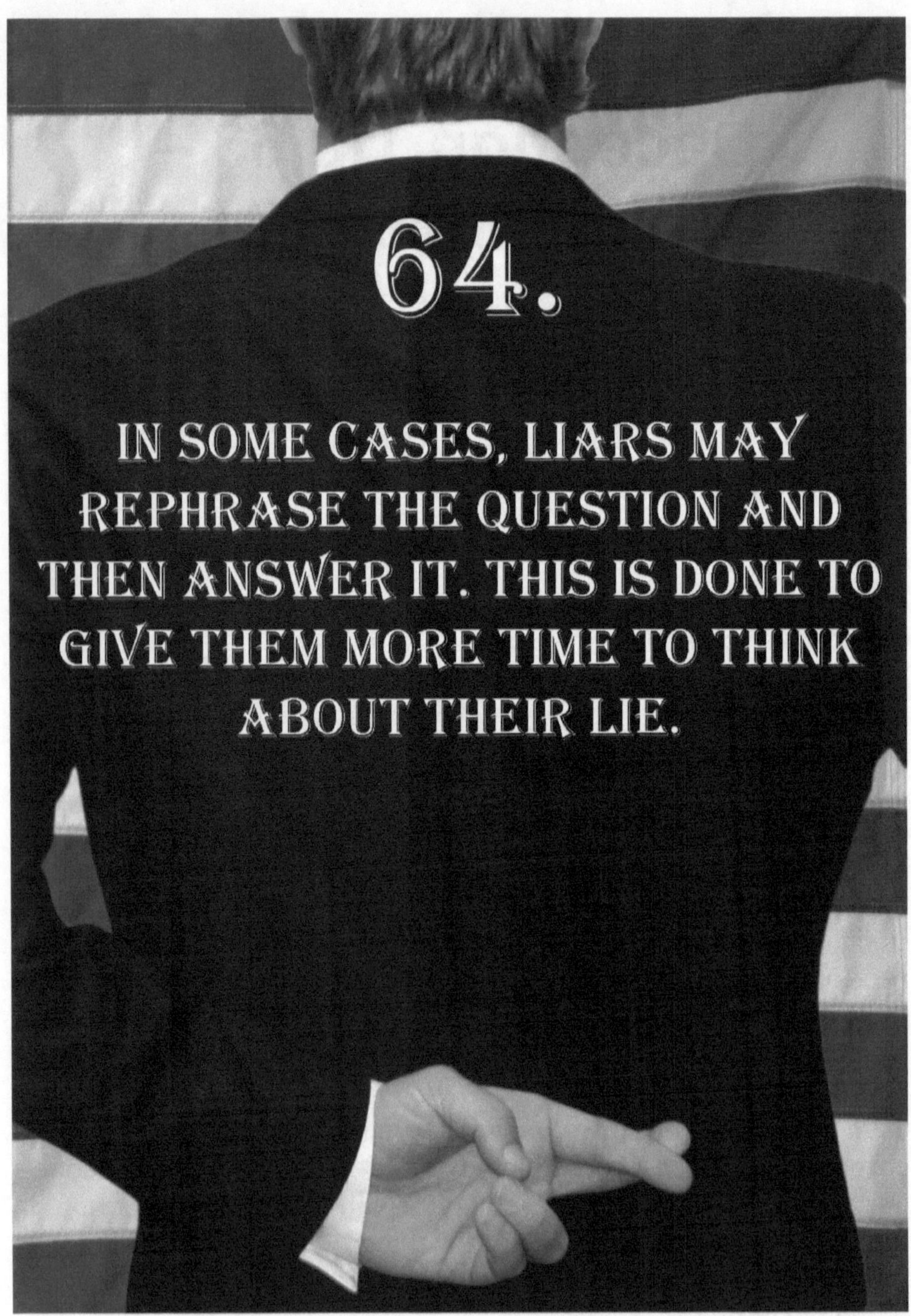
64.

IN SOME CASES, LIARS MAY REPHRASE THE QUESTION AND THEN ANSWER IT. THIS IS DONE TO GIVE THEM MORE TIME TO THINK ABOUT THEIR LIE.

Deception Tip 64 – Rephrase The Question

In some cases, liars may rephrase the question and then answer it. This is done to give them more time to think about their lie.

When people tell lies they want to have as much time as they can, especially in the heat of the moment. When someone is questioning them, they need time to take a mental break and prepare to deliver their lie. This is why there are so many stalling tactics seen in deceptive behaviors. We've gone over at least five different types.

This tip is another variation of a stalling tactic. Once again, a stalling tactic is anything that the liar does to give him or herself more time to respond. In this example, the liar may rephrase the question in an effort to have a little more time to deliver the lie. Remember, that it isn't much time. We're only talking a few seconds, simply enough for a mental break.

In addition, rephrasing the question allows them to think about the question in a different way. Therefore, sometimes, they will give themselves more than a few seconds. It is very similar to Deception Tip 43 Repeat The Question. Basically, anytime you notice someone is using a stalling tactic, ask yourself why he or she is stalling.

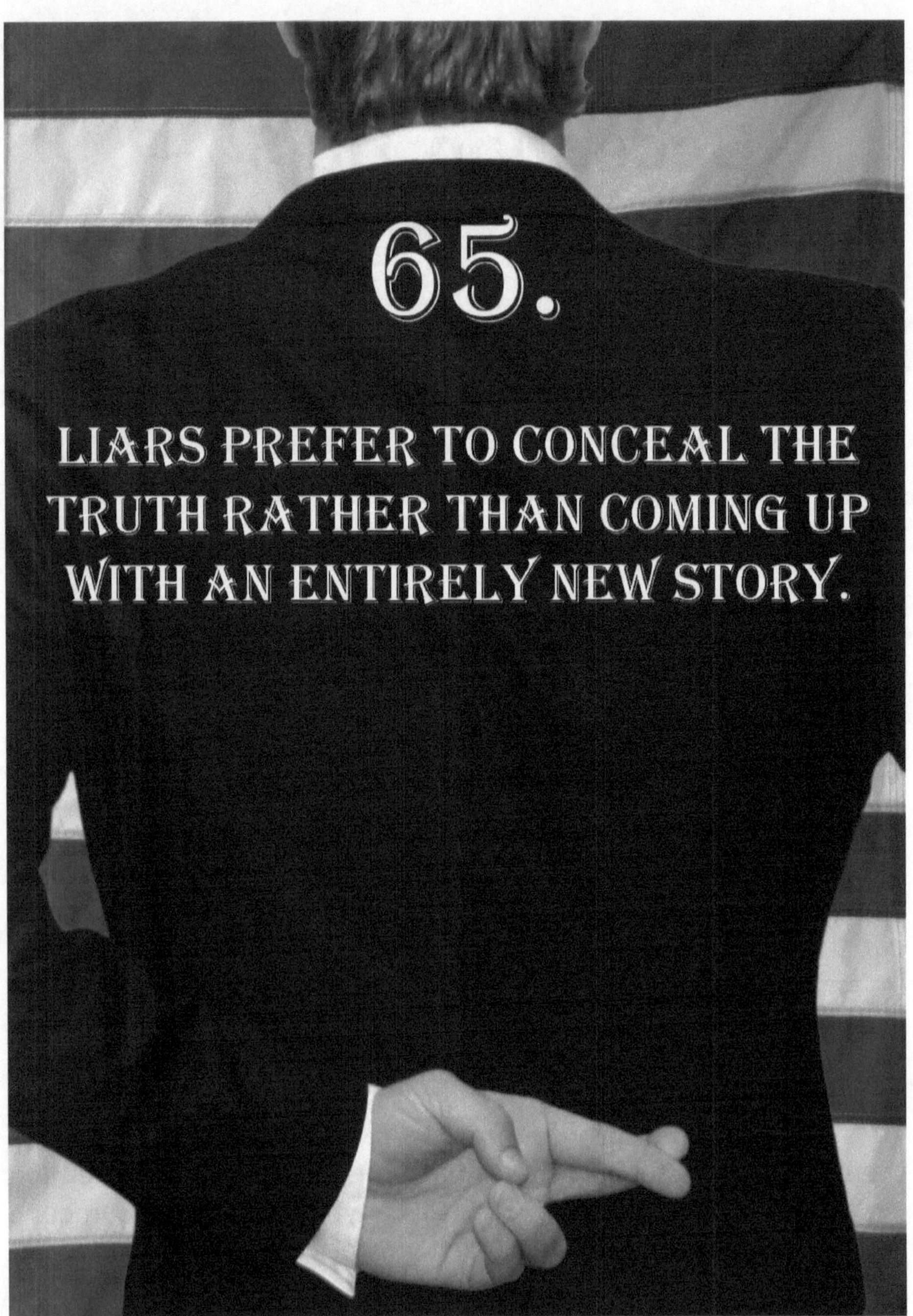
65.

LIARS PREFER TO CONCEAL THE
TRUTH RATHER THAN COMING UP
WITH AN ENTIRELY NEW STORY.

Deception Tip 65 – Conceal The Truth

Liars prefer to conceal the truth rather than coming up with an entirely new story.

Telling lies can require a lot of memory. The liar must remember all kinds of fictitious details and events in order to convince others that the event really happened as they say. For this reason, liars like to stick close to the truth and conceal the lie rather than coming up with an entirely false story.

This is something that you can use to your advantage. Chances are that many liars are dancing on the line of truth and falsity. Therefore, you can step on that line with them and use some tactics to make them fall. We've gone over a few of these before. Some examples include accusing them of something else or giving them a lie to use in their story.

In any case, if you know there is some truth to their lie then you may be able to add some of your own details and get them to start talking about things that you know for certain are false. This way you will certainly be able to catch them in their lie.

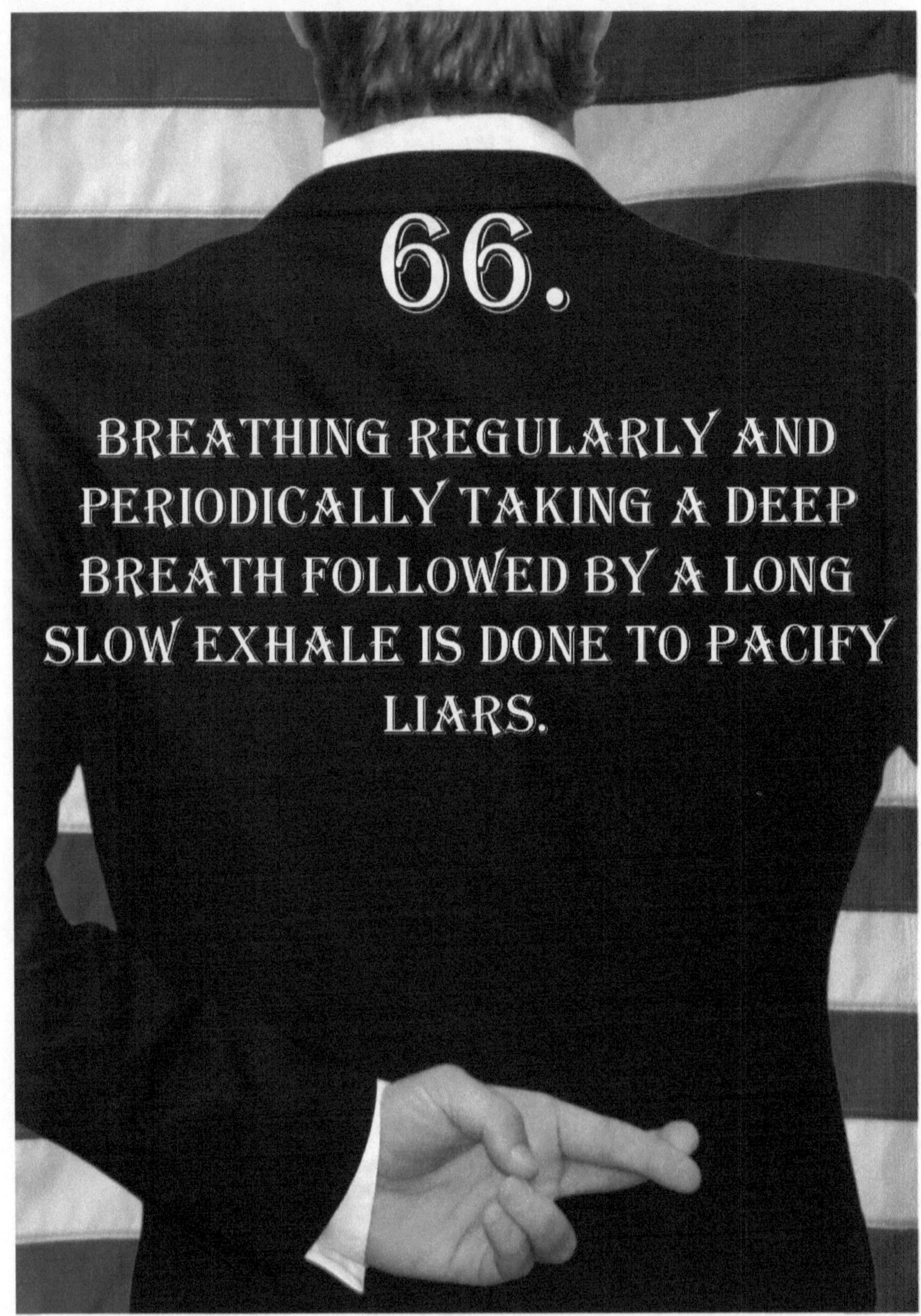
66.
BREATHING REGULARLY AND
PERIODICALLY TAKING A DEEP
BREATH FOLLOWED BY A LONG
SLOW EXHALE IS DONE TO PACIFY
LIARS.

Deception Tip 66 – Deep Breath

Breathing regularly and periodically taking a deep breath followed by a long slow exhale is done to pacify liars.

Remember that breathing is something that everyone must do. In addition, it is something with which you should be very familiar. Therefore, when people start to breathe differently than normal, you should be able to notice it. Remember, there are only a couple reasons why breathing would be abnormal. One is that there is some medical explanation and the other is deception.

If you can rule out medical reasons, including panting, exercise, tiredness, asthma, et cetera, then the only thing that is left is deception. Liars may hold their breath, exhale in relief, breathe as if hyperventilating, et cetera. There are all kinds of different breathing patterns that can be displayed by people who are being deceptive.

If someone is breathing regularly and taking a deep breath once in a while and then slowly exhaling, then this could be a sign of deception. It is a breath of stress relief. In addition, if it is being done with pursed lips or chimpanzee lips like in Deception Tips 46 and 63 then you really need to be on the lookout for other signs of deception.

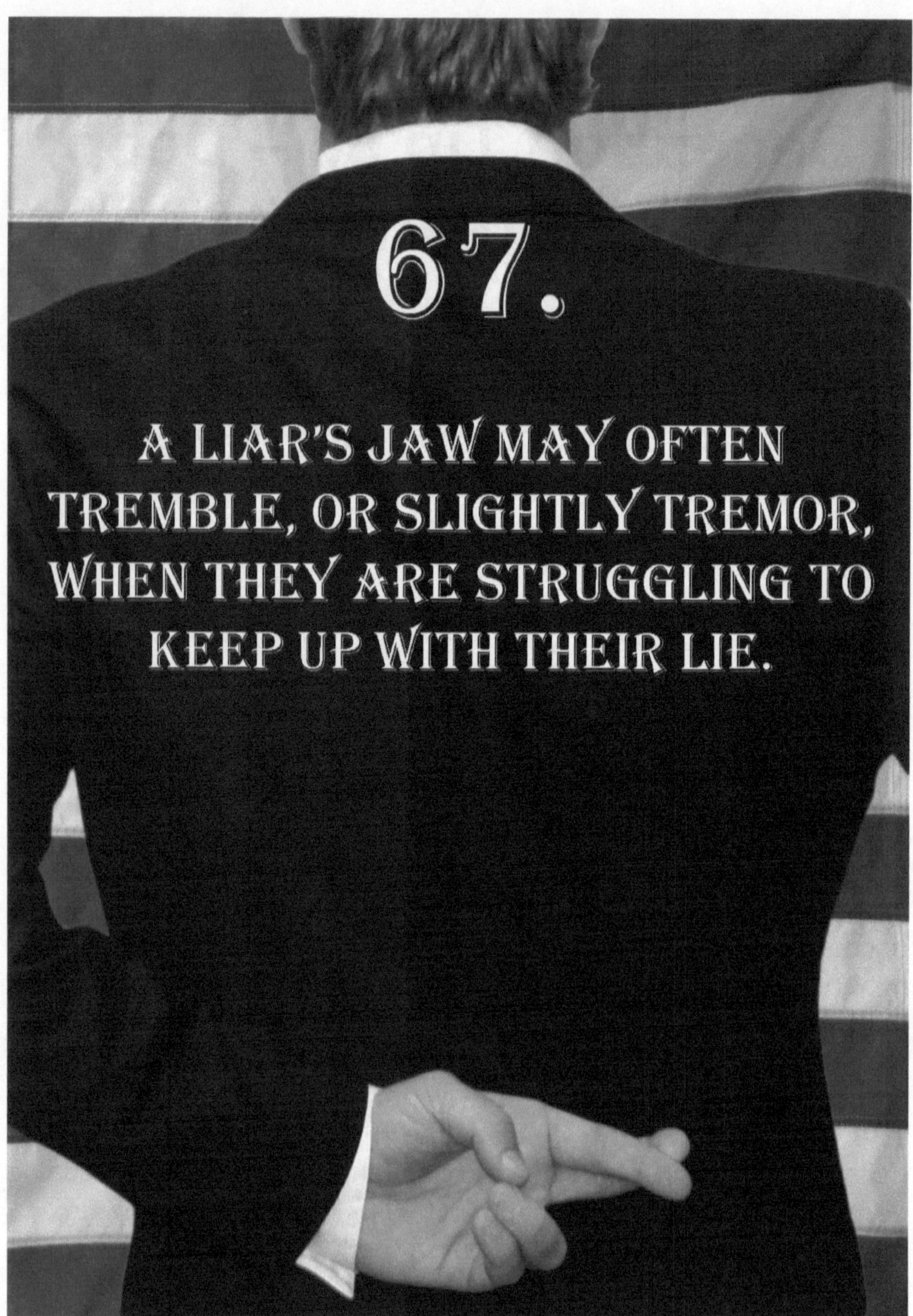

67.
A LIAR'S JAW MAY OFTEN TREMBLE, OR SLIGHTLY TREMOR, WHEN THEY ARE STRUGGLING TO KEEP UP WITH THEIR LIE.

Deception Tip 67 – Jaw Tremble

A liar's jaw may often tremble, or slightly tremor, when they are struggling to keep up with their lie.

Fear is a common emotion that can be displayed when a liar is afraid of being caught. In addition, if you begin to question a liar's story and poke holes in it, then he or she may display fear as well. They are afraid of the consequences of the truth and even more afraid of the added consequences of lying about it.

Thus, you may see a liar's jaw tremble when he or she is trying to keep up with telling a lie. The person may be trying to salvage their broken position and when they realize that it is a losing battle, this display of fear may occur. It is a sign of struggling and can be accompanied with stuttering or stammering as they try to speak.

No matter what, if you see someone's jaw tremble there is something going on. The person may be afraid, sad, or something else. The point is, that some form of emotion is happening. It is up to you to determine the cause of that emotion. Is it due to lying or some other factor? Look for other signs of deception to help your conclusion.

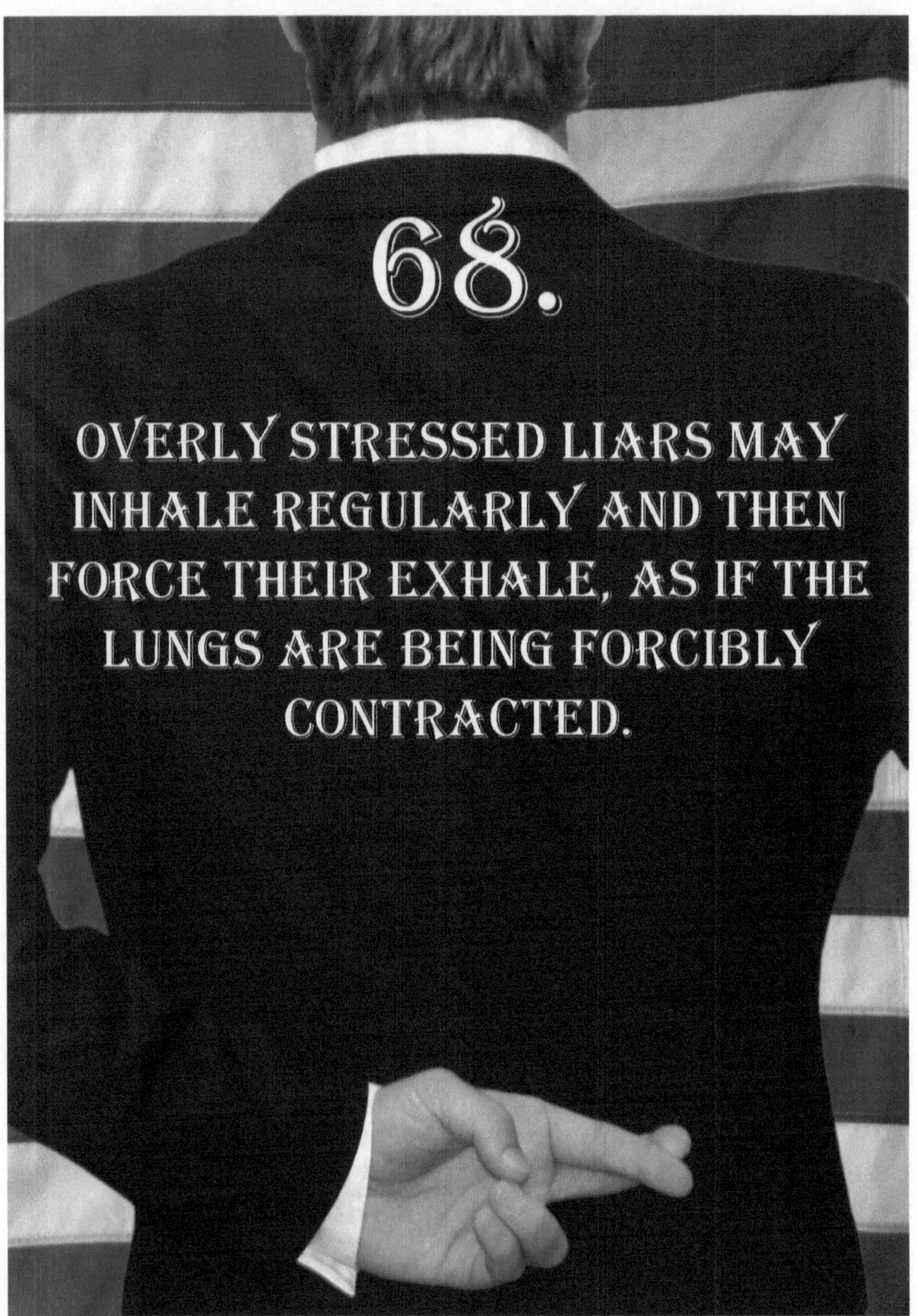
68.

OVERLY STRESSED LIARS MAY INHALE REGULARLY AND THEN FORCE THEIR EXHALE, AS IF THE LUNGS ARE BEING FORCIBLY CONTRACTED.

Deception Tip 68 – Force Exhale

Overly stressed liars may inhale regularly and then force their exhale, as if the lungs are being forcibly contracted.

We've been talking a lot about breathing and the different breathing things that liars may do when they are stressed. In addition, remember that their lips may take on all kinds of different shapes when they are breathing. Know that when people have breathing problems that it can be due to a medical reason as well.

Breathing exercises are a great way to relieve stress and that is why liars use them when they are in the midst of telling a lie. This particular breathing exercise occurs when a person is regularly breathing and then, all of a sudden, they exhale very forcefully. This is almost like someone pushed all of the air out of them.

The bottom line is that breathing is something that everyone has to do. Therefore, you should pay attention to it. In addition, since you have to do it yourself, you should be aware of your own breathing. Then, when you notice irregularities in other people or yourself, see if you can find out the reason behind them.

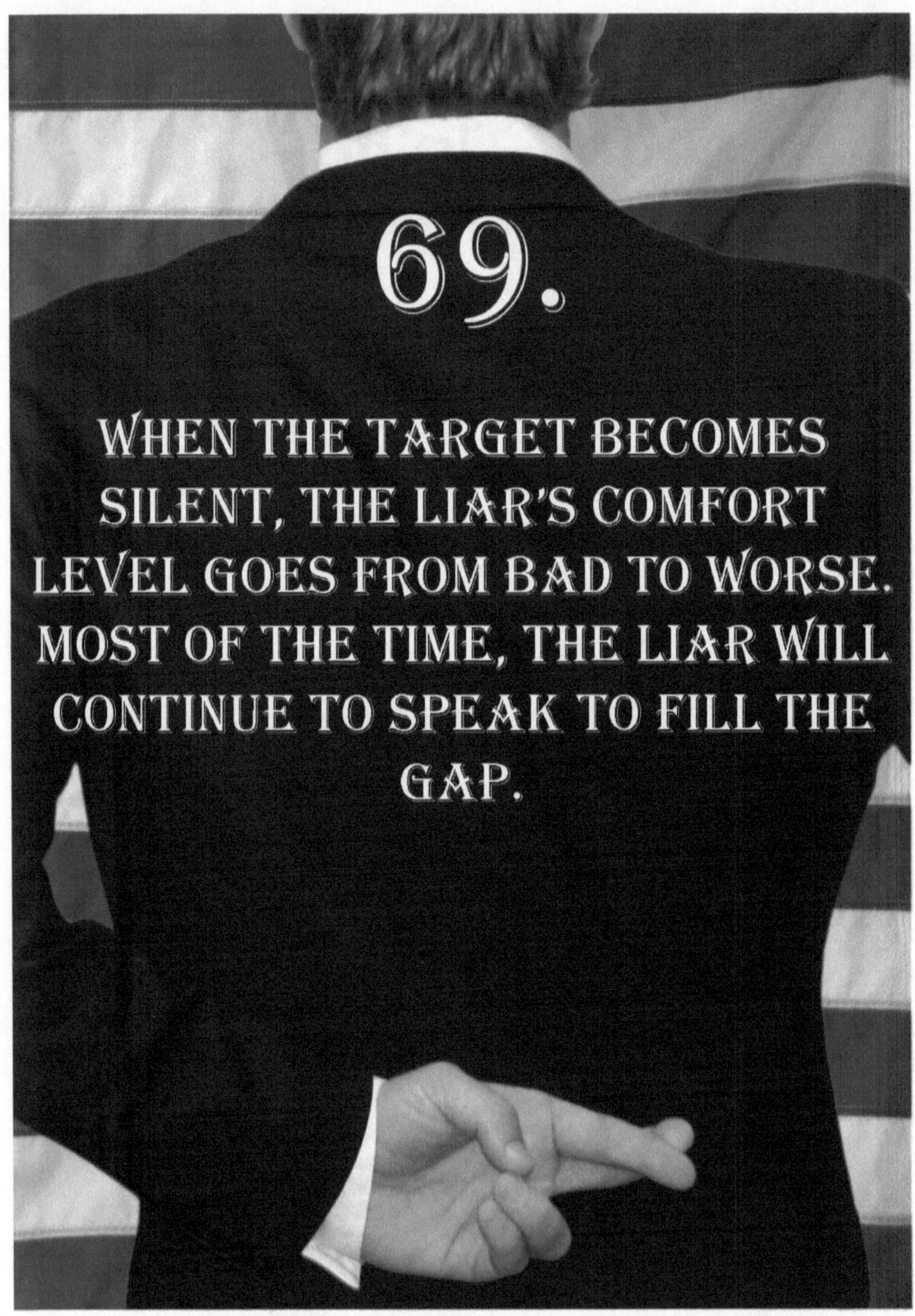
69.
WHEN THE TARGET BECOMES SILENT, THE LIAR'S COMFORT LEVEL GOES FROM BAD TO WORSE. MOST OF THE TIME, THE LIAR WILL CONTINUE TO SPEAK TO FILL THE GAP.

Deception Tip 69 – Become Silent

When the target becomes silent, the liar's comfort level goes from bad to worse. Most of the time, the liar will continue to speak to fill the gap.

Way back in Deception Tip 13 Stay Silent, you learned about how keeping your mouth shut will encourage the liar to continue to talk. This is because they want you to believe the lie. That is one of the liar's primary goals. They want you to believe them. Therefore, they will often continue to talk until they are convinced you believe their lie.

This is very similar. Silence can be a very uncomfortable thing. You are no doubt familiar with awkward silence. You can use it to your advantage by becoming silent during the conversation. The liar is already uncomfortable. Now you have elevated this discomfort. As a result, you may start to witness many more signs of deception.

In addition, the liar will probably start speaking more in an effort to fill this silence. Often times, they will trip over their tongue and contradict their story. This will reveal the holes in the story and help you determine the truth.

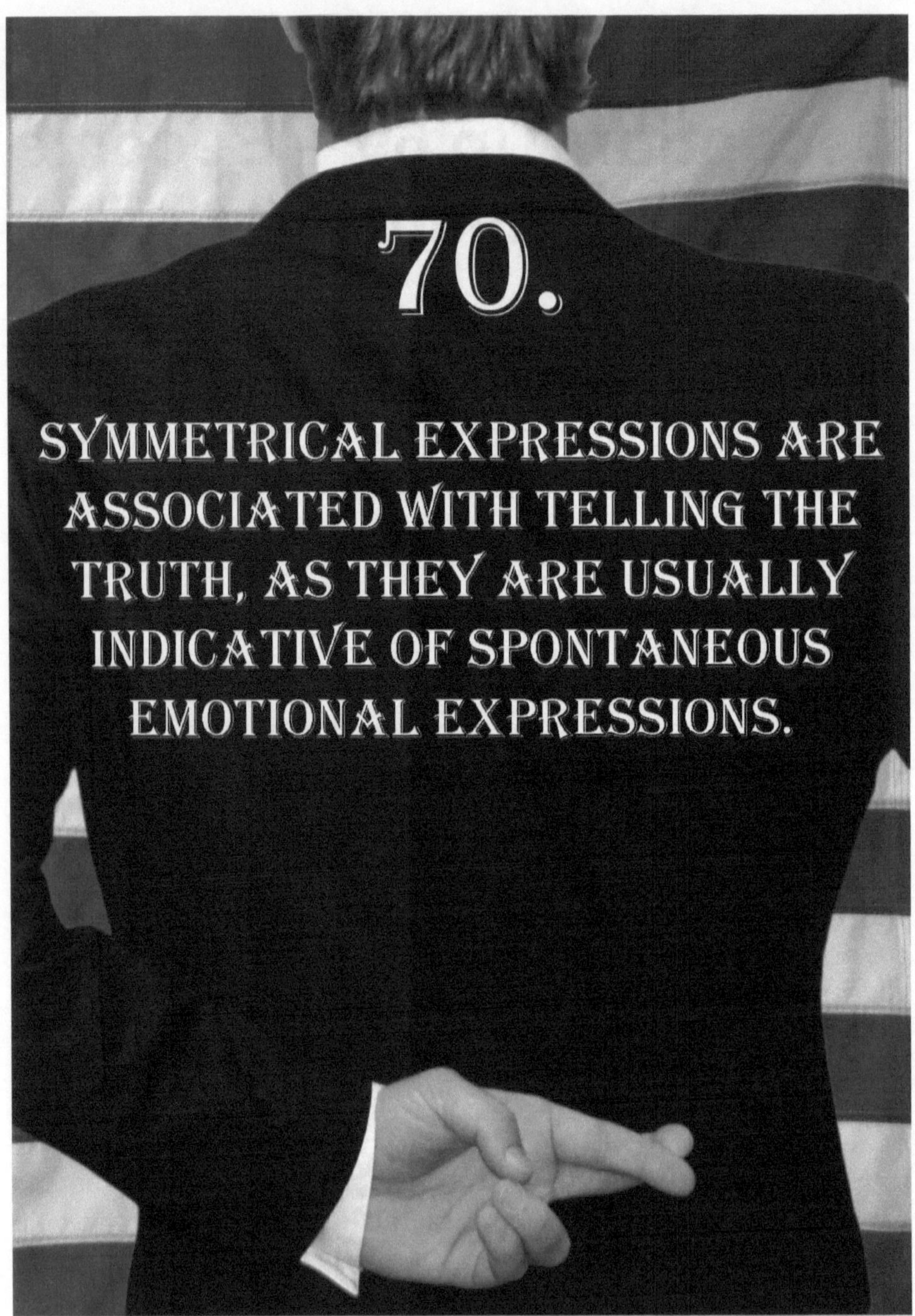
70.

SYMMETRICAL EXPRESSIONS ARE
ASSOCIATED WITH TELLING THE
TRUTH, AS THEY ARE USUALLY
INDICATIVE OF SPONTANEOUS
EMOTIONAL EXPRESSIONS.

Deception Tip 70 – Symmetrical And Spontaneous

Symmetrical expressions are associated with telling the truth, as they are usually indicative of spontaneous emotional expressions.

We've talked a lot about symmetrical and asymmetrical gestures and expressions. Remember that truthful expressions are symmetrical and false expressions are asymmetrical. In addition, truthful expressions are also spontaneous whereas false expressions are non-spontaneous. Truthful behaviors must also be congruent and not contradict one another.

If you need a little review on the different symmetrical tips we've gone over here they are. Deception Tip 3 Contradictory Behaviors, Deception Tip 12 Simultaneous Gestures, Deception Tip 14 Symmetrical Expressions, Deception Tip 16 Symmetrical Gestures, and Deception Tip 57 Asymmetrical Expressions.

I know this is a lot of information centered around one topic. However, it is important. In addition, it's pretty simple. All you need to do is remember that truthful behaviors will appear more natural. They will happen in synchronization with speech and gestures. On the other hand, deceptive behaviors will not.

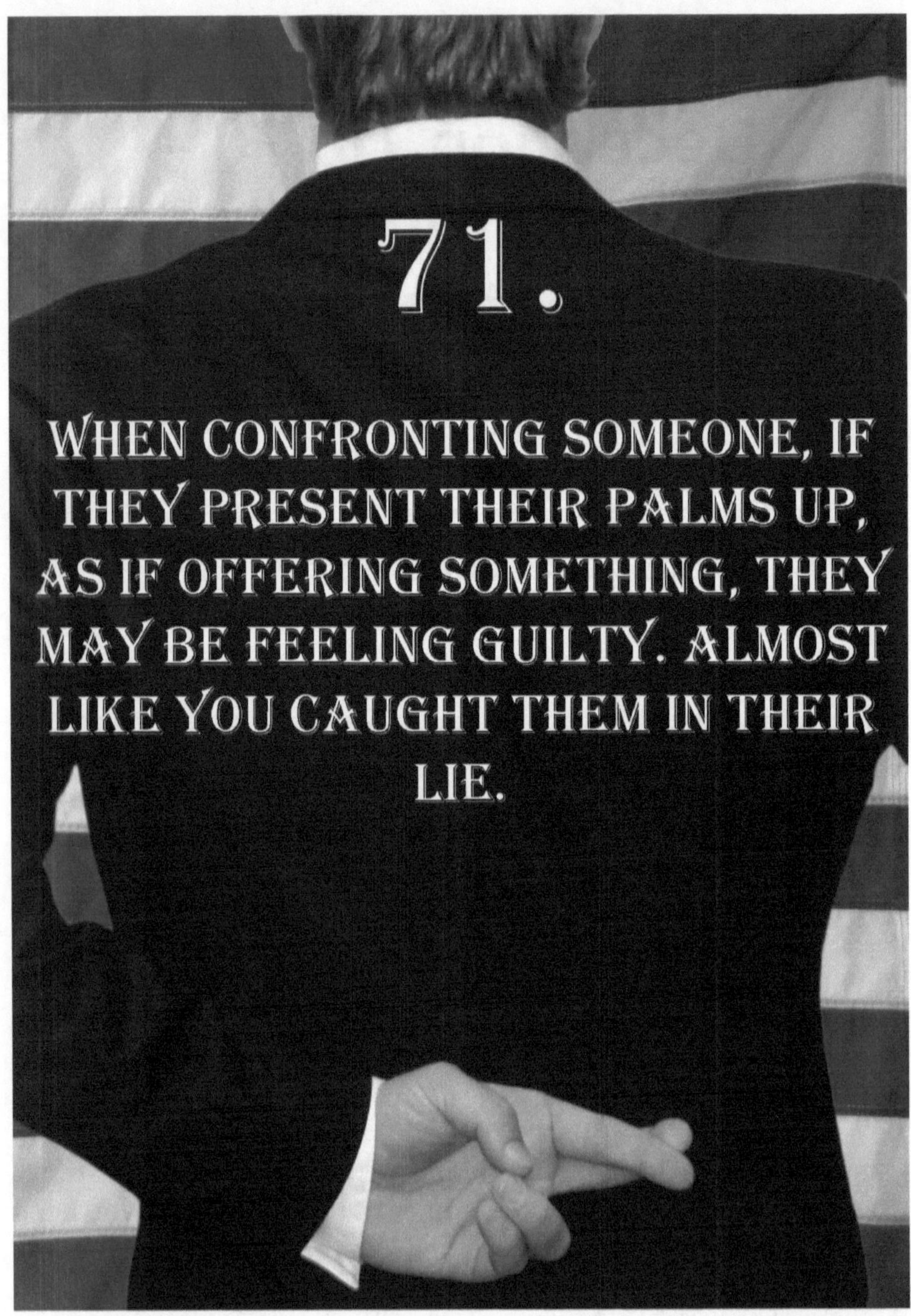
71.

WHEN CONFRONTING SOMEONE, IF THEY PRESENT THEIR PALMS UP, AS IF OFFERING SOMETHING, THEY MAY BE FEELING GUILTY. ALMOST LIKE YOU CAUGHT THEM IN THEIR LIE.

Deception Tip 71 – Palms Up

When confronting someone, if they present their palms up as if offering something they may be feeling guilty. Almost like you caught them in their lie.

Unconscious body language can tell you a lot about what a person is feeling. In addition, it can also help you more effectively communicate with him or her. We've gone over a few behaviors that are similar to this one. Namely Deception Tip 48 Slight Shoulder Shrug.

It is similar in the fact that it is a way of shrugging off the weight of knowledge or guilt. When someone slightly shrugs a shoulder it means they don't firmly believe what they are saying. When someone raises his or her hands it is a direct statement of disassociation. They are saying that they are not a part of whatever is happening.

Remember Deception Tip 29 Step Backward, how some people may raise their hands to ward off the accusation? Anytime someone turns up their hands, they are silently telling you that they are warding off whatever is happening. It can also be a sign of guilt if their hands are lower like at the bottom of a shoulder shrug.

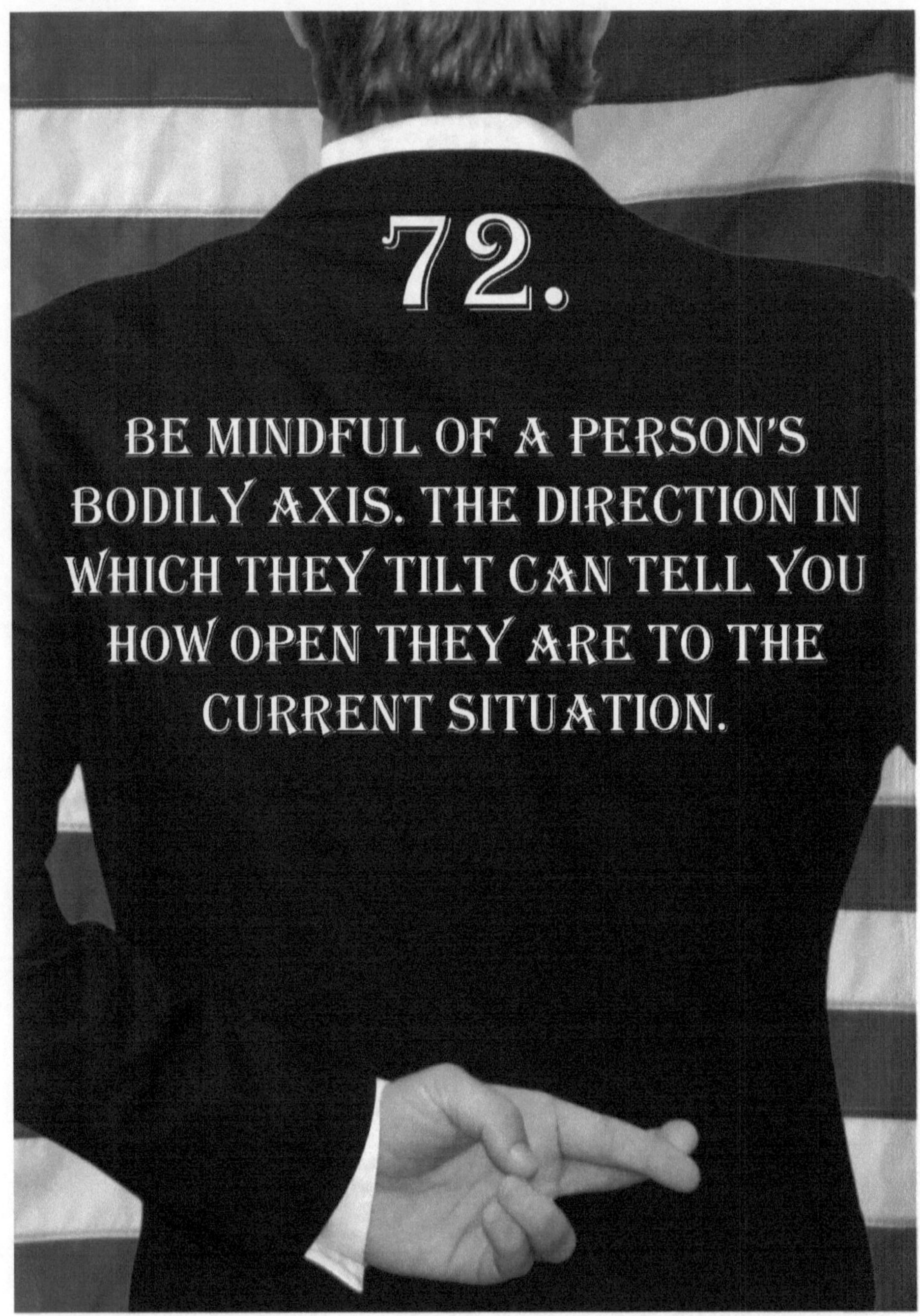

72.

BE MINDFUL OF A PERSON'S
BODILY AXIS. THE DIRECTION IN
WHICH THEY TILT CAN TELL YOU
HOW OPEN THEY ARE TO THE
CURRENT SITUATION.

Deception Tip 72 – Bodily Axis

Be mindful of a person's bodily axis. The direction in which they tilt can tell you how open they are to the current situation.

People can be very expressive, and if you pay attention you will know right away whether or not someone is interested in whatever is happening, or whether they don't care about it at all. People are always trying to do what's best for themselves. We are inherently selfish and want to preserve ourselves. You'll see this in body language.

When in conversations with others, pay attention to how their bodies are positioned. Are people leaning in? Are they engaged in the conversation? Or are they pointed toward the exit as mentioned in Deception Tip 50? You can drastically improve your communication skills if you take notice of this.

When people are positioned away from the speaker then you know they are looking for a chance to leave. They want out of the conversation. They have tuned out. However, when they are positioned toward the speaker they are engaged and interested in whatever is going on.

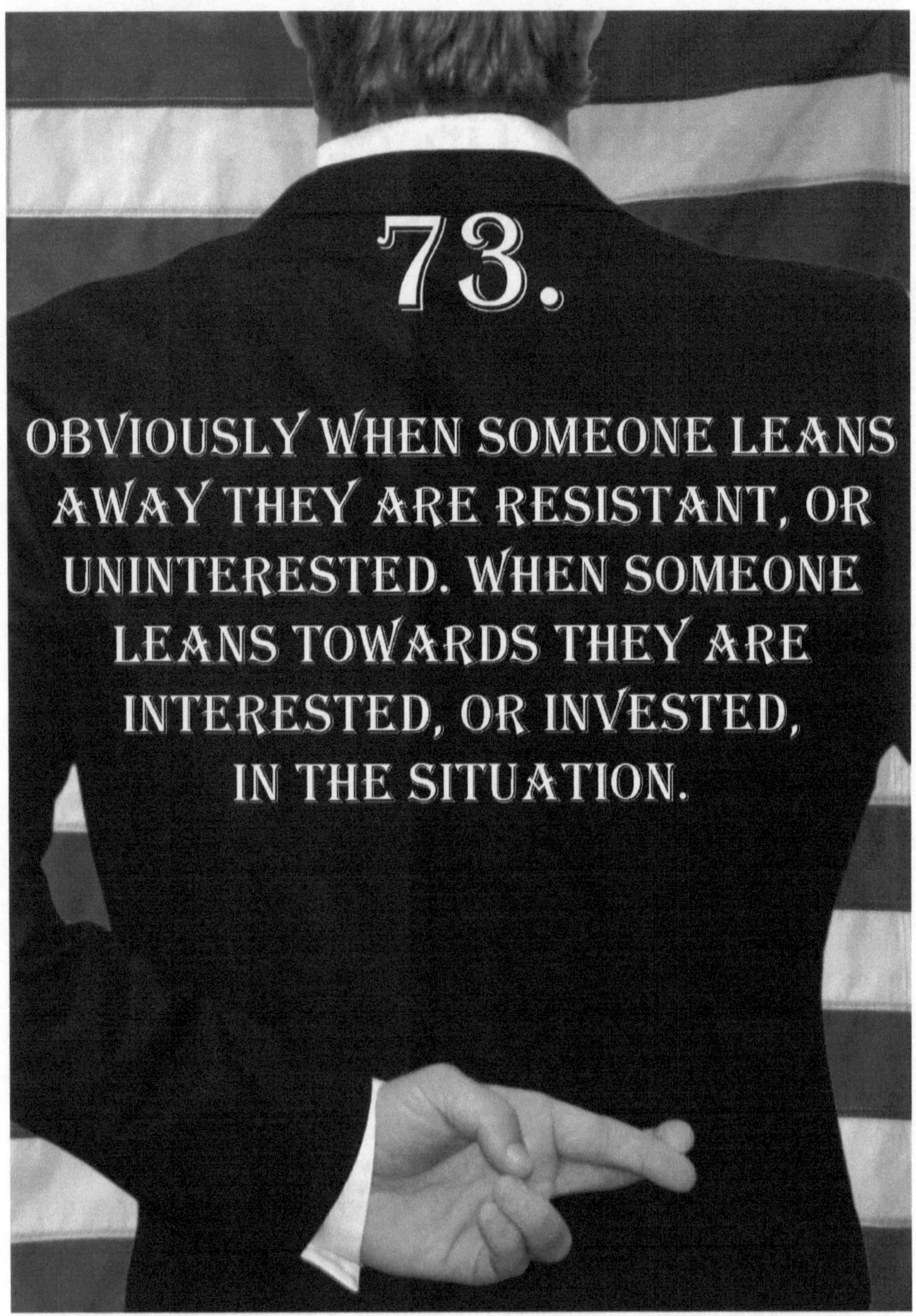
73.
OBVIOUSLY WHEN SOMEONE LEANS AWAY THEY ARE RESISTANT, OR UNINTERESTED. WHEN SOMEONE LEANS TOWARDS THEY ARE INTERESTED, OR INVESTED, IN THE SITUATION.

Deception Tip 73 – Leaning

Obviously when someone leans away they are resistant, or uninterested. When someone leans towards they are interested, or invested, in the situation.

This tip is directly related to Deception Tip 72 Bodily Axis and Deception Tip 50 Towards The Exit. A person who points his or her torso toward the exit is looking to escape the situation. They want to leave and are waiting for the right moment to do so.

In addition, a person's bodily orientation can tell you a lot about whether or not someone is interested and engaged in the conversation. You'll know based upon where they are directing the majority of their bodily attention. Therefore, if someone is leaning away from the conversation then you can reason that he or she is uninterested.

On the other hand, if someone is leaning toward the conversation then they are interested. That person wants to be engaged in whatever is happening and is leaning forward in anticipation of what will happen next. Therefore, pay attention to the orientation of peoples' bodies. It will tell you a lot about what they are thinking.

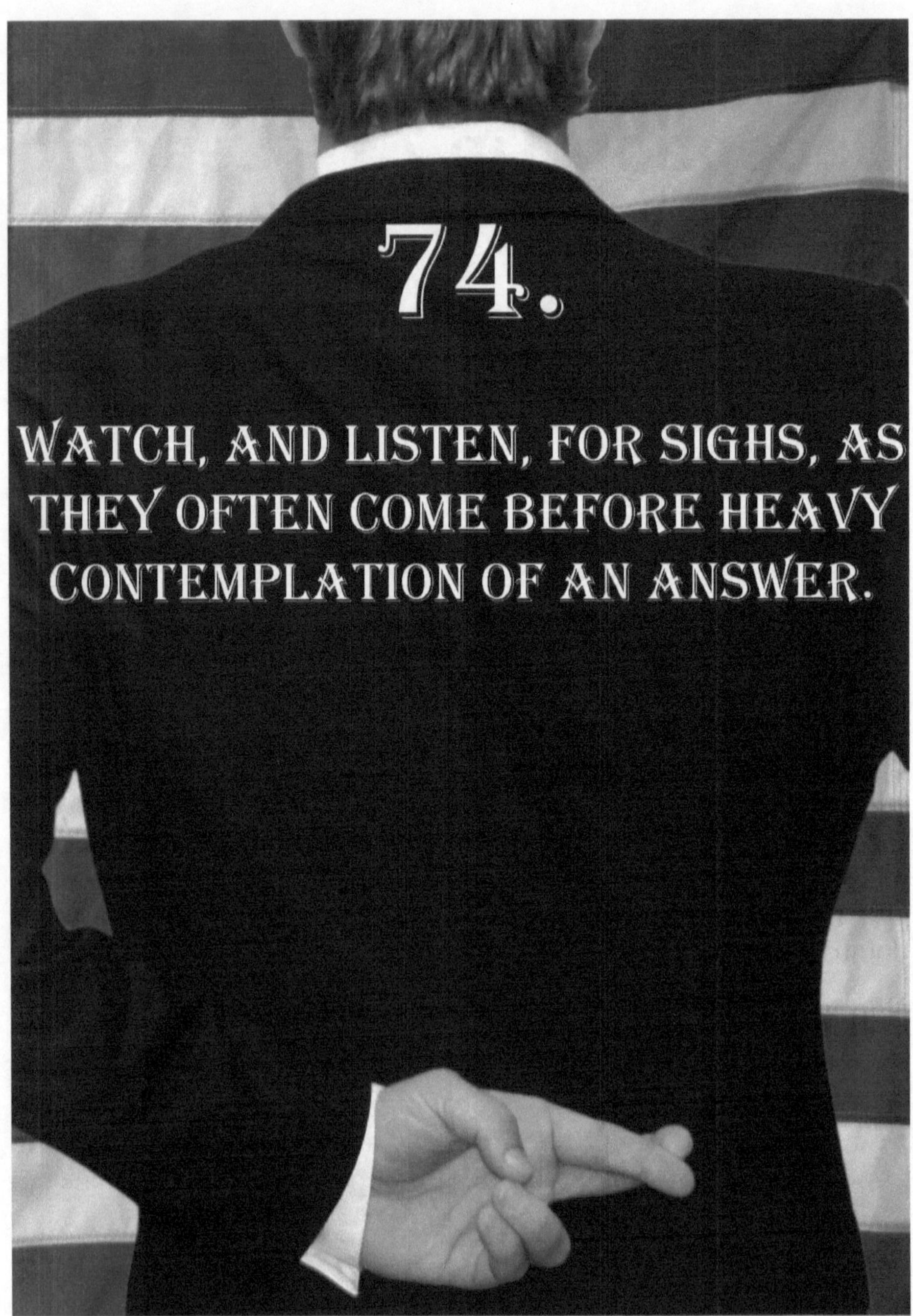
74.
WATCH, AND LISTEN, FOR SIGHS, AS
THEY OFTEN COME BEFORE HEAVY
CONTEMPLATION OF AN ANSWER.

Deception Tip 74 – Sighs

Watch, and listen, for sighs, as they often come before heavy contemplation of an answer.

Breathing is something that everyone must do and there are a lot of different emotions that can be conveyed through breathing. Of course, you can only know of the emotions based upon the sound of the breathing. This is why it is important for you to listen for different types of breathing and know what they mean.

Remember that deep breaths are often associated with stress-relief and can be used to pacify the stress and tension involved in lying. Of course, they could be pacifying other stress and tension as well. This is why it is essential for you to look for patterns and clusters of behavior in order to determine what the behaviors mean.

When people sigh, it is usually as a means of some form of relief. The person is relieved and the sigh is an outward expression of that relief. In addition, sighs may also come before an answer. The person is letting you know that there was a lot of contemplation involved in the decision and that they will be relieved when it's over.

75.

STEEPLING FINGERS MEAN
CONFIDENCE. LIARS MAY DISPLAY
THIS WHEN THEY BELIEVE THEY
HAVE FOOLED THE TARGET.

Deception Tip 75 – Steepling Fingers

Steepling fingers mean confidence. Liars may display this when they believe they have fooled the target.

This is a pretty popular behavior when people think they know what they are talking about. It is a gesture of superiority and seniority and is very similar to leaning back in the chair and putting your feet on the table. You are signifying that you are the boss.

When it comes to deception, this behavior may be displayed when a liar believes that they have fooled you. They think that they've one-upped you or pulled the wool over your eyes. It is very possible that you might notice contempt right before this gesture. They may also be smiling or grinning. This type of enjoyment is commonly known as "duping delight".

Of course, when you see someone steepling his or her fingers, it could be nothing significant at all. This is why you should be on the lookout for other behaviors that might accompany it. Chances are pretty good that if someone is steepling his or her fingers that the person is feeling pretty confident about something.

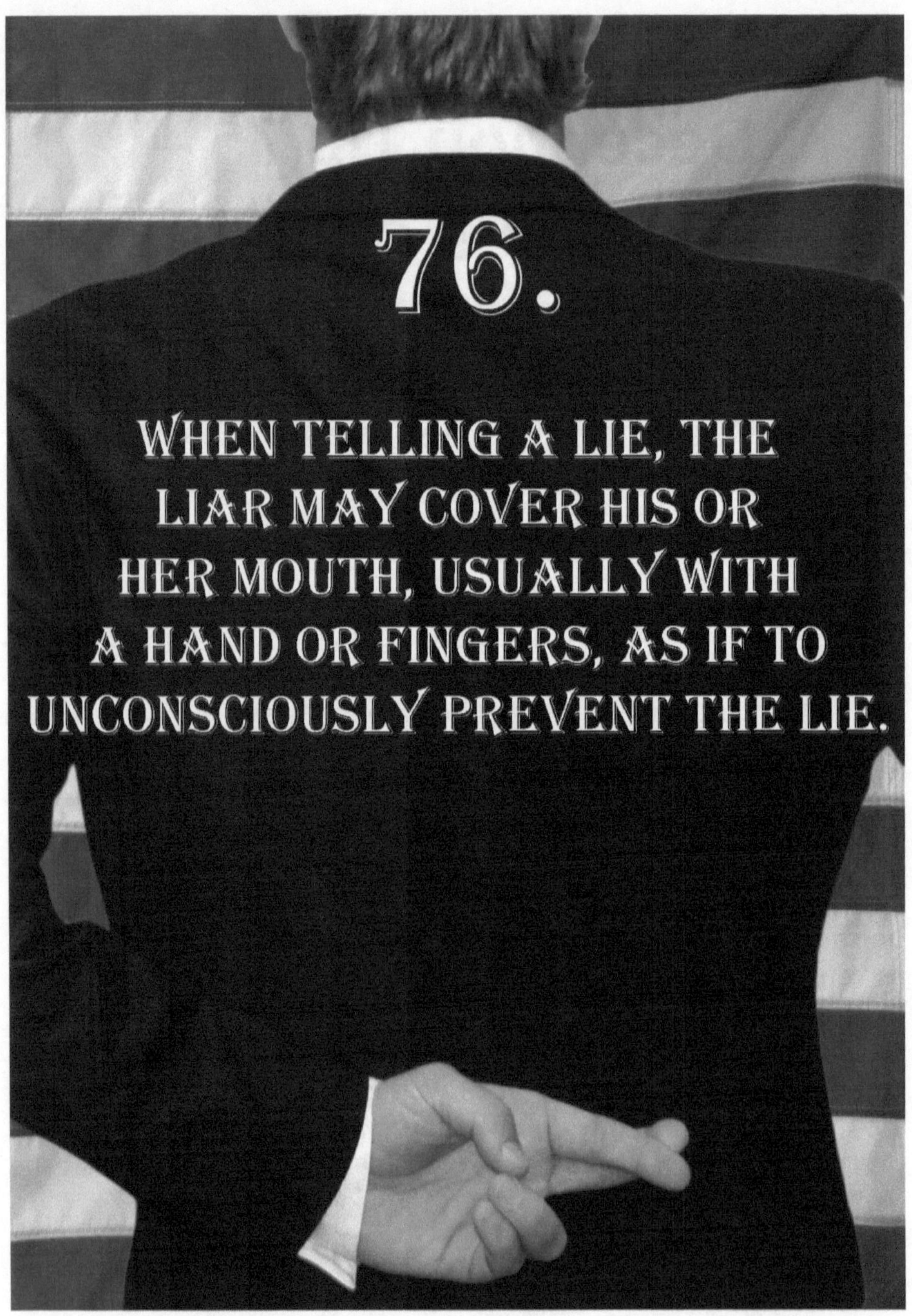

76.
WHEN TELLING A LIE, THE
LIAR MAY COVER HIS OR
HER MOUTH, USUALLY WITH
A HAND OR FINGERS, AS IF TO
UNCONSCIOUSLY PREVENT THE LIE.

Deception Tip 76 – Cover Mouth

When telling a lie, the liar may cover his or her mouth, usually with a hand or fingers, as if to unconsciously prevent the lie.

The conscious and the unconscious constantly battle back and forth when someone engages in deception. The conscious wants to get the lie over with and the unconscious wants the truth to be revealed. For this reason, when someone is lying, there will always be more than one sign of deception.

Some of these signs may occur before the lie is even told. Some examples are the signs of anxiety, stress, tension, et cetera. This is also a sign that may happen before the lie is told. The unconscious wants to prevent the lie. Therefore, it may unconsciously cover the person's mouth in an attempt to silence the lie.

Deception Tip 45 Hushing Lips is very similar to this. The current sign is a little more drastic in that the mouth may be entirely covered. This can happen with the person's hand clasped over the lips or it may be with different objects such as paper, a folder, or something else. Either way, when the mouth is covered you should always be asking why.

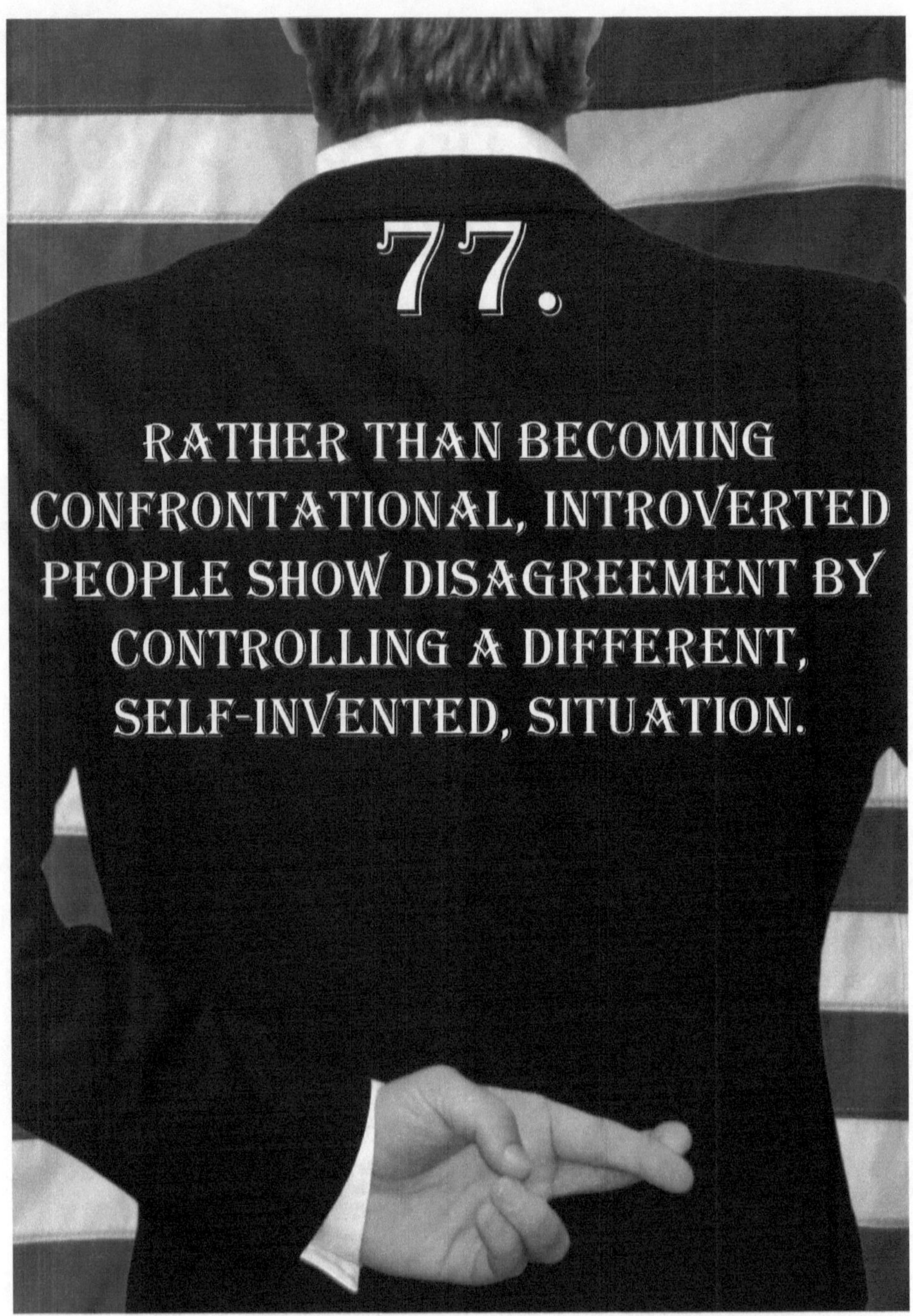
77.
RATHER THAN BECOMING CONFRONTATIONAL, INTROVERTED PEOPLE SHOW DISAGREEMENT BY CONTROLLING A DIFFERENT, SELF-INVENTED, SITUATION.

Deception Tip 77 – Introverted People

Rather than becoming confrontational, introverted people show disagreement by controlling a different, self-invented, situation.

It's no secret that introverted people are more reserved than other people. They don't enjoy social interaction like extroverted people. In some cases, they may not even want to tolerate social interaction like "normal" people. Let me be clear, there's nothing abnormal about introverted people. I'm simply demonstrating that there are three types: introvert, middle, extrovert.

When a liar is questioned, this is a form of conflict. It is important to understand that introverted people and extroverted people will respond very differently to this conflict. How you respond to them will play a significant factor in whether or not you are able to continue speaking with them.

Introverted people do not like confrontation. Therefore, they will generally not directly argue their point. They may not even state their position or defend themselves. Rather, they may either do nothing, or they may show their disagreement by inventing a situation or problem that they can control. Examples could be minor things like making you get them coffee or picking apart your fashion choices. Or it could be something major like feelings of paranoia, stalking, or believing someone is in love with them.

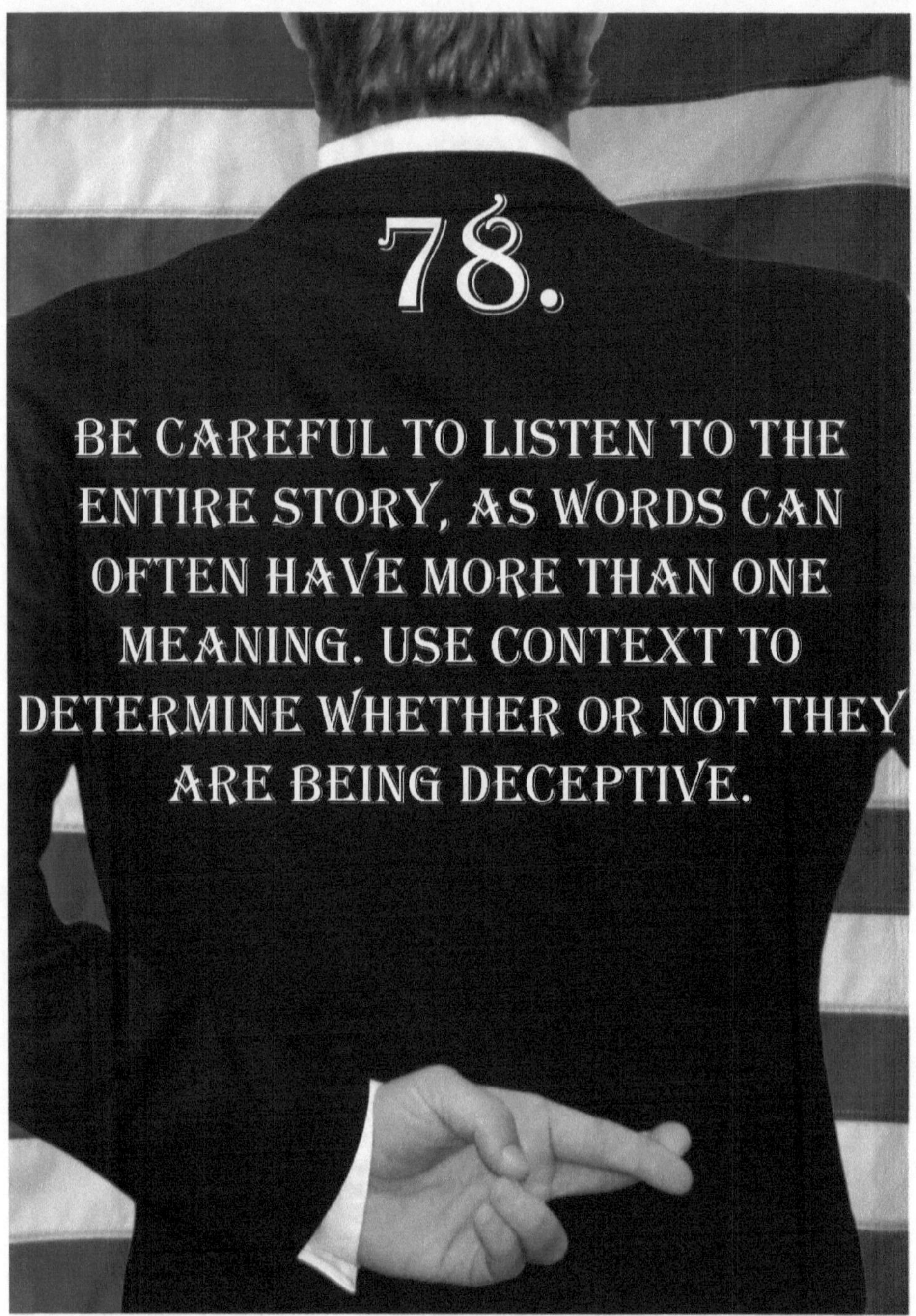
78.
BE CAREFUL TO LISTEN TO THE
ENTIRE STORY, AS WORDS CAN
OFTEN HAVE MORE THAN ONE
MEANING. USE CONTEXT TO
DETERMINE WHETHER OR NOT THEY
ARE BEING DECEPTIVE.

Deception Tip 78 – Entire Story

Be careful to listen to the entire story, as words can often have more than one meaning. Use context to determine whether or not they are being deceptive.

Remember it is very important to allow the liar to speak. They have one main goal and that is to tell you a lie so that you believe them. Therefore, they want to speak. Deception Tip 13 Stay Silent and Deception Tip 69 Become Silent informed you of this. Make sure you know them because they are great tactics to use in deception detection.

Be patient and allow the liar to tell the entire story. Then ask to hear it again if you want. Words can have multiple meanings and the context of the situation makes a huge difference in how you interpret what they are saying. Therefore, make sure you understand. Ask for clarification if you need it. In addition, you can also repeat what they said back to them to make sure you fully understand.

The bottom line is that you want to make sure you have all the facts before you start making any judgments. You need to be sure that you know they are lying because you witnessed multiple signs of deception. Always look for patterns and clusters of behavior.

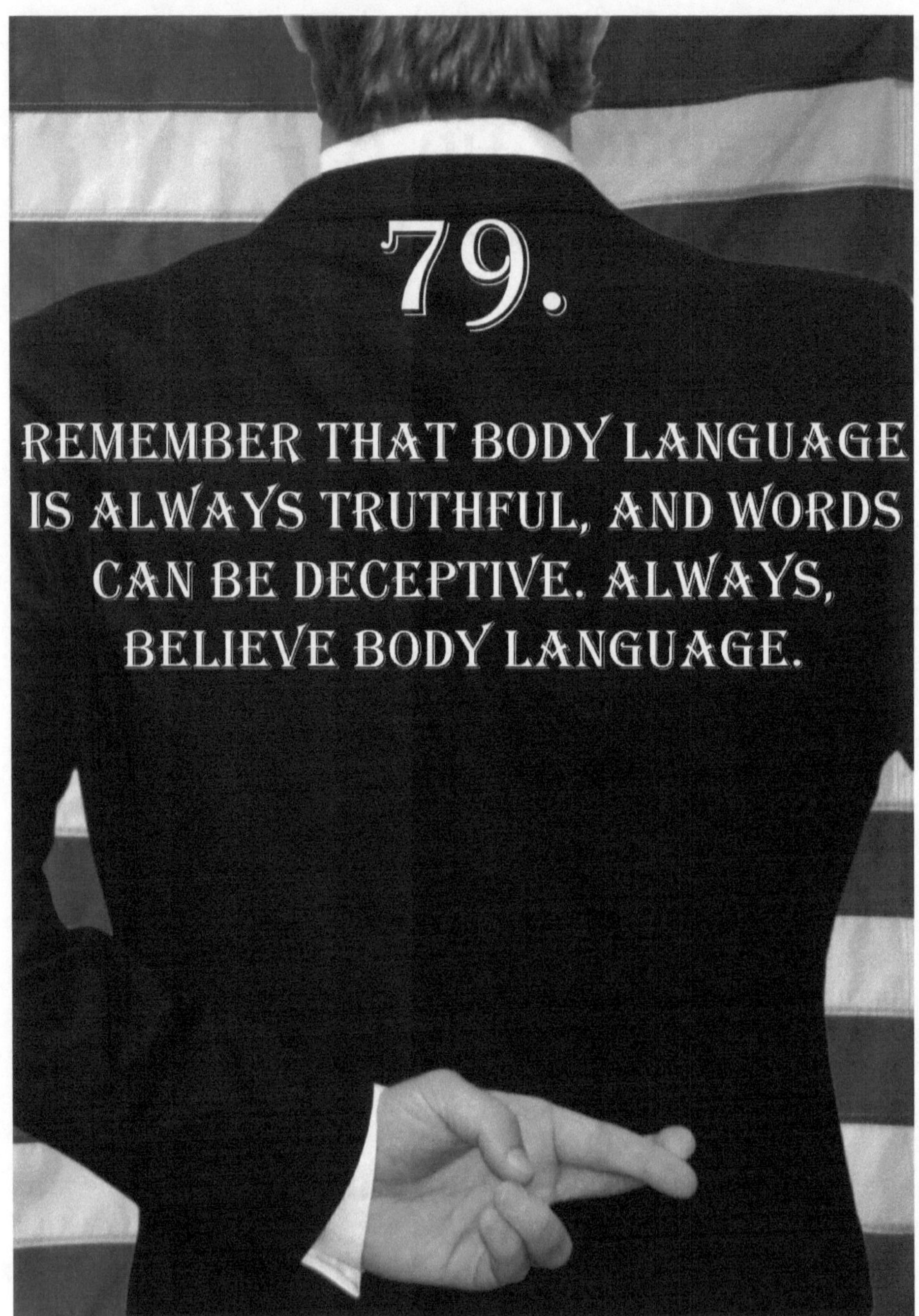
79.
REMEMBER THAT BODY LANGUAGE IS ALWAYS TRUTHFUL, AND WORDS CAN BE DECEPTIVE. ALWAYS, BELIEVE BODY LANGUAGE.

Deception Tip 79 – Believe Body Language

Remember that body language is always truthful, and words can be deceptive. Always, believe body language.

When it comes to detecting deception, in general, words are produced by the conscious and body language is produced by the unconscious. As you know, the conscious can be very deceptive and the unconscious is always truthful. Therefore, words produced by the conscious have the potential to be deceptive. However, body language produced by the unconscious is always truthful.

Keep in mind, that some body language may be produced by the conscious. Therefore, stating that ALL body language is truthful is not accurate. Most body language is truthful and all unconscious body language is truthful. Generally, you will be pretty accurate in your assessments if you base them on body language.

Remember, it is extremely important to look for patterns and clusters of behavior. This is how you'll be able to tell the conscious body language from the unconscious body language. Unconsciously, there will always be more than one sign. Watch for them and take note of them. Then you will be better able to understand what every body is really saying.

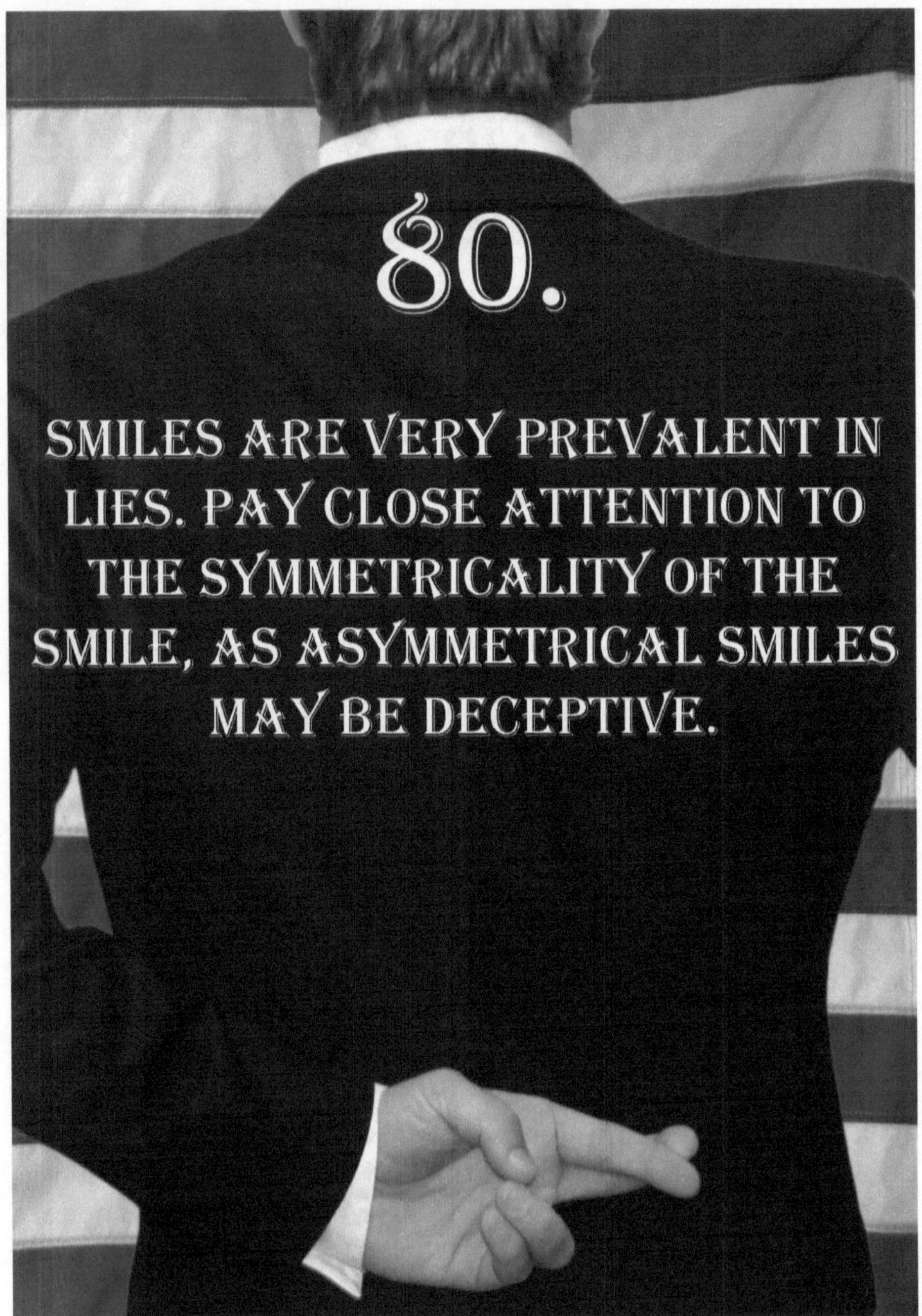
80.
SMILES ARE VERY PREVALENT IN
LIES. PAY CLOSE ATTENTION TO
THE SYMMETRICALITY OF THE
SMILE, AS ASYMMETRICAL SMILES
MAY BE DECEPTIVE.

Deception Tip 80 – Smiles In Lies

Smiles are very prevalent in lies. Pay close attention to the symmetricality of the smile, as asymmetrical smiles may be deceptive.

The smile is probably the most noticed facial expression. This is because it is also probably the most frequent facial expression. In addition, smiles can occur in a variety of different situations. In fact, smiles are not always indicative of happiness! People can smile for all sorts of reasons. They can be afraid, shy, irritated, or even sad.

When people lie, smiling usually takes the form of a masking expression. This means that it is used to cover up other facial expressions. Remember it is easier to conceal facial expressions rather than stop them or fake them entirely. Since a smile is such a large facial expression it is a very popular mask.

Being able to tell the difference between a real smile and a fake smile is very important. Fake smiles may last longer on the face. In addition, they will often be asymmetrical, like other false emotions. Another very important aspect of smiling is the involvement of the eyes. You'll see more wrinkles around the eyes in real smiles. Therefore, keep your eyes on smiles. If you notice a fake one, see if you can find out why.

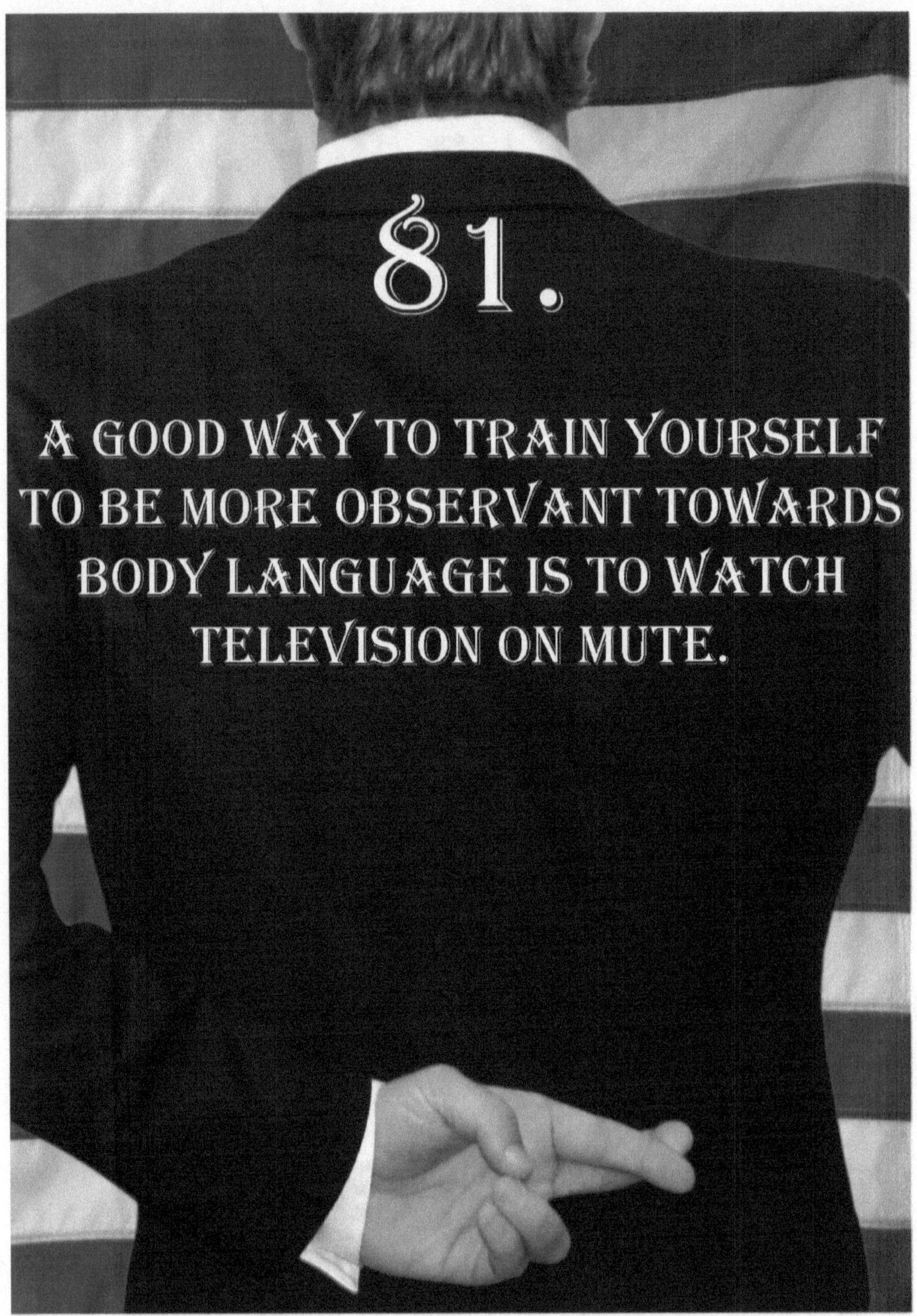
81.
A GOOD WAY TO TRAIN YOURSELF
TO BE MORE OBSERVANT TOWARDS
BODY LANGUAGE IS TO WATCH
TELEVISION ON MUTE.

Deception Tip 81 – Mute The TV

A good way to train yourself to be more observant towards body language is to watch television on mute.

If you want to become an expert at reading people and detecting deception then you need to practice. However, sometimes practicing in public can be a little strange. People might wonder what you're doing and you may make others uncomfortable when you're first starting out. They'll wonder why you aren't looking them in the eye et cetera.

Therefore, a great way for you to practice reading people is to watch TV on mute. The reason you should watch it on mute is so that you focus on the body language instead of what is being said. You can do this with any TV program. However, you may wish to start out with the boring city council meetings on your local station. News anchors, reporters, and politicians are other great people to watch.

Eventually, you can watch soap operas and other TV shows. However, since that is acting you will be better off watching "real life TV" instead. Later on, flip the volume on to see if you notice any verbal cues to deception in addition to the body language.

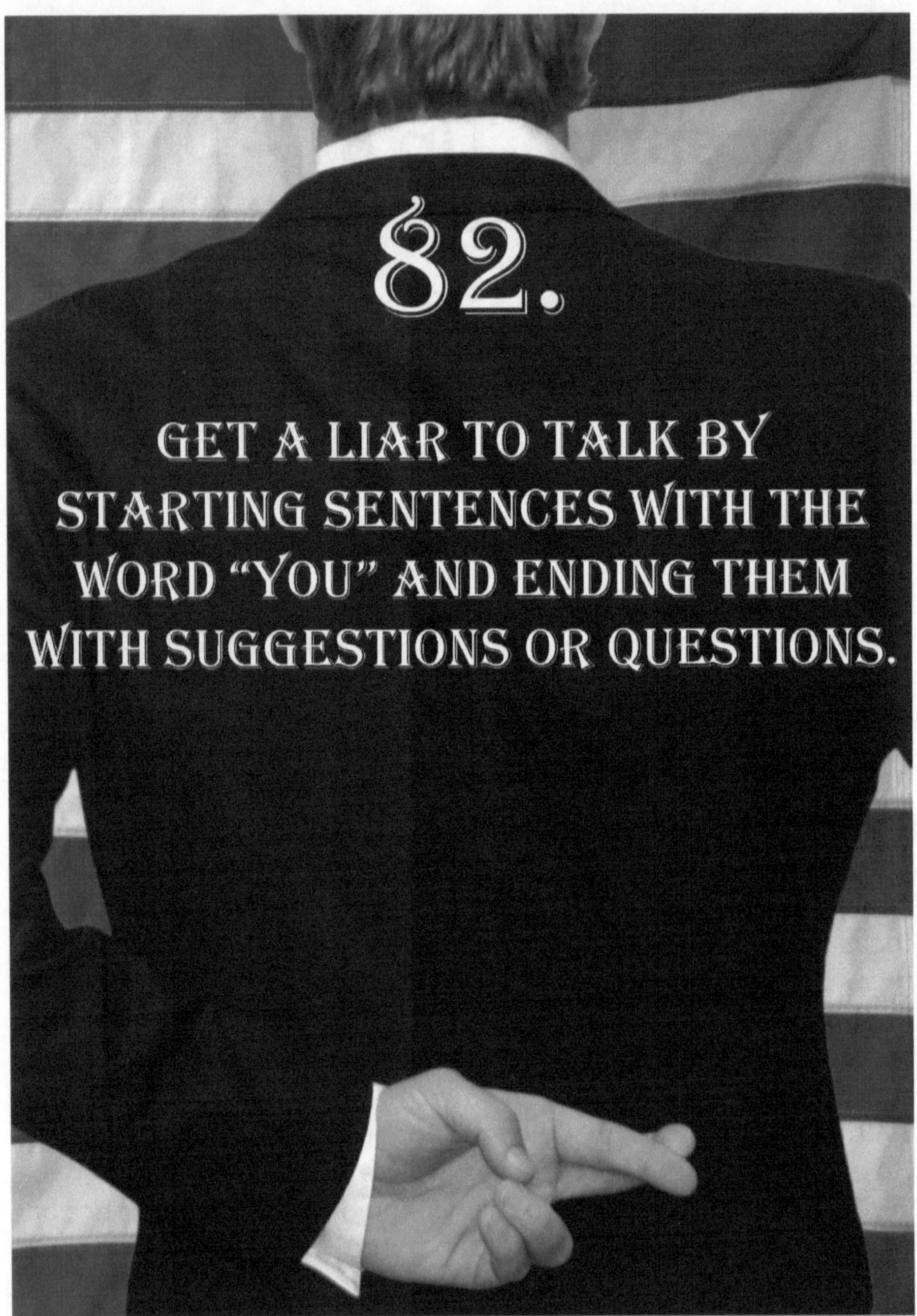
82.
GET A LIAR TO TALK BY
STARTING SENTENCES WITH THE
WORD "YOU" AND ENDING THEM
WITH SUGGESTIONS OR QUESTIONS.

Deception Tip 82 – Starting Sentences

Get a liar to talk by starting sentences with the word "you" and ending them with suggestions or questions.

If you are questioning someone who isn't cooperating very well then you need to get him or her to speak. One way of doing this is to entice them to talk. Make them feel like they have something to explain. You must insinuate things and put them on the spot so that they feel like they have to defend themselves or justify their situation.

A great way to do this is by starting your sentences with the word "you" and finishing them with a question or some form of suggestive statement. For example, "you went to work and then what happened" or something like that would be a great question. In addition, "so you decided to take matters into your own hands instead of letting more qualified people take care of it" would be another example.

Either way, you need to make the person feel like they have to answer for something. Like you've got it all wrong and they need to straighten it out so that you understand what is going on. When they feel like this, they will often start telling you the whole story to make sure you understand.

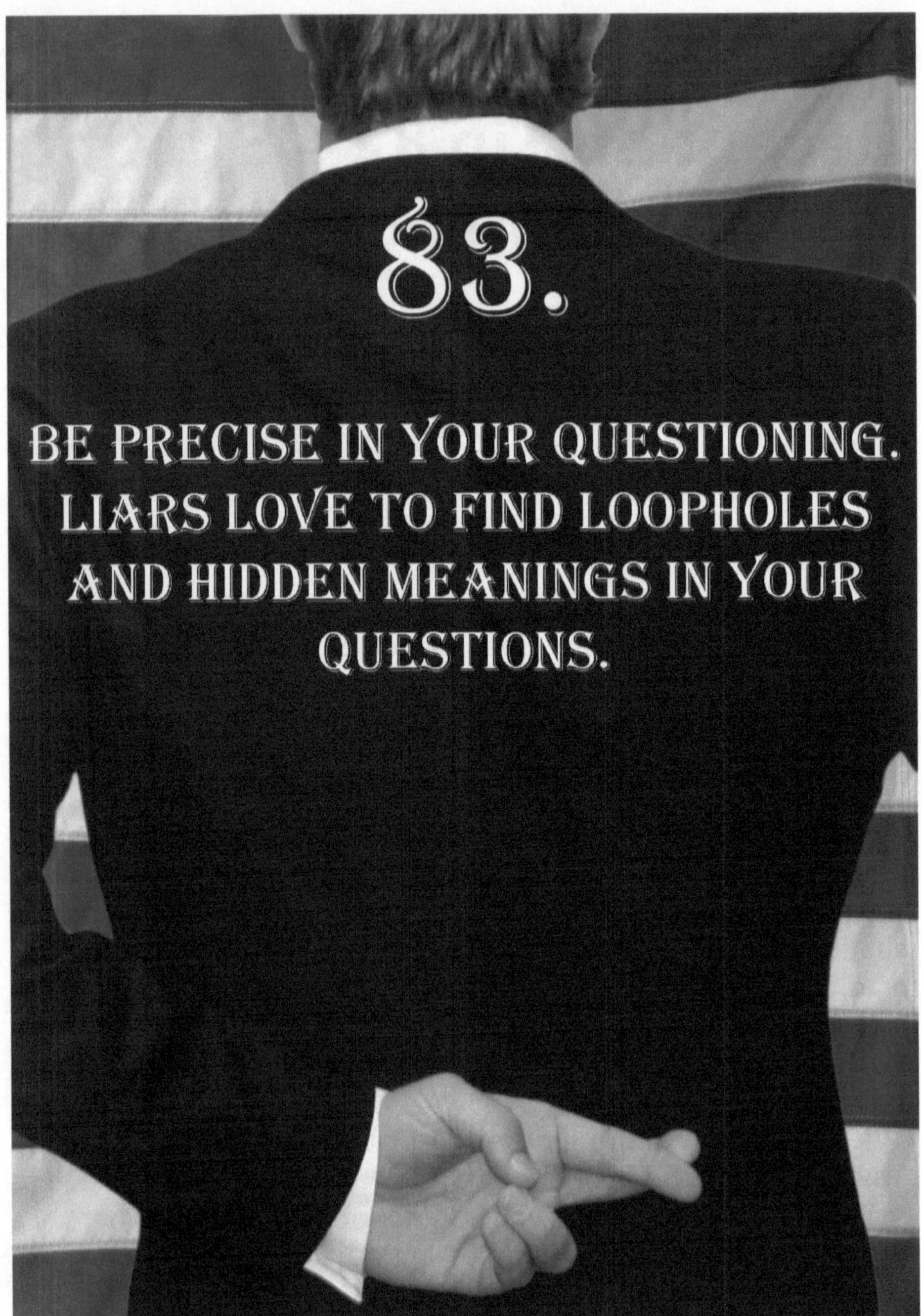
83.
BE PRECISE IN YOUR QUESTIONING.
LIARS LOVE TO FIND LOOPHOLES
AND HIDDEN MEANINGS IN YOUR
QUESTIONS.

Deception Tip 83 – Be Precise

Be precise in your questioning. Liars love to find loopholes and hidden meanings in your questions.

If you're dealing with someone who doesn't like to give you straight answers, then you need to refine your questions. You need to ask more direct questions that only have one possible answer. Yes or no questions are a great example of this. In addition, using some direct response questions will also be helpful in making sure you receive the answers you seek.

Some people love to be evasive and don't want you to know exactly what is going on. For this reason, they will find loopholes in your questions and only answer part of the question. Then they'll get you talking on something else so that you forgot that they didn't entirely answer. Continue pushing with your questions to refine their answers. Eventually, they will give you the answer you want.

A great example of a question to avoid is: "How do you feel when things are frustrating?" Although this seems like a pretty direct question, it isn't. The answer you hope for is an explanation of the person's feelings. That is what you'll most likely receive. However, a difficult person might simply answer "frustrated".

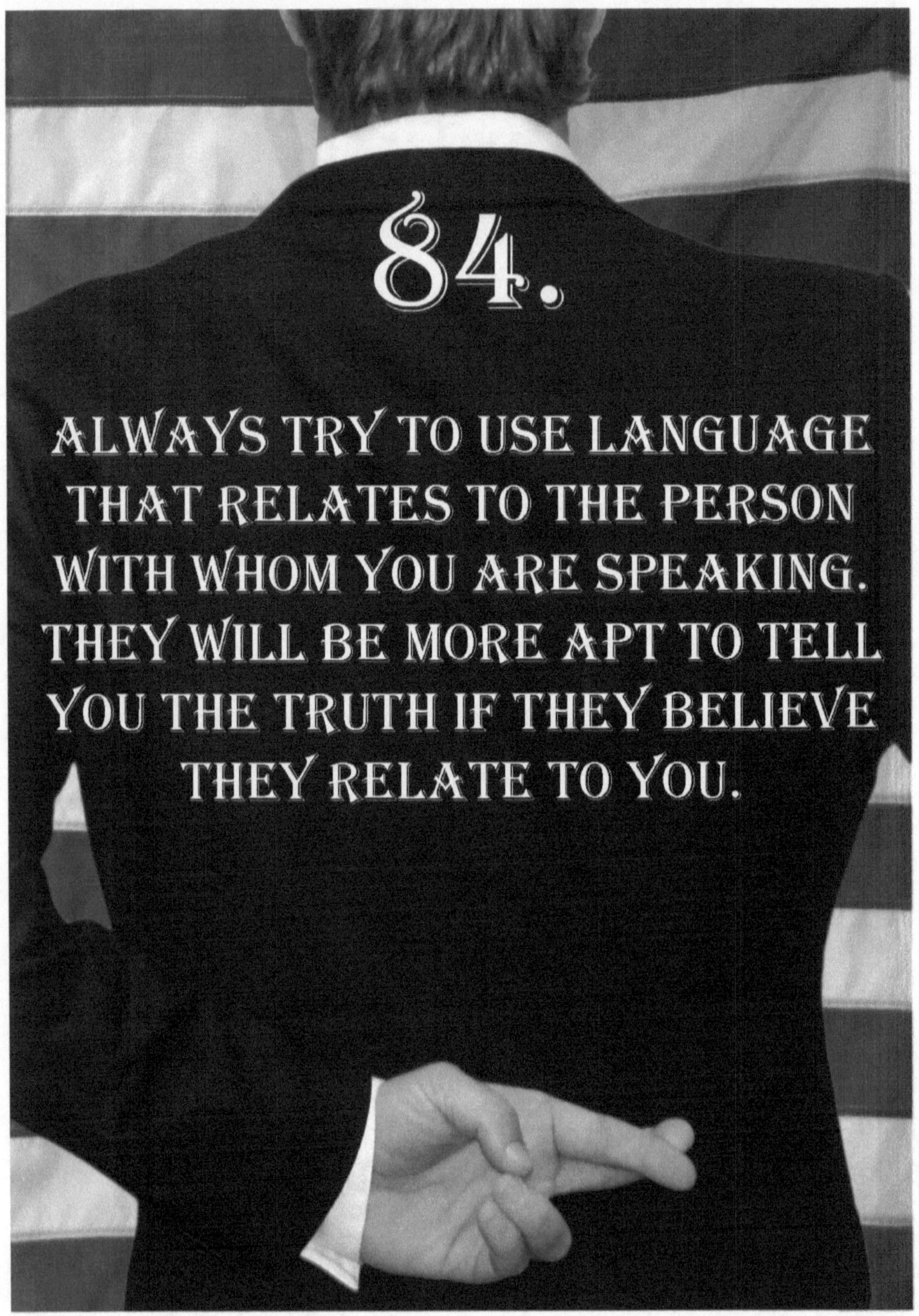
84.

ALWAYS TRY TO USE LANGUAGE
THAT RELATES TO THE PERSON
WITH WHOM YOU ARE SPEAKING.
THEY WILL BE MORE APT TO TELL
YOU THE TRUTH IF THEY BELIEVE
THEY RELATE TO YOU.

Deception Tip 84 – Relating Language

Always try to use language that relates to the person with whom you are speaking. They will be more apt to tell you the truth if they believe they relate to you.

Relating to others is a very common negotiation tactic. People often want to do business with other people that they believe relate to them. The more you have in common with someone the better you'll get along with them. It is human nature. It's one of the first things negotiators try to establish in dangerous situations.

When people feel like they have something in common with you, then they may be more apt to open up. They may have a desire to share with you because they feel like you understand them. You'll be able to understand why they do what they do when no one else will. They want to relate to you. Everyone wants to fit in.

If you can make people believe that they relate to you and that you have things in common with them. Then you will be more able to effectively communicate with them. Humans are social creatures and want to fit in with one another. No one wants to be left out. Therefore, use language terms that include others and you'll be a more effective communicator.

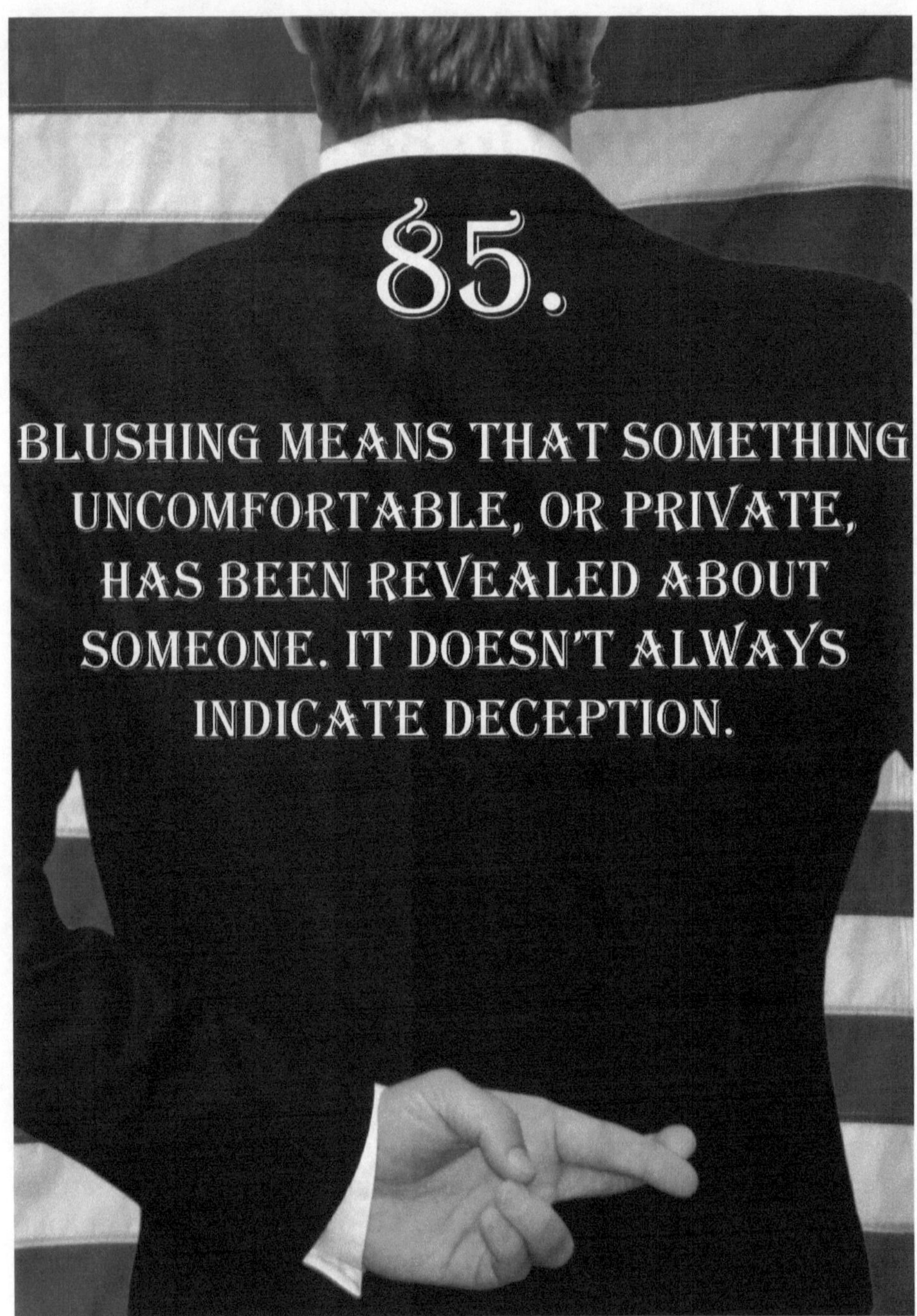
85.

BLUSHING MEANS THAT SOMETHING
UNCOMFORTABLE, OR PRIVATE,
HAS BEEN REVEALED ABOUT
SOMEONE. IT DOESN'T ALWAYS
INDICATE DECEPTION.

Deception Tip 85 – Blushing

Blushing means that something uncomfortable, or private, has been revealed about someone. It doesn't always indicate deception.

People may blush for all kinds of reasons. The most commonly known reason is thought to be when someone likes someone else. However, this isn't always the case. The main reason behind why a person blushes is because they have been exposed. Something secret, or private, has been revealed and now they are bashful about it and blush.

For this reason, you may also witness covering private areas of the body as mentioned in Deception Tip 6 Covering Genitals. In addition, some people may curl up and reduce the amount of space they take up – Deception Tip 40. Others may create defensive barriers as discussed in Deception Tip 8.

Either way, blushing is a form of embarrassment. It may not even be something that physically happened. It could be something that the person thought of. Therefore, when you see someone blush, examine the situation and see what's going on. You may be able to assist that person with something or catch them in a lie.

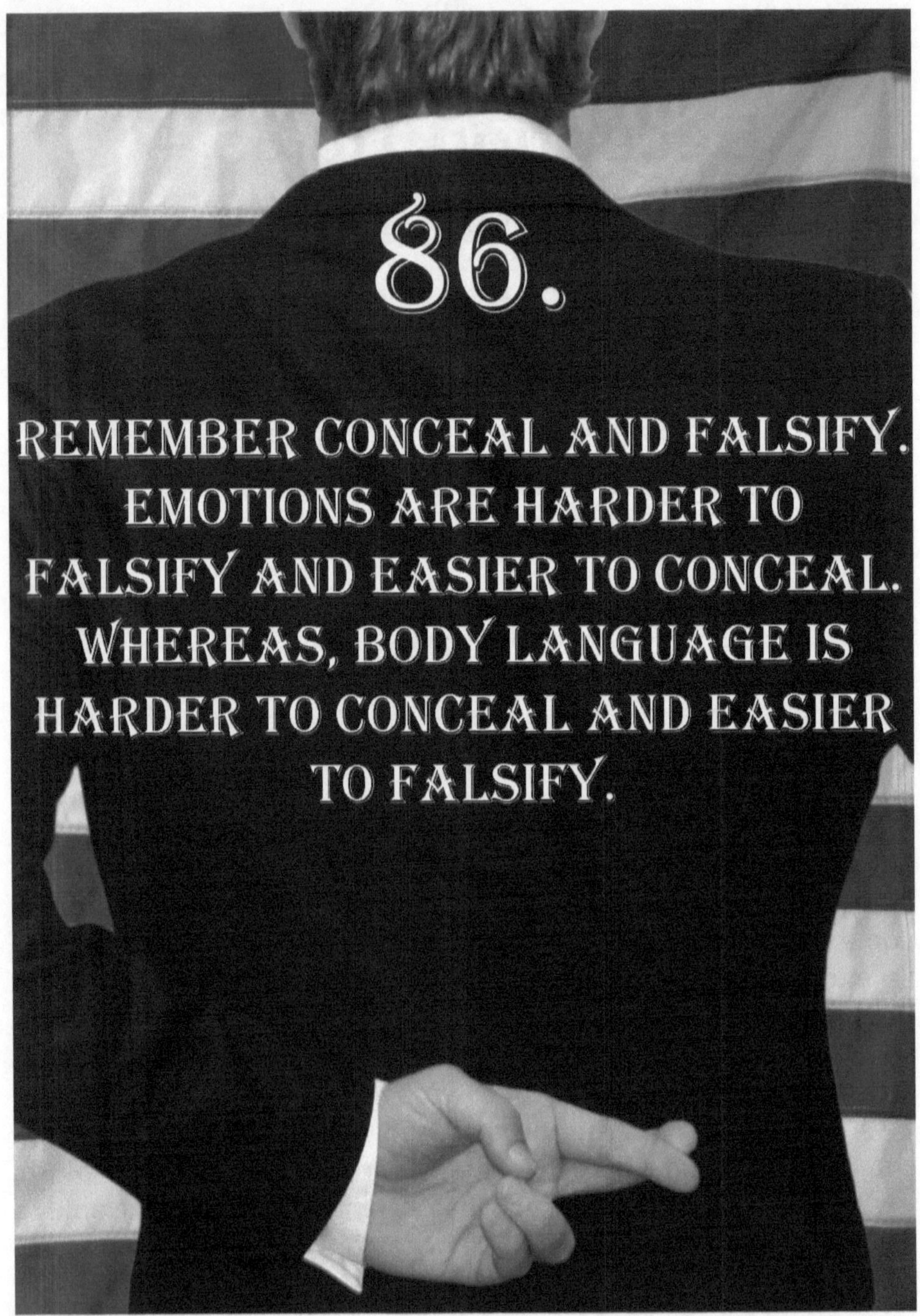
86.

REMEMBER CONCEAL AND FALSIFY.
EMOTIONS ARE HARDER TO
FALSIFY AND EASIER TO CONCEAL.
WHEREAS, BODY LANGUAGE IS
HARDER TO CONCEAL AND EASIER
TO FALSIFY.

Deception Tip 86 – Conceal And Falsify

Remember conceal and falsify. Emotions are harder to falsify and easier to conceal. Whereas, body language is harder to conceal and easier to falsify.

We've talked about this before. Deception Tip 37 Mask The Face is about how liars prefer to mask the face over the body. They attempt to conceal their emotions. In addition, Deception Tip 65 Conceal The Truth is about how people prefer to conceal the story rather than invent an entirely new story.

Concealing emotions is much easier than falsifying them. This is why you must be on the lookout for masking emotions such as the smile discussed in Deception Tip 80. Emotional expressions are very quick and happen with a lot of little muscles. They are spontaneous and hard to fake. Therefore, liars prefer to conceal them rather than try to fake them.

Body language is something that is easier to falsify rather than conceal. This is because it is much larger than a facial expression so the chances of covering it up are less likely. More people would notice if you cover up body language. Think of faking a yawn to put an arm around someone. However, you could easily consciously fake doing that. The reason is because it's a gesture. Therefore, liars prefer to fake body language rather than conceal it.

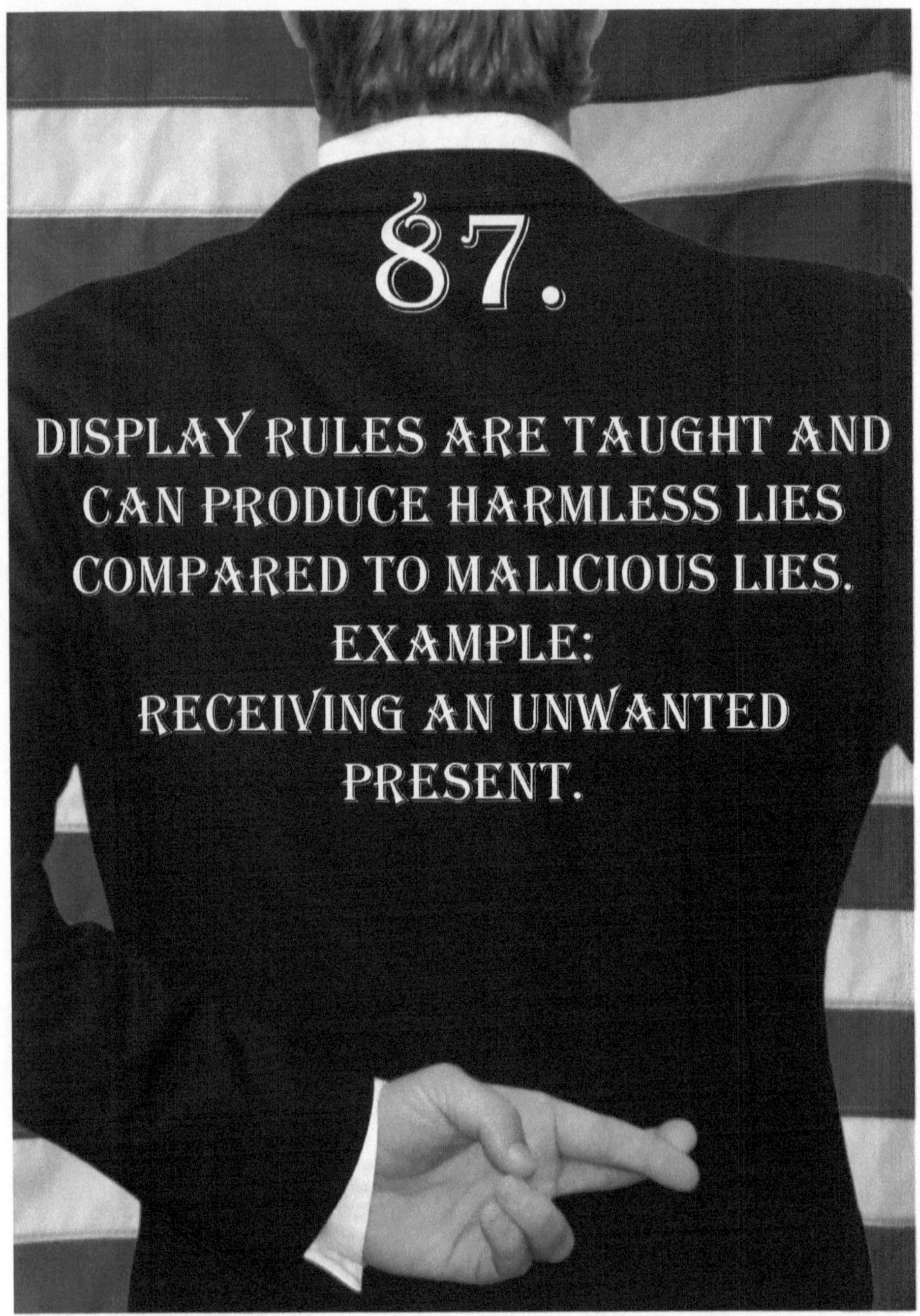
87.
DISPLAY RULES ARE TAUGHT AND
CAN PRODUCE HARMLESS LIES
COMPARED TO MALICIOUS LIES.
EXAMPLE:
RECEIVING AN UNWANTED
PRESENT.

Deception Tip 87 – Display Rules

Display rules are taught and can produce harmless lies compared to malicious lies. Example: receiving an unwanted present.

Remember that not all lies are told with the intent to harm other people. In addition, people lie a lot. There are a variety of statistics out there that say people lie around 200 times per day. Are all of these lies done with the intent to harm others? Certainly not! You may not even be aware of all the lies you tell. Still, you are telling them.

Think of answering simple questions like "how are you today?" or "do you like my haircut?" These questions require simple answers that are automatic. You're most likely going to respond with favorable answers such as "good" and "it's nice". The reason is because you are a polite person and you don't want to hurt someone's feelings.

Many lies told are polite, social, lies. They are done in conversation and there really isn't much significance to them. They are pretty harmless and often encouraged. Think of how a parent teaches a child to thank people for the presents they receive even if they don't like them or already have them.

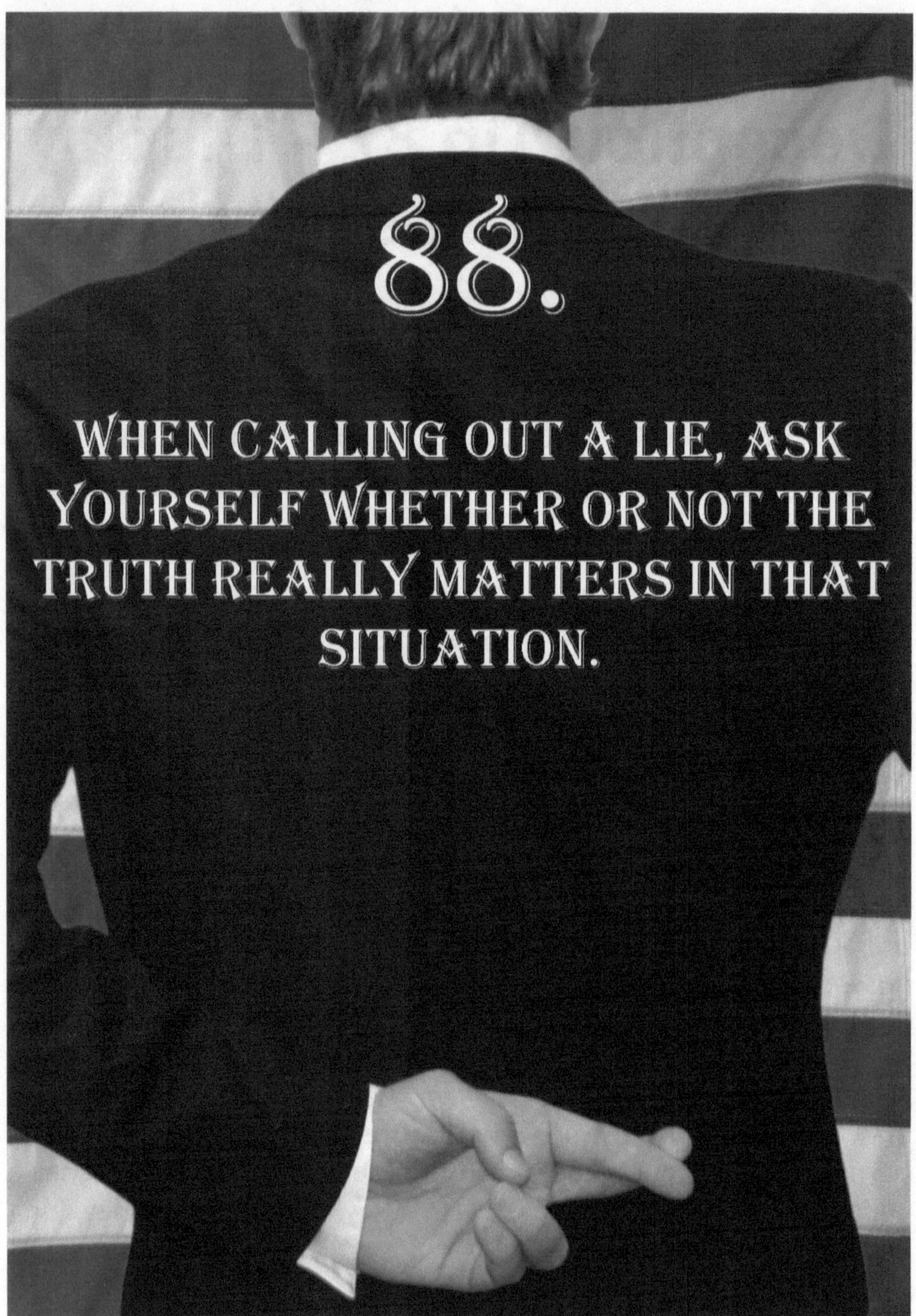

88.

WHEN CALLING OUT A LIE, ASK
YOURSELF WHETHER OR NOT THE
TRUTH REALLY MATTERS IN THAT
SITUATION.

Deception Tip 88 – Calling Out Lies

When calling out a lie, ask yourself whether or not the truth really matters in that situation.

This tip is closely related to Deception Tip 87. Remember that people lie many times a day and that the majority of these lies are done due to display rules and polite society. "The food was great", "I'm doing well", et cetera. These lies don't cause harm and are told to avoid seeming rude and hurting someone's feelings.

Nevertheless, they are lies and, therefore, there will most likely be signs of deception. As a result, you'll probably be able to notice the signs of deception and pick up on these lies. Now, the question is whether or not you feel the need to call out the liar and expose the lie. You must ask yourself whether or not the truth really matters.

Remember that the lie was told to avoid the possibility of someone's feelings being hurt. If you expose the lie, then the person may have hurt feelings. In addition, the liar that you expose might feel hurt as well. Now you've successfully made two people feel bad. What did that accomplish? If it isn't something beneficial, then you might as well not say anything.

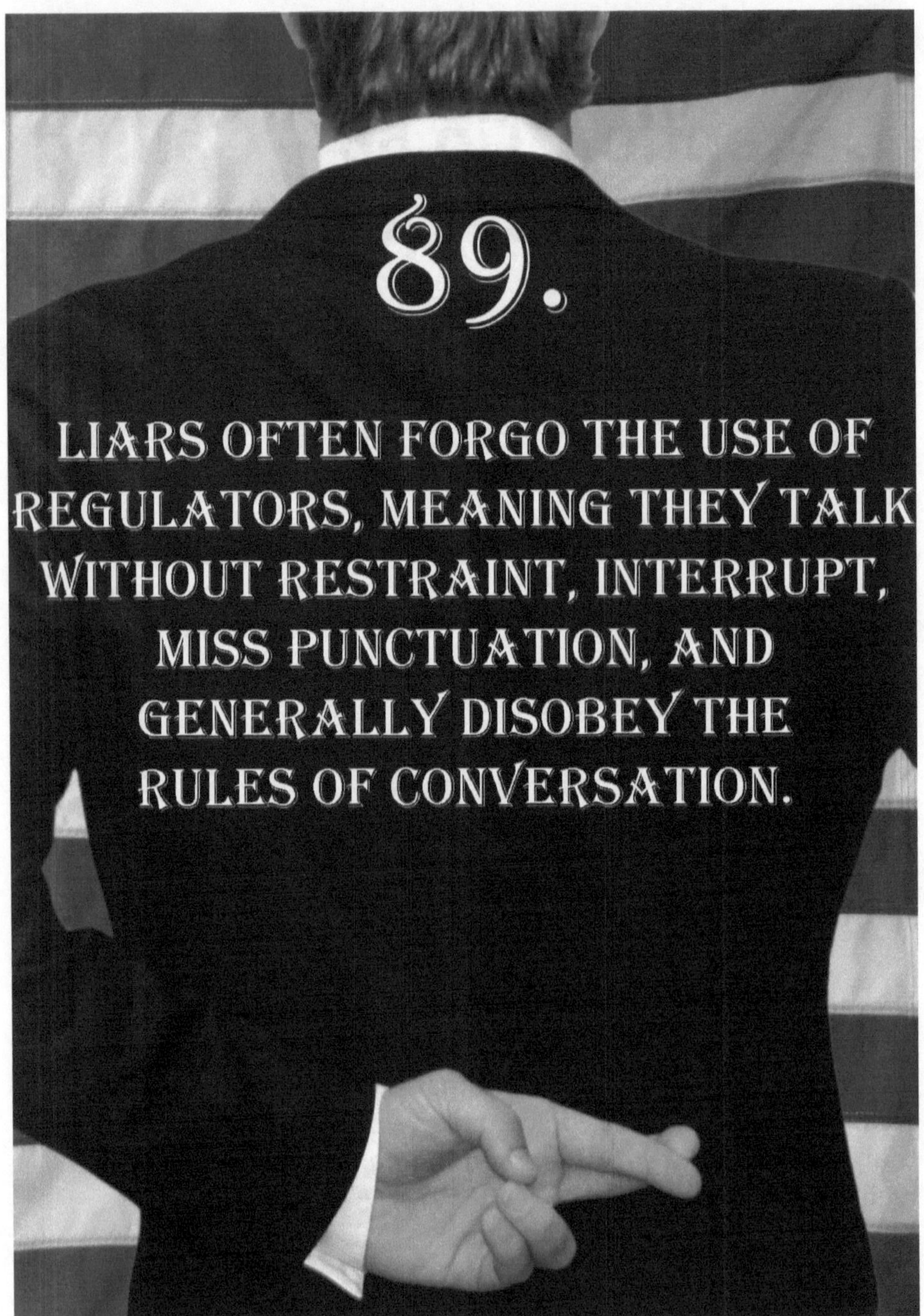
89.

LIARS OFTEN FORGO THE USE OF
REGULATORS, MEANING THEY TALK
WITHOUT RESTRAINT, INTERRUPT,
MISS PUNCTUATION, AND
GENERALLY DISOBEY THE
RULES OF CONVERSATION.

Deception Tip 89 – Forgo Regulators

Liars often forgo the use of regulators, meaning they talk without restraint, interrupt, miss punctuation, and generally disobey the rules of conversation.

Liars cannot wait to get their story out. They want to tell the lie. It is boiling up inside of them causing all kinds of stress, tension, and anxiety. In addition, they want you to believe the lie. That means, in order for you to believe it, they have to tell it. Therefore, they are on a mission to speak and tell their lie.

We've discussed several tips relating to this on how the liars want to speak due to the stress boiling up inside them. Therefore you must stay silent Deception Tip 13 and become silent Deception Tip 69. The current tip is one that is more related to speech patterns like Deception Tip 5 Contractions.

Due to the fact that liars are so motivated to tell their lie, they will often forgo using regulators in conversation. In other words, the normal rules of polite conversation don't really apply to them. They may speak at length with long run-on sentences or continually interrupt you. So if you can't seem to get a word in edgewise, start looking for other potential signs of deception.

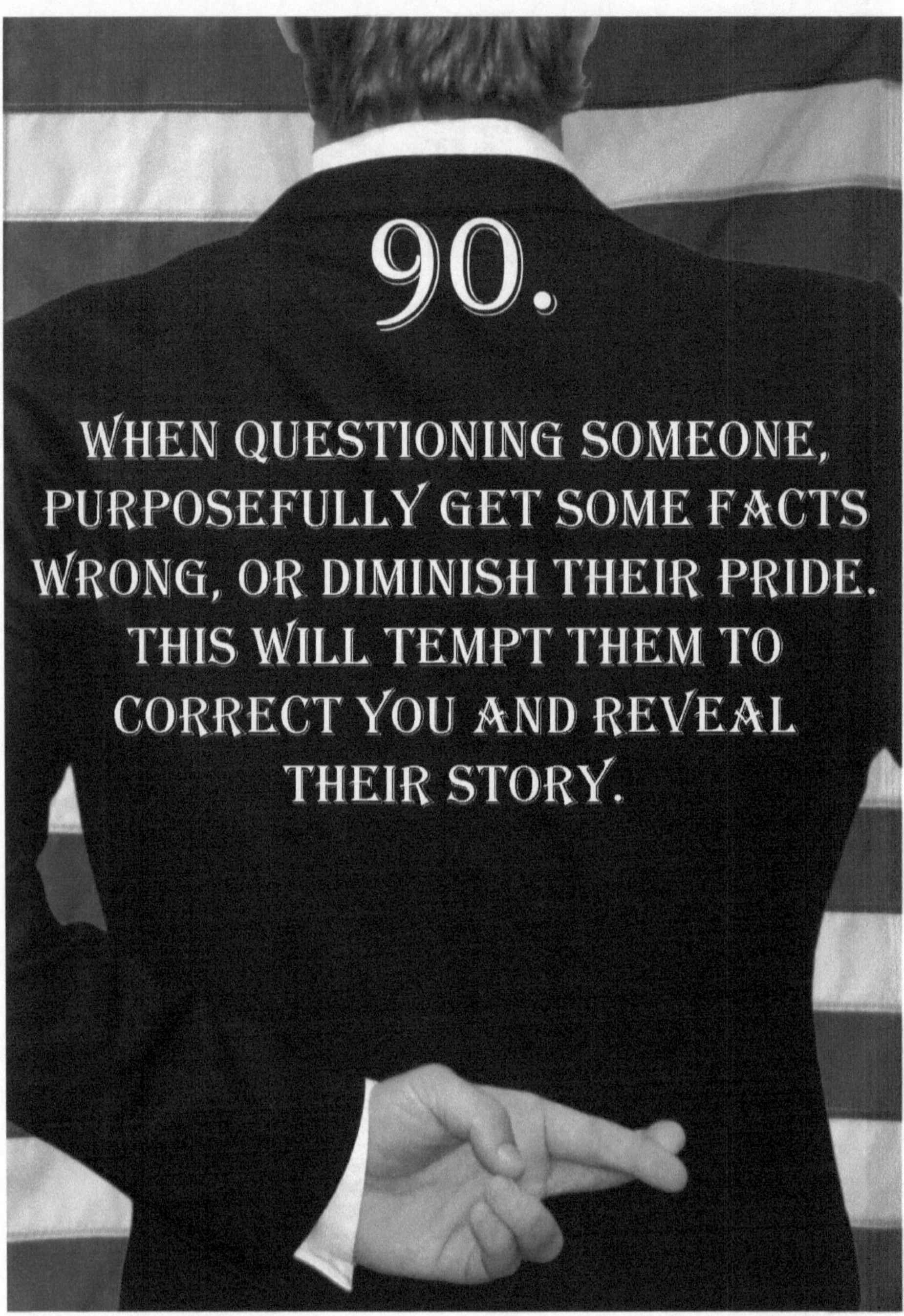
90.
WHEN QUESTIONING SOMEONE,
PURPOSEFULLY GET SOME FACTS
WRONG, OR DIMINISH THEIR PRIDE.
THIS WILL TEMPT THEM TO
CORRECT YOU AND REVEAL
THEIR STORY.

Deception Tip 90 – Wrong Facts

When questioning someone, purposefully get some facts wrong, or diminish their pride. This will tempt them to correct you and reveal their story.

Liars want to make sure you understand exactly what they are talking about. They want you to get it right. Therefore, if you don't understand what is going on, then they will continue to talk to try to convince you of their lie. Remember, one of their main goals is to get you to believe the lie.

In Deception Tip 26 Accusing Liars, we discussed how accusing a liar of a more serious crime might get them to fess up to a lesser crime. They want to make sure they are getting the best deal and that you believe exactly what they want you to believe. Therefore, if you purposefully mess up some facts that they tell you, they will leap to correct those facts.

When you do this, keep your eye out for contempt. The liar may display it if you state facts that they told you that are actually false. However, when you mess up their story, they may become frustrated and continue to explain it. Chances are, if it is a lie, they may mess up sooner or later and therefore, reveal the truth.

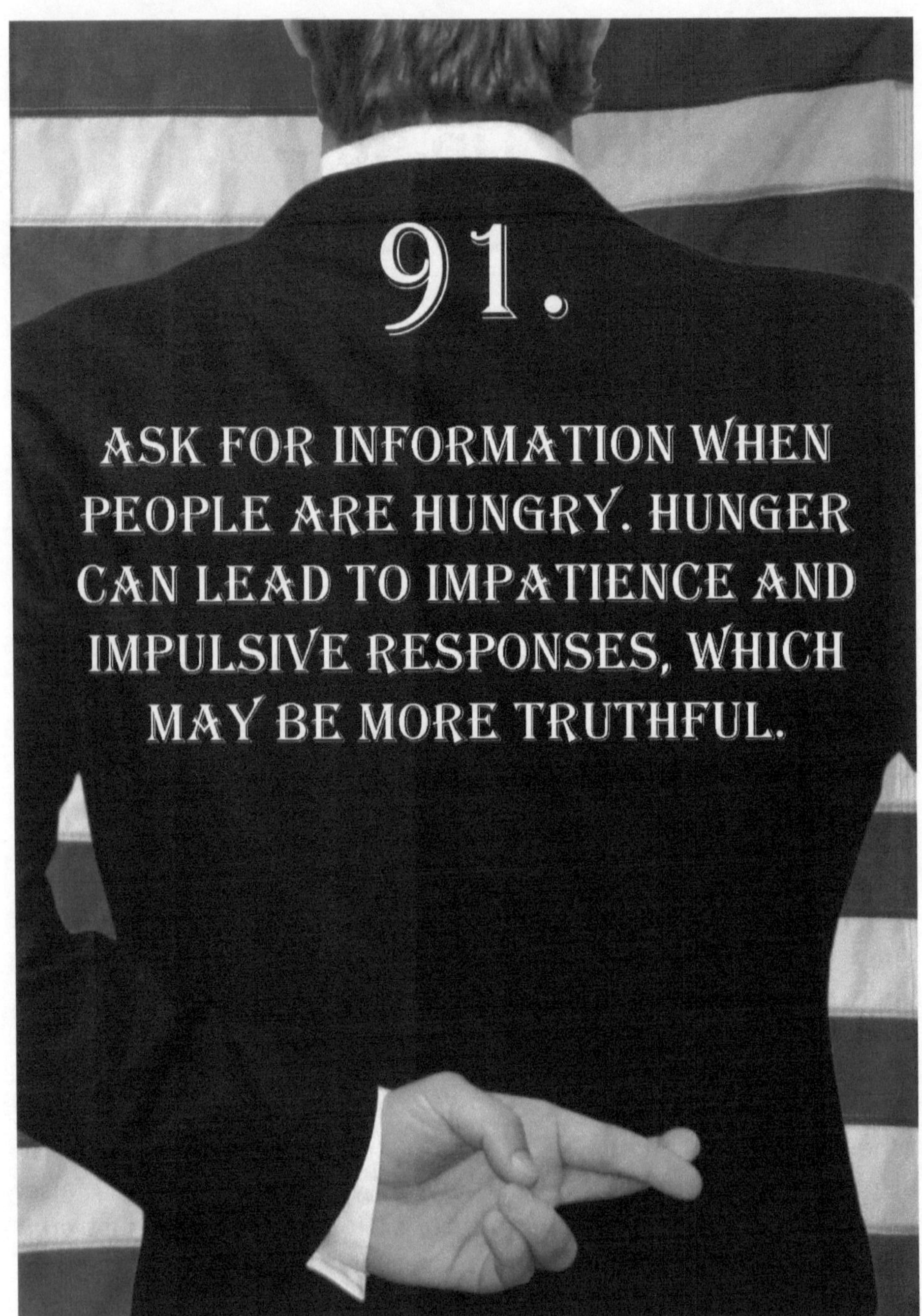
91.
ASK FOR INFORMATION WHEN
PEOPLE ARE HUNGRY. HUNGER
CAN LEAD TO IMPATIENCE AND
IMPULSIVE RESPONSES, WHICH
MAY BE MORE TRUTHFUL.

Deception Tip 91 – Hunger

Ask for information when people are hungry. Hunger can lead to impatience and impulsive responses, which may be more truthful.

Never go to the grocery store when you are hungry. You've no doubt done this before and you find that you always end up buying more than you need. This is because you were hungry and everything looked good. In addition, you've probably also been angry or short-tempered when you were hungry. The common term for this is "hangry".

You can use this to your advantage when you need information from someone. If you know that the person is hungry, then use that chance to ask them your questions. When people are hungry they are often thinking about how they can no longer be hungry and how soon they can eat. Therefore, they may be apt to give you quicker, more truthful, responses.

This is because they are probably thinking about getting food instead of thinking about the lie. It is important to note that this method can also work if someone has to use the bathroom. Of course, you may find that depending on the situation; the person may not need a bathroom in order to relieve him or herself.

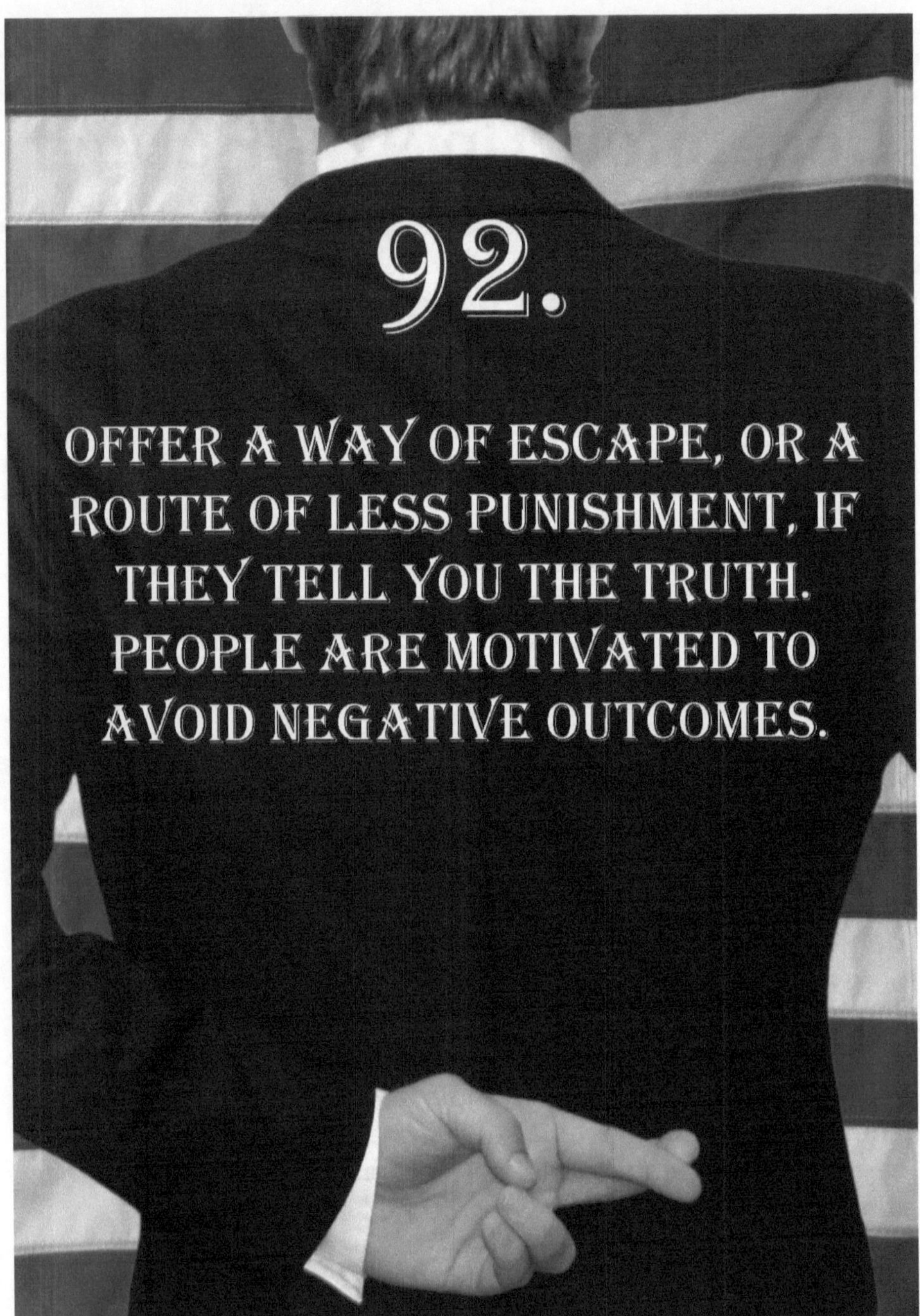
92.

OFFER A WAY OF ESCAPE, OR A
ROUTE OF LESS PUNISHMENT, IF
THEY TELL YOU THE TRUTH.
PEOPLE ARE MOTIVATED TO
AVOID NEGATIVE OUTCOMES.

Deception Tip 92 – Avoid Negative Outcomes

Offer a way of escape, or a route of less punishment, if they tell you the truth. People are motivated to avoid negative outcomes.

People are always motivated to avoid negative outcomes. Freud said that humans are motivated to seek pleasure and avoid pain. Whether or not you are a Freudian, this statement holds true. People want to do things that are enjoyable. No healthy person wants to be in pain all of the time. Thus, liars are also motivated to avoid negative outcomes.

Remember Deception Tip 26 Accusing Liars? When you accuse a liar of doing something with a more serious consequence it may get them to fess up to whatever they did so that they will take the lesser consequence. The current tip is similar in that you are providing the liar a lesser consequence if he or she tells you the truth.

Offer them a way out or give them a deal. Make it a one-time offer so there is a sense of urgency and let them know exactly what the outcome will be. In addition, be sure to inform them of the outcome if they don't take the deal. Make that outcome be much worse than your deal.

93.
REAL MEMORIES ARE RECORDED
USING ALL SENSES. WHEREAS LIES
ARE MAINLY VISUAL. QUESTION
LIARS BY ASKING ABOUT HOW
SOMETHING SMELLED, FELT,
SOUNDED, TASTED, ET CETERA.

Deception Tip 93 – Real Memories

Real memories are recorded using all senses. Whereas lies are mainly visual. Question liars by asking about how something smelled, felt, sounded, tasted, et cetera.

When people invent lies, they are created visually. They are not a real memory so they are memorized and rehearsed. However, remember that in Deception Tip 65 you learned that liars prefer to conceal the truth rather than coming up with an entirely fictitious story. Therefore, some parts of their story will probably be real.

Of course, the difficult part will be determining what part of the story is fiction and what part is truth. This is where your other deception detection skills will come in handy. Look for signs of deception that cluster around a specific part of the story. That should help you hone in on the lie.

If you suspect that someone is lying about something, begin asking him or her about their other senses. See if you can determine how the situation was around them. What it felt like, how it sounded, what the smells were, et cetera. Yes, it may be a little strange, however, when real memories are recorded, they are recorded with all of the senses.

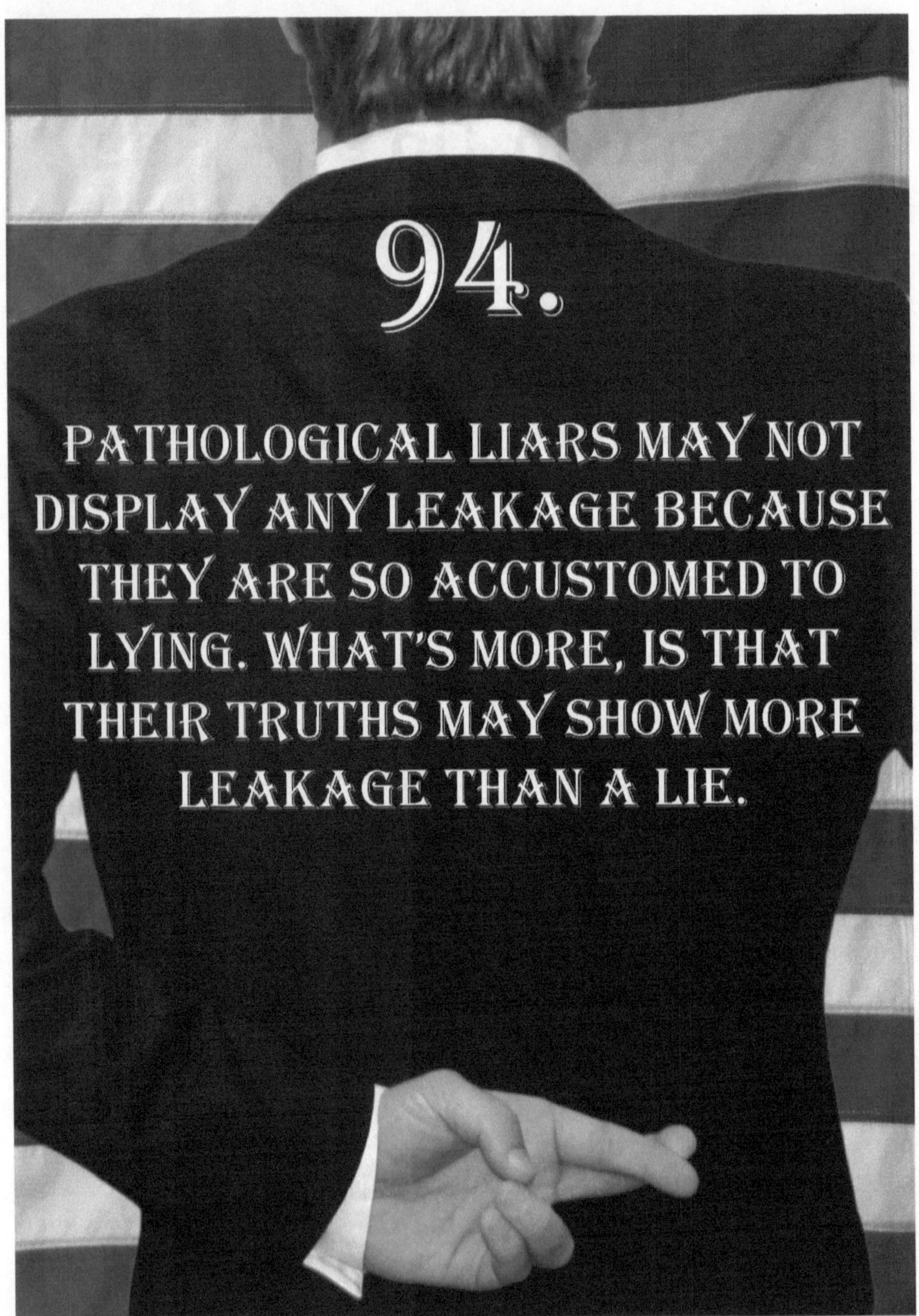
94.

PATHOLOGICAL LIARS MAY NOT
DISPLAY ANY LEAKAGE BECAUSE
THEY ARE SO ACCUSTOMED TO
LYING. WHAT'S MORE, IS THAT
THEIR TRUTHS MAY SHOW MORE
LEAKAGE THAN A LIE.

Deception Tip 94 – Pathological Liars

Pathological liars may not display any leakage because they are so accustomed to lying. What's more is that their truths may show more leakage than a lie.

Most people are uncomfortable when telling a lie, unless it is a social or polite lie, of course. In that case, they may not even realize that they are lying. On the other hand, some people are so accustomed to lying that it is a natural part of their behavior. These people are usually termed as sick because they are pathological liars.

When they lie, you may not notice signs of deception leakage because they are so used to lying. It doesn't make them uncomfortable. There is nothing in their conscience that tells them lying is wrong. They believe it is a natural way of life and they can't go without it.

As a result, they may still leak signs of deception. However, it will probably be when they are not lying. This is because they are so comfortable telling lies that when they tell the truth they experience stress and anxiety. Don't worry, these people are outliers. They are the exception to the rule and are not as common as you might think.

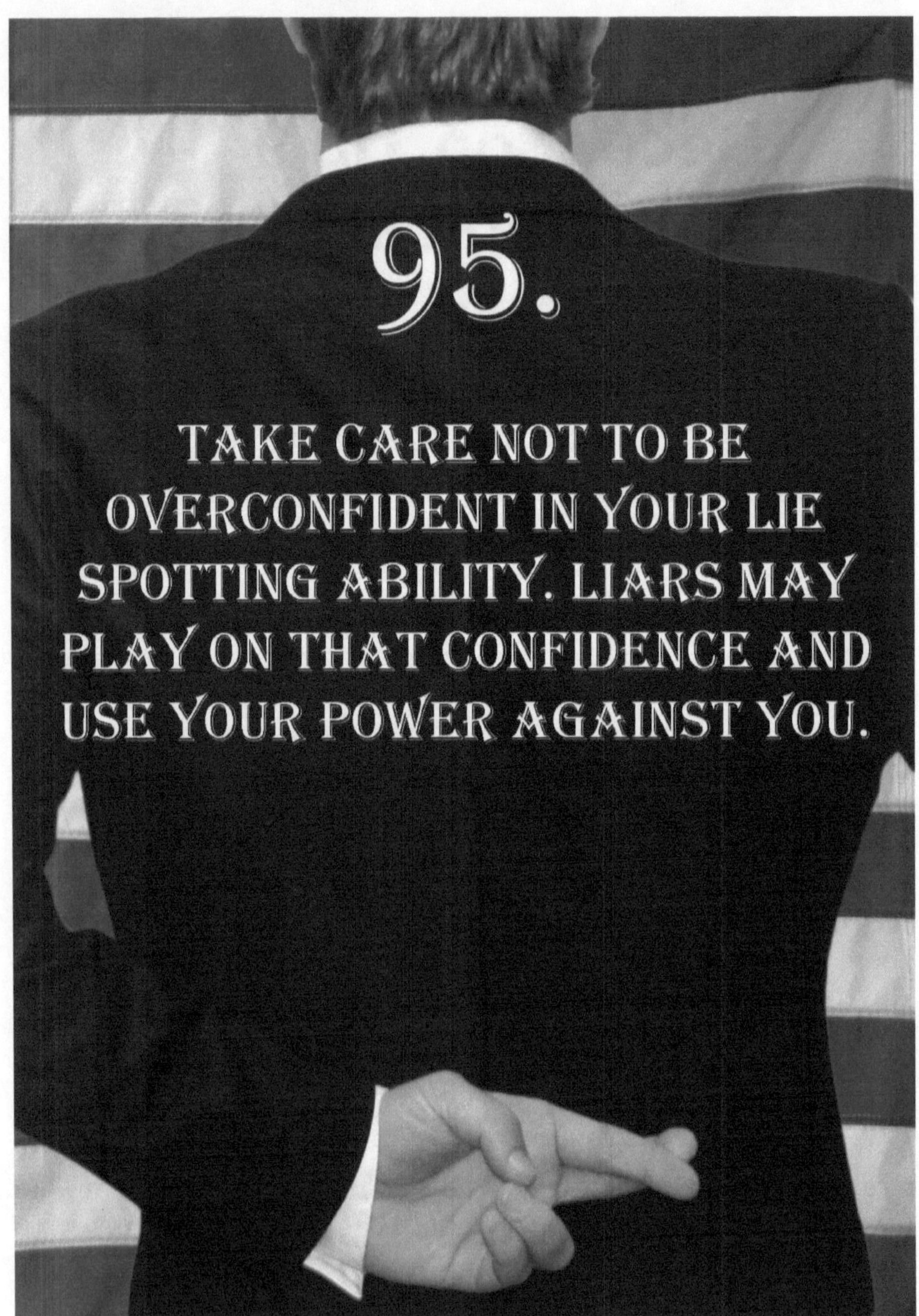
95.

TAKE CARE NOT TO BE
OVERCONFIDENT IN YOUR LIE
SPOTTING ABILITY. LIARS MAY
PLAY ON THAT CONFIDENCE AND
USE YOUR POWER AGAINST YOU.

Deception Tip 95 – Overconfidence

Take care not to be overconfident in your lie spotting ability. Liars may play on that confidence and use your power against you.

You have learned a lot about the different signs of deception and how to tell whether or not someone is lying. Hopefully, you are starting to notice those signs on other people and even on yourself. Be careful not to become too confident in your lie detection ability. If you do, you may fall harder than you think.

It is generally best to remain humble and not tell anyone and everyone about your new ability. Allow it to remain behind the scenes. If people start to believe that you are some kind of mind reader then they may be uncomfortable. In addition, if they feel like you are always analyzing them, they will definitely be uncomfortable.

In some cases, there will be people who put you on the spot and test you in your ability to read them. This is never a good thing because now you may have anxiety and they will take extra care to prevent any leakage. It is an unnatural situation where you'll be set up to fail. Therefore, remain humble and don't flaunt your ability.

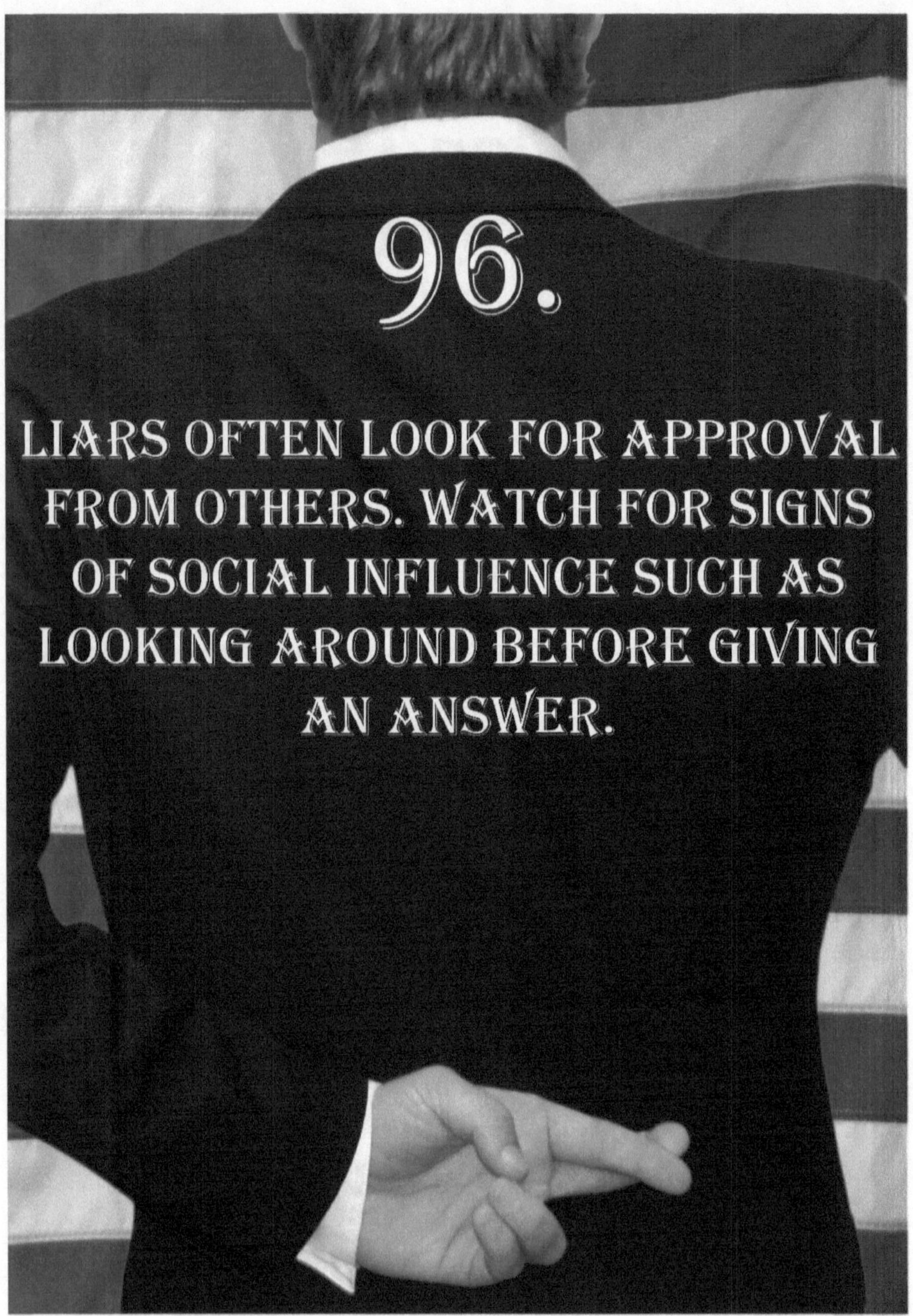
96.

LIARS OFTEN LOOK FOR APPROVAL
FROM OTHERS. WATCH FOR SIGNS
OF SOCIAL INFLUENCE SUCH AS
LOOKING AROUND BEFORE GIVING
AN ANSWER.

Deception Tip 96 – Social Influence

Liars often look for approval from others. Watch for signs of social influence such as looking around before giving an answer.

Humans are social creatures. We want to fit in with others and want to be a part of the group. In Deception Tip 35 Mirror Movements, you learned how truthful people tend to mirror the movements of others. This is because they want to be connected. In addition, in Deception Tip 84 Relating Language you learned that relating to others might help you learn the truth.

The point is that humans want to feel like they belong. Therefore, watch for signs of social influence that may occur before someone gives you an answer. The person may look at someone else in the room or even see if anyone else is in the room.

These social signs of influence may help you determine whether or not the person is being deceptive. Looking at someone else in the room may mean that you need to speak to that other person. Looking around the room to see if anyone is there may mean that the information is highly sensitive. Either way, social influence can be an important factor in detecting deception.

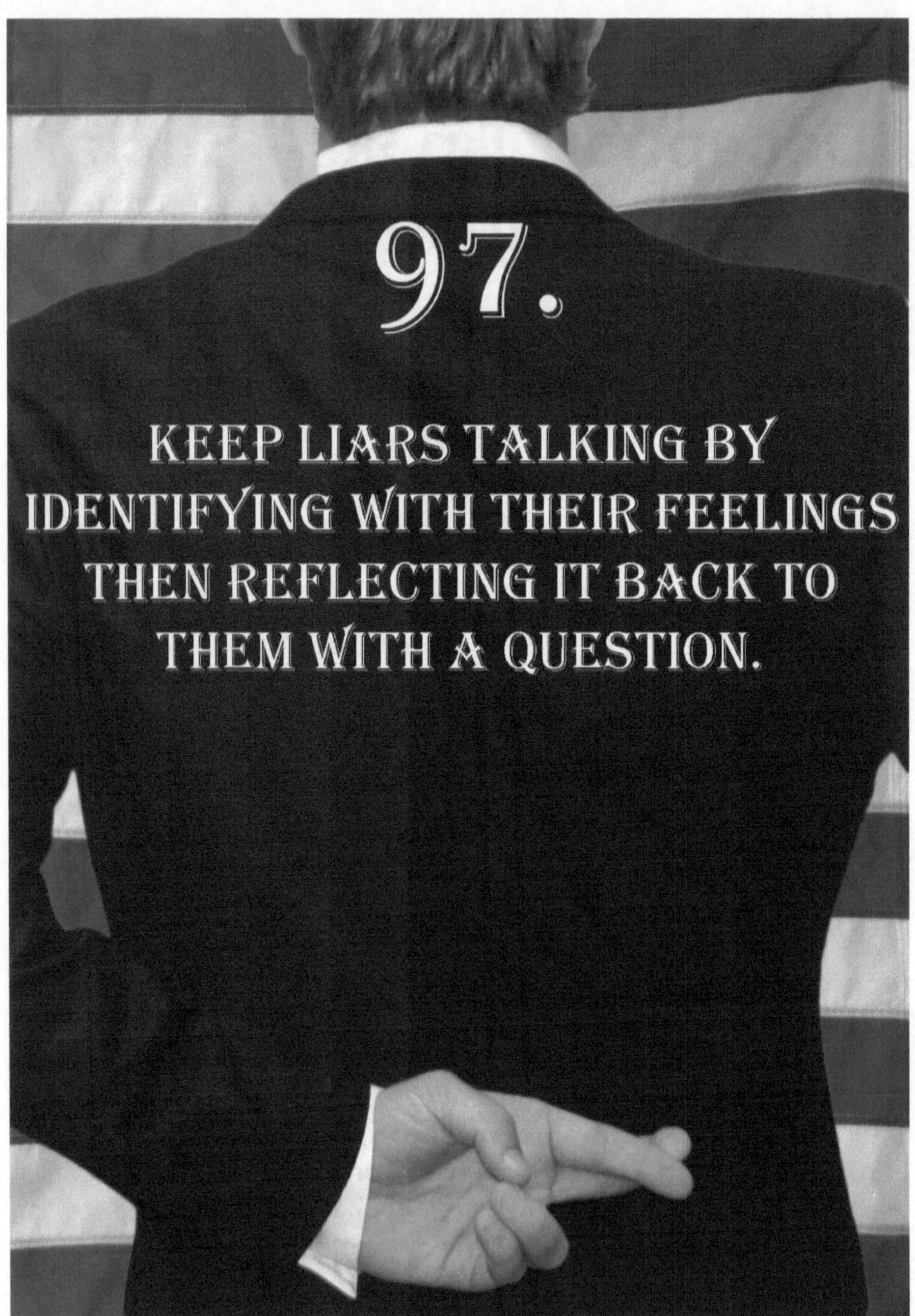
97.
KEEP LIARS TALKING BY
IDENTIFYING WITH THEIR FEELINGS
THEN REFLECTING IT BACK TO
THEM WITH A QUESTION.

Deception Tip 97 – Keep Liars Talking

Keep liars talking by identifying with their feelings then reflecting it back to them with a question.

Liars want to talk. They want to tell their story so that you will believe it. Remember, they are under a lot of stress and tension. In addition, the more they talk the better the chance of them revealing the truth. Therefore, do everything you can to keep them talking.

That means you may have to stay silent (Deception Tip 13), become silent (Deception Tip 69), or engage in conversation. You can use any number of the different tactics you've learned throughout these deception tips. Remember to use starting sentences mentioned in Deception Tip 82 and relate to them as discussed in Deception Tip 84.

The more you can do to keep them talking the better. Identify with their feelings and reflect them back to them. Make them feel like you care and you are on their side. Place their feelings in a question and ask them more about their experiences, thoughts, or feelings. Of course, this tactic won't work with all liars. However, it is a good one to have in your repertoire.

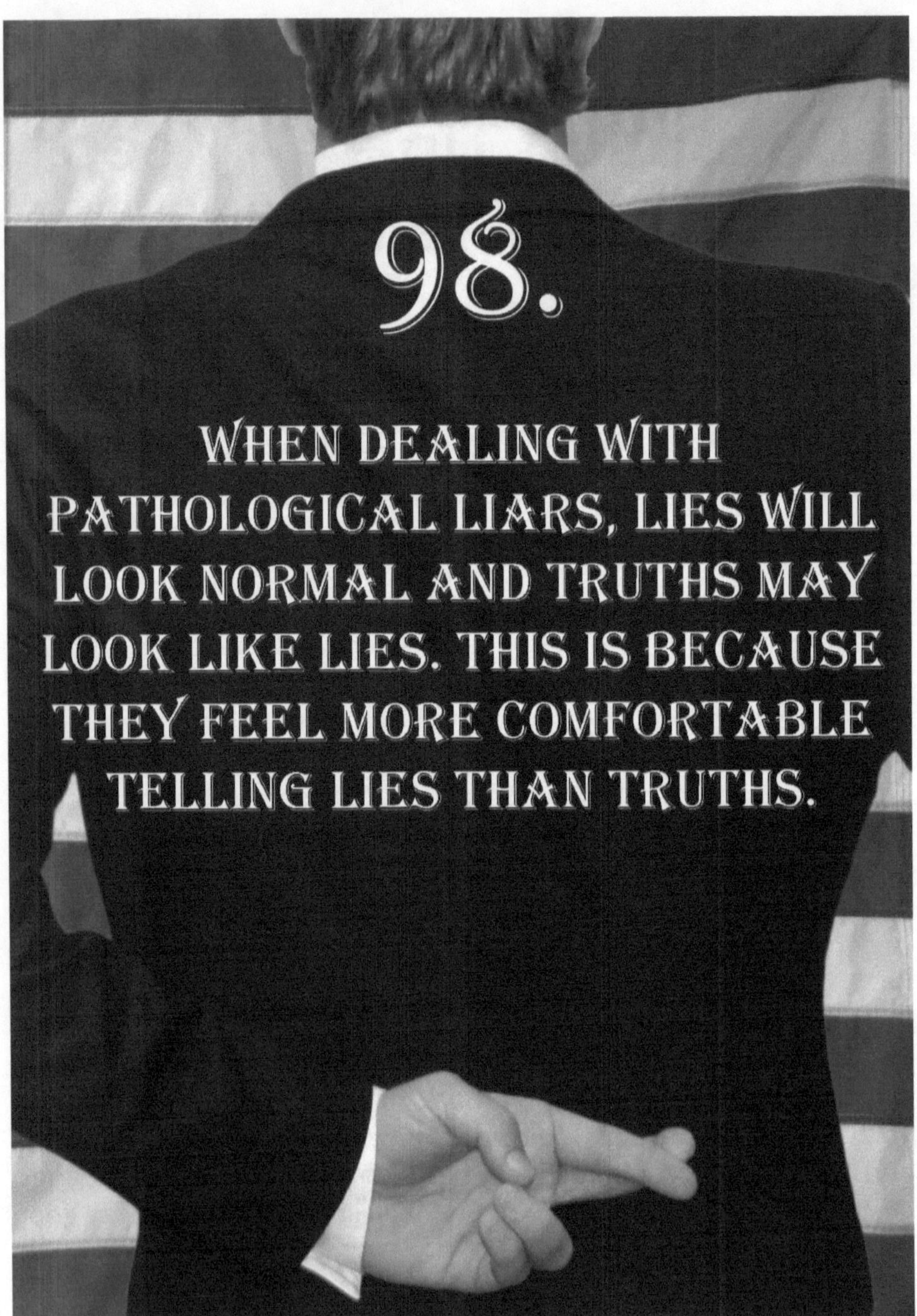
98.

WHEN DEALING WITH
PATHOLOGICAL LIARS, LIES WILL
LOOK NORMAL AND TRUTHS MAY
LOOK LIKE LIES. THIS IS BECAUSE
THEY FEEL MORE COMFORTABLE
TELLING LIES THAN TRUTHS.

Deception Tip 98 – Truths Like Lies

When dealing with pathological liars, lies will look normal and truths may look like lies. This is because they feel more comfortable telling lies than truths.

In Deception Tip 94, you learned about pathological liars and how they are very comfortable telling lies. In fact, they might be considered sick by some doctors and are definitely abnormal. Most people do not enjoy lies and their conscience tells them that lying is wrong and that they should tell the truth whenever possible.

Pathological liars, on the other hand, enjoy telling lies. They don't feel any stress or anxiety when they lie. It is natural for them. As a result, when they tell the truth, they may feel stressed or anxious. Therefore, you may witness signs of stress and tension leaked through body language.

It is important for you to remember that these people are not a common occurrence. They are a minority and the odds of you continually running into them are slim. However, you must be aware of the fact that they are out there. So keep your mind sharp and always look for patterns and clusters of behavior.

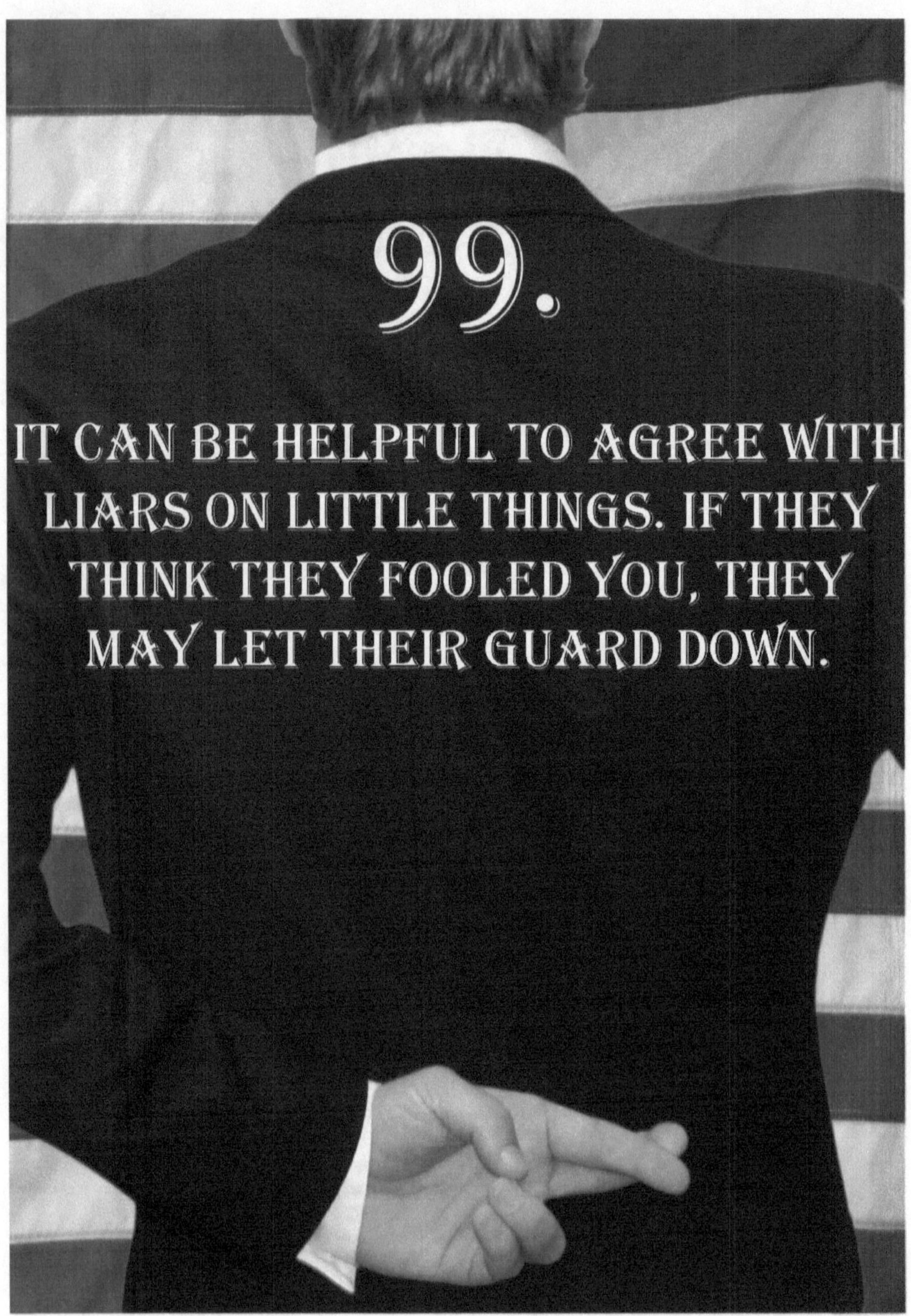
99.

IT CAN BE HELPFUL TO AGREE WITH
LIARS ON LITTLE THINGS. IF THEY
THINK THEY FOOLED YOU, THEY
MAY LET THEIR GUARD DOWN.

Deception Tip 99 – Agree With Liars

It can be helpful to agree with liars on little things. If they think they fooled you, they may let their guard down.

Liars want to be believed. This is the entire point of telling a lie. They want someone to believe it. Of course, they also want to cover up, or get away with, whatever the lie is about. However, in order to do that, they need someone to believe the lie. Therefore, that is the main goal.

In Deception Tip 11 Accepting Lies, you learned that liars will seize any opportunity to be believed. They may even accept lies told by the target to go along with their story. The current tip is very similar. If you agree with some of their lies then they may relax a little bit. They may believe that they have gotten you to believe their lie.

In addition, when you accept one of their lies, watch for signs of contempt. They may believe they have fooled you and display it or even a smile of duping delight. In addition, they may begin to relax a little bit thereby exposing a thread for you to pull and unravel their entire lie.

100.
LIARS TRY TO SOUND SMARTER, AND MORE CREDIBLE, THAN THEY ACTUALLY ARE. TRIP THEM UP BY USING THEIR OWN JARGON AGAINST THEM.

Deception Tip 100 – Liar's Jargon

Liars try to sound smarter, and more credible, than they actually are. Trip them up by using their own jargon against them.

Deception Tip 17 Detailed Stories and Deception Tip 31 Unconventional Language are closely related to this tip. Therefore, if you don't remember them I encourage you to go back and examine them once again. Liars like to use lots of detail and statistics in an effort to sound more credible. In addition, they like to use unconventional language so that they sound more knowledgeable.

Remember, most people do not remember all kinds of detail. People can hardly remember the date of their anniversary let alone the dates and times of specific events. In addition, most people speak using five and ten cent words. Therefore, when you hear long multiple syllable words, start looking for other signs of deception.

Liars also like to use jargon in an effort to make it seem like they are the only ones who know about whatever it is being discussed. They want others to feel inferior so that they will simply believe the lie rather than try to understand what is going on. If you use this jargon against them, their lie may be exposed. Especially, if they don't really understand the jargon.

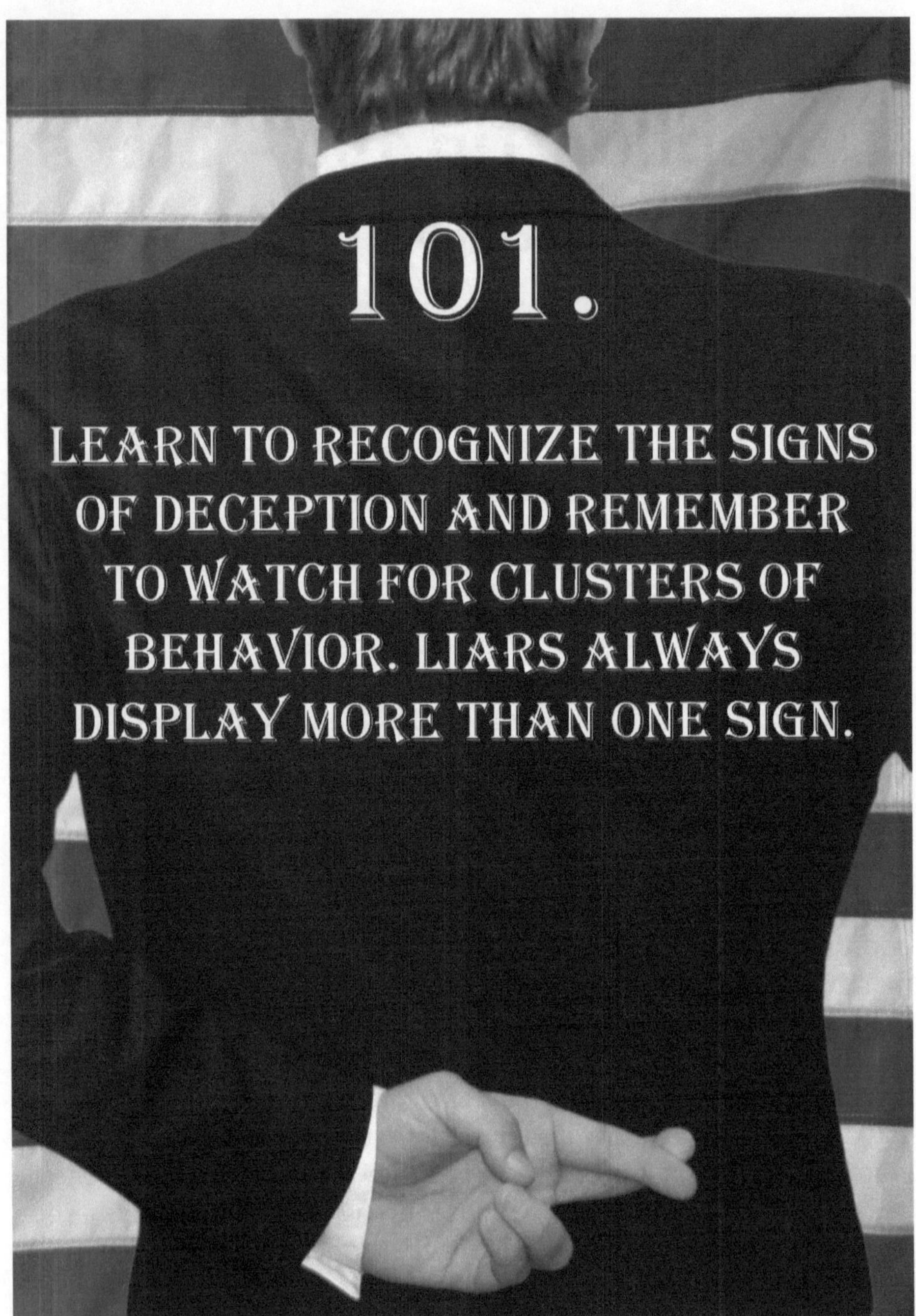
101.
LEARN TO RECOGNIZE THE SIGNS
OF DECEPTION AND REMEMBER
TO WATCH FOR CLUSTERS OF
BEHAVIOR. LIARS ALWAYS
DISPLAY MORE THAN ONE SIGN.

Deception Tip 101 – Signs Of Deception

Learn to recognize the signs of deception and remember to watch for clusters of behavior. Liars always display more than one sign.

Throughout all of these tips, the phrase "patterns and clusters of behavior" has been hammered into you. This is because it is very important. You must always watch for several signs of deception. Remember, when you see one sign it could mean anything. It could mean any number of things. Therefore, you must wait before coming to a conclusion.

You must look for additional signs of deception and see if any appear. If someone is lying, there will always be more than one sign. This is because the unconscious is very truthful. It wants the truth to come out and will continue leaking truthful body language in an effort to make that happen.

Therefore, if you pay attention, you will notice patterns and clusters of behavior. Then, once you put them together, you will be able to tell for certain whether or not someone is lying. Then it is up to you whether or not you wish to expose that lie.

Conclusion

Hopefully, you have enjoyed the deception tips images as well as reading a little more about each tip. I really hope you have learned more about reading people and detecting deception. You're probably familiar with the other books I've written in addition to the Deception Tips Blog and the Deception Tips Videos.

However, in case you aren't, then I encourage you to take a look at the A Guide To Deception book. Check out the Deception Tips eBook for a quick reference guide of each one of these tips without the descriptions. You may also wish to start listening to the Deception Tips Podcast and watch the Deception Tips Videos. They will help you stay sharp and continue to recognize the signs of deception so that you can read people and know the truth.

The more you review this material and study it the better you will become at spotting lies. I encourage you to share it with your friends and discuss it with them. Practice reading these signs and help others do the same.

Best of luck,
Spencer Coffman

About The Author

Spencer has been studying human emotions and the meaning behind body language since 2010. He has been certified at the expert level in both the Micro-Expression Training Tool (METT) and the Subtle Expression Training Tool (SETT). Doctor Paul Ekman, who is arguably the founding father of micro-expression research, created these tools.

In 2013, Spencer published new findings regarding humans' ability to interpret smiles and in 2015 he published A Guide To Deception, which teaches people how to spot lies. He has also created the Deception Tips Blog, the Deception Tips eBook, the Deception Tips Podcast, and the Deception Tips Videos. To learn more about Spencer, visit his website SpencerCoffman.com. You may also wish to check out DeceptionTips.com.

About The Author